Dan Gartner

THIRD EDITION

Physical Best Activity Guide

Middle and High School Levels

THIRD EDITION

Physical Best
Activity Guide

Middle and High School Levels

National Association for
Sport and Physical Education

*an association of the American Alliance for Health,
Physical Education, Recreation and Dance*

Human Kinetics

Library of Congress Cataloging-in-Publication Data

Physical Best (Program)
  Physical best activity guide : middle and high school levels / National Association for Sport and Physical Education. -- 3rd ed.
    p. cm.
  Includes bibliographical references.
  ISBN-13: 978-0-7360-8118-4 (soft cover)
  ISBN-10: 0-7360-8118-6 (soft cover)
  1. Physical education and training--Study and teaching (Elementary)--United States. I. National
Association for Sport and Physical Education.
  GV365.P49915 2010
  613.7071'2--dc22
                                        2010030727

ISBN-10: 0-7360-8118-6 (print)
ISBN-13: 978-0-7360-8118-4 (print)

The Web addresses cited in this text were current as of October 2010, unless otherwise noted.

Acquisitions Editors: Scott Wikgren and Sarajane Quinn; **Developmental Editor:** Ragen E. Sanner; **Assistant Editor:** Anne Rumery; **Copyeditor:** Bob Replinger; **Permission Manager:** Dalene Reeder; **Graphic Designer:** Joe Buck; **Graphic Artists:** Kathleen Boudreau-Fuoss and Dawn Sills; **Cover Designer:** Keith Blomberg; **CD Face Designer:** Susan Rothermel Allen; **Photographer (cover):** © Human Kinetics; **Photographer (interior):** © Human Kinetics, unless otherwise noted; **Photo Production Manager:** Jason Allen; **Art Manager:** Kelly Hendren; **Associate Art Manager:** Alan L. Wilborn; **Illustrator:** © Human Kinetics; **Printer:** Versa Press

Printed in the United States of America   10   9   8   7   6

The paper in this book is certified under a sustainable forestry program.

Human Kinetics
Website: www.HumanKinetics.com

United States: Human Kinetics
P.O. Box 5076
Champaign, IL 61825-5076
800-747-4457
e-mail: humank@hkusa.com

Canada: Human Kinetics
475 Devonshire Road Unit 100
Windsor, ON N8Y 2L5
800-465-7301 (in Canada only)
e-mail: info@hkcanada.com

Europe: Human Kinetics
107 Bradford Road
Stanningley
Leeds LS28 6AT, United Kingdom
+44 (0) 113 255 5665
e-mail: hk@hkeurope.com

Australia: Human Kinetics
57A Price Avenue
Lower Mitcham, South Australia
5062
08 8372 0999
e-mail: info@hkaustralia.com

New Zealand: Human Kinetics
P.O. Box 80
Torrens Park, South Australia 5062
0800 222 062
e-mail: info@hknewzealand.com

E4738

CONTENTS

ACTIVITY AND REPRODUCIBLES FINDER

Activity number	Activity title	Activity page	Concept	Middle school	High school	Reproducibles (on CD-ROM)
3.1	Clean Out Your Arteries	23	Health benefits	•		None
3.2	Aerobic Benefit Hunt	26	Health benefits	•		Aerobic Benefit Cards
						Aerobic Benefit Student Worksheet
3.3	Chart Your Heart Rate	28	Intensity		•	Chart Your Heart Rate Worksheet
3.4	Aerobic Fitness Is FITT	31	Intensity		•	Aerobic Fitness Worksheet
3.5	Fitting in Fitness	33	Frequency	•		Fitting in Fitness Sport Handouts
3.6	Heartbeat Stations	36	Intensity and time	•		Heartbeat Stations Scoresheet
3.7	Cross-Training Trio	38	Time and type	•	•	Aerobic Fitness: Cross-Training Benefits and Guidelines
						Aerobic Fitness: Cross-Training Activities Log
3.8	Continuous Relay	41	Intensity and time		•	Individual Workout Log
3.9	Mini Triathlon	44	Intensity and time	•	•	None
3.10	1,000 Reps	46	Growth and development	•	•	1,000 Reps and Seconds Chart
						Estimated Energy Expenditure for Common Activities Chart
3.11	Aerobic FITT Log	49	Progression	•	•	FITT Log
						FITT Log Worksheet
4.1	Go for the Team Gold	55	Health benefits	•		Go for the Team Gold Task Cards
						Go for the Team Gold Handout
4.2	Safely Finding the 8- to 12-Rep Range	57	Intensity		•	Weight Training Chart
4.3	Warm Up With Weights	60	Warm-up and cool-down		•	Weight Training Chart
4.4	Muscle FITT Bingo	62	Specificity	•	•	Muscle FITT Bingo Cards
4.5	Muscles in Action	64	Specificity	•		Muscle Cards
						Labeled Muscle Diagram
						Muscles in Action Plan Worksheet
4.6	Mission Push-Up Possible	67	Intensity and progression	•		Mission Push-Up Possible Card
						Mission Push-Up Possible Chart
						Individual Push-Up Progress Sheet

(continued)

Activity Finder *(continued)*

Activity number	Activity title	Activity page	Concept	Middle school	High school	Reproducibles (on CD-ROM)
4.7	Get Fit	70	Specificity	•		Get Fit Worksheet
						Get Fit Exercise Signs
4.8	Muscle Up	72	Specificity		•	Muscle Groups Diagram
						Muscle Up Classification Chart
4.9	Muscular Fitness Scavenger Hunt	75	Specificity	•	•	Muscular Fitness Scavenger Hunt Handout
						Muscular Fitness Scavenger Hunt Puzzle
						Muscular Fitness Scavenger Hunt Station Cards
4.10	Know Your Way Around the Weight Room	78	Type		•	Know Your Way Around the Weight Room: Peer Teaching Exercise Descriptions
						Know Your Way Around the Weight Room Peer Assessment
						Know Your Way Around the Weight Room Exercises
						Common Weight Room Errors
4.11	Muscular Strength and Endurance FITT Log	80	Progression	•	•	FITT Log
						FITT Log Worksheet
5.1	Stretch Marks the Spot	87	Specificity	•		Stretch Marks the Spot Handout
						Flexibility Task and Benefit Cards
5.2	All-Star Stretches	89	Health benefits	•	•	Flexibility Task and Benefit Cards
						Guidelines for Safe Stretching Poster
						Benefits of Good Flexibility Poster
5.3	Flexibility Puzzles	92	Flexibility benefits	•	•	Benefits of Good Flexibility Poster
						Flexibility Puzzle
						Flexibility Word Search Answer Key
						Flexibility Word Search Worksheet
						Stretch Station Cards
5.4	Type Cast	95	Specificity	•	•	Flexibility Task and Benefit Cards
						Benefits of Good Flexibility Poster
5.5	Sport Spectacular	98	Specificity		•	Sport Stretch Pages
5.6	Introduction to Yoga	100	Frequency and time	•	•	Yoga Signs
						Yoga Pose Cards
						Yoga Log
5.7	Flexibility FITT Log	103	Progression	•	•	FITT Log
						FITT Log Worksheet
6.1	All-Sport Body Composition Quizzo	109	Body composition	•		Body Composition Quizzo Chart
						Body Composition Quizzo Term Cards
						All-Sport Body Composition Activity List

Activity number	Activity title	Activity page	Concept	Middle school	High school	Reproducibles (on CD-ROM)
6.2	Body Composition Survivor	112	Health benefits	•	•	Body Composition Survivor Challenges
						Benefits of Developing and Maintaining Ideal Body Composition Puzzle
						Risks of Having a High Percentage of Body Fat Puzzle
						Body Composition Facts Puzzle
						Super Survivor Questions
6.3	Frisbee Calorie Blaster	116	Health benefits	•		None
6.4	Nutrition Memory	118	Food and portion size	•		Food and Portion Memory Cards
						Food and Portion Memory Card Key
6.5	Cross-Training Triumph	120	Growth and development		•	Cross-Training Triumph Tasks
6.6	Health Quest	123	Nutrition	•	•	Checkpoint Signs
						Health Quest Answer Sheet
						Food Guide Pyramid
6.7	Fast-Food Frenzy	126	Nutrition	•		Fast-Food Frenzy Discovery Worksheet
						Calorie Chart
						Fast-Food Frenzy Station Signs
						Lunch Menu Suggestion Cards
						Health Behavior Contract
6.8	Calorie Balancing Act	131	Energy expenditure and weight management		•	Activity and Calorie Information Sheet
						Eat the Food, Do the Time Worksheet
6.9	Jump Rope Digestion	134	Nutrition and digestion	•		Digestive System Component Chart
						Food Guide Pyramid
7.1	Health-Related Fitness Warm-Up	141	Health benefits	•		Team Health-Related Fitness Warm-Up Answer Sheet
						Health-Related Fitness Warm-Up Station Signs
7.2	Fitness Bingo	143	Defining health- and skill-related fitness	•		Fitness Bingo Task Cards
						Fitness Bingo Card
7.3	Component Countdown	145	Defining health- and skill-related fitness	•	•	Component Countdown Recording Sheet
						Component Countdown Fitness Tags
						Component Countdown Team Task Cards
						Component Countdown Teacher Key
7.4	Monopoly Fitness	148	Health-related fitness	•	•	Monopoly Fitness Station Signs
7.5	Health and Fitness Treasure Hunt	150	Health benefits	•		Health and Fitness Treasure Hunt Task Cards
7.6	Fortune Cookie Fitness	152	Exploring options and making choices	•		Fitness Fortunes

(continued)

Activity Finder *(continued)*

Activity number	Activity title	Activity page	Concept	Middle school	High school	Reproducibles (on CD-ROM)
7.7	Circuit Training Choices	155	Exploring options and making choices		•	Circuit Training Choices Signs
7.8	Fitness Unscramble	157	Exploring options and making choices	•	•	Fitness Unscramble Task Signs
						Fitness Unscramble Worksheet
						Fitness Unscramble Worksheet Answer Key
7.9	Jump Band Fitness	160	Exploring options and making choices	•	•	None
7.10	Partner Racetrack Fitness	163	Exploring options and making choices	•	•	Racetrack Signs
7.11	12 Ways to Fitness	166	Exploring options and making choices	•		Add-On Cards
7.12	Sporting Fitness	169	Exploring options and making choices	•	•	Sporting Fitness Activity Cards
						Sporting Fitness Soccer Drills
7.13	Basketball Skills Fitness	171	Understanding health-related fitness	•	•	Circuit Station Cards
7.14	Mat Exercise Stations	174	Exploring options and making choices	•	•	None
7.15	Speed Circuit	177	Exploring options and making choices	•	•	None
7.16	Medicine Ball Circuit	179	Exploring options and making choices	•	•	Medicine Ball Circuit Station Signs
7.17	Fitness Adventure	182	Exploring options and making choices	•		Fitness Adventure Station Cards
						Fitness Adventure Worksheet
						Fitness Adventure Answer Key
7.18	Racetrack Fitness Using Stability Balls	185	Exploring options		•	Racetrack Fitness Station Signs
7.19	Know the Risks and Benefits	187	Healthy behaviors	•	•	Health Risk Station Signs
						Healthy Behavior Station Signs
						Health Risks and Benefits Worksheet
7.20	Body Image Museum Tour	189	Quackery and body image	•		Media Representation of Sport and Physical Activity
8.1	Learning Self-Management Skills	195	Self-management skills	•	•	What Stage Am I?
						Physical Activity Pyramid for Teens
	Enrichment Activity: Fitness Trail	198	Exercise	•	•	Fitness Trail Station Signs
8.2	Goal Setting	200	Goal setting	•	•	Setting Goals
						Short-Term Versus Long-Term Goals
8.3	Using Pedometers to Set Goals and Assess Physical Activity	202	Pedometer use and goal setting		•	Assessment Record Sheet

Activity number	Activity title	Activity page	Concept	Middle school	High school	Reproducibles (on CD-ROM)
8.4	Using Heart Rate Monitors	204	Heart rate monitor use and goal setting	•	•	Activity Template and Record Sheet
8.5	Fitness Olympics	206	Goal setting	•		Fitness Olympics Scorecard
						Basketball Station Cards
8.6	Power Team Training	208	Goal setting		•	Power Team Challenge Scorecard
						Power Team Challenge Station Task Cards
9.1	Health and Fitness Quackery	213	Quackery and passive exercise	•	•	Evaluating Exercise Devices
						Fitness-Related Experts
9.2	Evaluating Health Products	215	Quackery and self-motivated exercise	•	•	Sense and Nonsense
						Evaluating Health and Fitness Information and Services
	Enrichment Activity: Exercise at Home	216	Exercise	•	•	Exercising at Home Worksheet
10.1	Program Planning	221	Fitness profile	•	•	Developing Your Personal Plan
10.2	Sticking to a Plan	223	Nonactive versus physically active	•	•	Personal Exercise Word Puzzle
						Fitness Review Crossword Puzzle
						Overcoming Barriers
10.3	Evaluating a Physical Activity Program	225	Personal fitness plan	•	•	Reproducibles for this activity are specific to each self-assessment or activity idea.
	Self-Assessment Idea: Evaluating Your Physical Activity Program	225	Evaluation	•	•	Evaluating Your Physical Activity Program Worksheet
	Activity Idea: Perform Your Plan	226	Evaluation and change	•	•	Performing Your Plan
	Activity Idea: Your Exercise Circuit	226	Development	•	•	Your Exercise Circuit
	Activity Idea: Your Health and Fitness Club	227	Evaluation	•	•	Your Health and Fitness Club Worksheet
	Activity Idea: Heart Rate Target Zones	227	Heart rate and aerobic fitness		•	Aerobic Fitness: How Much Activity Is Enough?
	Activity Idea: Sports Stars	228	Exercise	•	•	Sports Stars Program
10.4	Schoolwide Special Event: Exercise Your Rights	230	Advocacy	•	•	Exercise Your Rights Poster

Additional Handouts

Chapter	Page	Concept	Reproducibles (on CD-ROM)
2	10	Building physical fitness	Building Physical Fitness
2	12	Principles of training	Principles of Training Poster
2	12	FITT guidelines	FITT Guidelines

PREFACE

This guide contains information that you need to help sixth through twelfth grade students gain the knowledge, skills, appreciation, and confidence to lead physically active, healthy lives. The easy-to-use instructional activities have been developed and used successfully by physical educators across the United States. You will find competitive and noncompetitive activities, demanding and less demanding activities, and activities that allow maximum time on task.

ABOUT PHYSICAL BEST

Physical Best is a comprehensive health-related fitness education program developed by physical educators for physical educators. Physical Best was designed to educate, challenge, and encourage all young people in the knowledge, skills and attitudes needed for a healthy and fit life. The goal of the program is to help students move from dependence to independence for their own health and fitness by promoting regular, enjoyable physical activity. The purpose of Physical Best is to educate all children, regardless of athletic talent, physical and mental abilities, or disabilities. Physical Best implements this goal through quality resources and professional development workshops for physical educators. Physical Best is a program of the National Association for Sport and Physical Education (NASPE). NASPE is a nonprofit membership organization of over 15,000 professionals in the sport and physical education fields. NASPE is an association of the American Alliance for Health, Physical Education, Recreation and Dance, which is dedicated to strengthening basic knowledge about healthy lifestyles among professionals and the public. Putting that knowledge into action in schools and communities across the nation is critical to improved academic performance, social reform, and the health of individuals.

OVERVIEW OF PHYSICAL BEST RESOURCES

New to this edition will be suggestions found within various activities for incorporating special types of equipment such as heart rate monitors, stability balls, and stretch bands. Also new to this edition is an appendix which lists Internet resources to use when developing special fitness events.

Above all, the activities are designed to be educational and fun. Packaged with the book is a CD-ROM that contains reproducible charts, posters, and handouts that accompany the activities of the third edition. Editable versions of some of the worksheets have been included.

This book has two companion resources:

▶ *Physical Education for Lifelong Fitness: The Physical Best Teacher's Guide, Third Edition* is a comprehensive guide to incorporating health-related fitness and lifetime physical activity into physical education programs. The guide provides a conceptual framework based on recent research covering topics such as behavior, motivation and goal setting, health-related fitness curriculum development and teaching methods, components and principles of fitness, and inclusion in health-related fitness and health-related fitness assessment. The guide also contains a wealth of practical information and examples from experienced physical educators. The third edition has streamlined and reorganized many of the chapters; added practical information, a glossary, and resources for physical educators; and updated information and references throughout the text.

▶ *Physical Best Activity Guide: Elementary Level, Third Edition* contains the information needed to help kindergarten through fifth grade students gain the knowledge, skills, appreciation, and confidence to lead physically active, healthy lives. The easy-to-use instructional activities have been developed and used successfully by physical educators across the United States. You will find both competitive and noncompetitive activities, demanding and less-demanding activities, and activities that allow maximum time on task. Above all, the activities are designed to be educational, fun, and inclusive. Packaged with the book is a CD-ROM of reproducible charts, posters, and handouts that accompany the activities included in the third edition.

RELATED RESOURCES

During a typical school year, many educators use more than one program and a variety of teaching resources, overlapping different approaches on a day-to-day basis. With this in mind, it may be reassuring to know that although Physical Best is designed to be used independently for teaching health-related fitness, the following resources can be used in conjunction with the Physical Best program. *Fitnessgram/Activitygram*, *Fitness for Life*, and the NASPE products listed in this section are suggested resources to complement Physical Best.

Fitnessgram/Activitygram

Fitnessgram/Activitygram (developed by the Cooper Institute) is a comprehensive health-related fitness and activity assessment as well as a computerized reporting system. All elements within *Fitnessgram/Activitygram* are designed to assist teachers in accomplishing the primary objective of youth fitness programs, which is to help students establish physical activity as a part of their daily lives.

Fitnessgram/Activitygram is based on a belief that extremely high levels of physical fitness, while admirable, are not necessary to accomplish objectives associated with good health and improved function. All children need to have adequate level of activity and fitness. *Fitnessgram/Activitygram* is designed to help all children and youth achieve a level of activity and fitness associated with good health, growth, and function.

Fitnessgram/Activitygram resources are published and available through Human Kinetics, as are the materials for the Brockport Physical Fitness Test, a health-related fitness assessment for students with disabilities.

Fitness for Life

Fitness for Life is a comprehensive K through 12 program designed to promote lifelong healthy lifestyles and associated health-related physical fitness, wellness, and other health benefits. The high school text, *Fitness for Life* (updated 5th ed.), was the first text for secondary personal fitness classes and earned a Texty Award for excellence. *Fitness for Life* has been shown to be effective in promoting physically active behavior after students finish school. *Fitness for Life: Middle School*, also a Texty Award winner, helps middle school students learn concepts of physical activity, fitness, nutrition, and wellness. Both texts are based on NASPE standards and have extensive ancillary packages to make teaching and learning easy and effective.

Fitness for Life: Elementary School, designed to be a significant part of the total school wellness program, features plug-and-play video activity routines for use in the classroom and in physical education classes. Guides for classroom teachers and school coordinators, as well as lesson plans for physical educators, are included along with DVD and CD resources. Students are active while learning important physical activey, fitness, and nutrition concepts. More than 28 activity routines and 160 videos containing grade-appropriate activities with nutrition and physical activity messages are included in the Fitness for Life: Elementary School program.

Both *Fitness for Life* and *Physical Best* are based on the HELP philosophy, which promotes **H**ealth for **E**veryone with a focus on **L**ifetime activity of a **P**ersonal nature. The two programs complement one another effectively, because the *Physical Best Activity Guides* (all levels) can be used before and after a *Fitness for Life* program, as well as during the program to provide supplemental activities. In fact, the two programs are so compatible that Physical Best offers teacher training for *Fitness for Life* course instructors.

NASPE Resources

NASPE publishes many additional useful and related resources that are available by calling 800-321-0789 or online through the AAHPERD store at www.aahperd.org.

Quality Physical Education Resources

- *Moving Into the Future: National Standards for Physical Education, 2nd edition.* (2004). Stock No. 304-10275.
- *PE Metrics: Assessing the National Standards.* (2008). Stock No. 304-10458.
- *Beyond Activities: Learning Experiences to Support the National Physical Education Standards: Elementary Volume.* (2003). Stock No. 304-10265.
- *Beyond Activities: Learning Experiences to Support the National Physical Education Standards: Secondary Volume.* (2003). Stock No. 304-10268.
- *Physical Activity for Children: A Statement of Guidelines for Children Ages 5–12.* (2003). Stock No. 204-10276.
- *Active Start: A Statement of Physical Activity Guidelines for Children From Birth to Five Years.* (2009). Stock No. 304-10488.

Appropriate Practice Documents

- *Appropriate Practices in Movement Programs for Children Ages 3–5.* (2009). Stock No. 304-10487.
- *Appropriate Instructional Practice Guidelines for Elementary School Physical Education.* (2009). Stock No. 304-10465.
- *Appropriate Instructional Practice Guidelines for Middle School Physical Education.* (2009). Stock No. 304-10464.
- *Appropriate Instructional Practice Guidelines for High School Physical Education.* (2009). Stock No. 304-10471.
- *Appropriate Instructional Practice Guidelines for High Education Physical Activity Programs.* (2009). Stock No. 304-10489.

Opportunity to Learn Documents

- *Opportunity to Learn Standards for Elementary Physical Education.* (2009). Stock No. 304-10484.
- *Opportunity to Learn Standards for Middle Physical Education.* (2009). Stock No. 304-10485.
- *Opportunity to Learn Standards for High School Physical Education.* (2009). Stock No. 304-10486.

Assessment Series

Assorted titles relating to fitness and heart rate.

PHYSICAL BEST CERTIFICATION

Physical Best provides accurate, up-to-date information and training to help today's physical educator create a conceptual and integrated format for health-related fitness education within their programs. NASPE-AAHPERD offers a certification program that allows physical education teachers to become a Physical Best Specialist. The Physical Best certification has been created specifically for the purpose of updating physical educators on the most effective strategies for helping their students gain the knowledge, skills, appreciation, and confidence needed to lead physically active, healthy lives. The program focuses on application—how to teach fitness concepts through developmentally and age-appropriate activities.

To earn certification as a Physical Best Health-Fitness Specialist, you will need to do the following:

- Attend the one-day Physical Best Health Fitness Specialist workshop.
- Read this book, *Physical Education for Lifelong Fitness: The Physical Best Teacher's Guide, Third Edition*, and *Fitnessgram/Activitygram Test Administration Manual, Fifth Edition*.
- Use the required resources to complete an online exam.

For more information, call Physical Best at 800-213-7193.

ACKNOWLEDGMENTS

Many educators contributed their time and expertise to this project. Besides being grateful for the overall guidance of the Physical Best Steering Committee, we especially want to thank Christina Sinclair and Jeff Carpenter for their roles in this revision.

The following individuals contributed new activities or significant editorial input to this edition.

Second Edition Contributors

Melissa Black, Ohio

Jeff Carpenter, Washington

Charles Corbin, Arizona

Darren Dale, Connecticut

Paul Darst, Arizona

Gary Feltman, Illinois

Marian Franck, Maryland

Jennie Gilbert, Illinois

Linda Hilgenbrinck, Illinois

Jill Humann, New Jersey

John Kading, Wisconsin

Margaret Kading, Wisconsin

Melody Kyzer, North Carolina

Judy Jagger-Mescher, Ohio

Nila Ledford, Maryland

Guy LeMasurier, Pennsylvania

Ray Martinez, Wisconsin

Carolyn Masterson, New Jersey

Karen McConnell, Washington

Jennifer Melnick, Maryland

Margie Miller, Missouri

Cindy Mitchell, Washington

Cynthia Naylor, Maryland

Kevin O'Brien, Ohio

Sarajane Quinn, Maryland

Mary Jo Sariscsany, California

Hosung So, California

Belinda Stillwell, California

Kathleen Thornton, Maryland

Linda Webbert, Maryland

Christopher Wunder, Maryland

Elizabeth Zinkand, Maryland

Third Edition Contributors

Robyn Bretzing, Utah

Mary Buddemeier, Maryland

Debbie Buenger, Maryland

Cathy Crabb, Washington

Hal Cramer, Maryland

Steffanie Engle, Maryland

Jill Goldman, New Jersey

Crystal Gorwitz, Wisconsin

Libby Leventry, Maryland

Maria Macarle, New York

Beth Marchione, Pennsylvania

Sally Nazelrod, Maryland

John Perna, Pennsylvania

Scott Ronspies, Illinois

Kelly Schattall, Maryland

Christina Sinclair, Colorado

Sheri Treadwell, Colorado

Pamela Williams, Colorado

Susan Wunder, Maryland

We would also like to thank the many anonymous contributors who gave their time and effort to this work.

Introduction

Galina Barskaya

OVERVIEW OF THE PRESIDENTIAL YOUTH FITNESS PROGRAM

The Presidential Youth Fitness Program (PYFP) is a voluntary program that includes a health-related assessment, as well as educational and motivational tools, to support educators and empower students to adopt an active lifestyle.

Launched in September 2012, PYFP offers a comprehensive school-based program that promotes physical activity and fitness for improving the health of America's young people.

PYFP is built around three pillars:

1. Professional development and education
2. Assessment
3. Recognition and awards

Although seemingly separate in nature, these pillars are linked by the expertise and contributions of the program's partners and their collective interest in equipping physical educators with the materials and information they need to deliver a high-quality, beneficial health-related fitness education experience to their students.

PYFP is built from a partnership of five organizations: American Alliance for Health, Physical Education, Recreation and Dance; Amateur Athletic Union; Centers for Disease Control and Prevention; The Cooper Institute; and President's Council on Fitness, Sports and Nutrition. These organizations came together with a goal to provide one national youth fitness test that focuses on health and equips educators with the resources and knowledge necessary for helping their students lead active lives.

The Three Pillars

Here is a closer look at the program's three pillars.

1. Professional development. PYFP will equip educators with the knowledge and tools required for implementing a high-quality fitness education experience for students and for promoting and engaging them in physical activity regardless of a school's physical education budget. That includes integrating elements of the Physical Best program, with access to resources to support the successful teaching of health-related fitness. Online and in-person training opportunities are available at www.presidentialyouthfitnessprogram.org.

2. Assessment. FITNESSGRAM® is the adopted assessment of PYFP. Developed in the early 1980s by The Cooper Institute, Fitnessgram includes a variety of health-related physical fitness assessments of aerobic capacity, muscle strength, muscle endurance and flexibility, and body composition. Scores from these assessments are compared to Healthy Fitness Zone® standards to determine students' overall physical fitness and to suggest areas for improvement when appropriate. Using Fitnessgram keeps the focus of fitness assessment on promoting and improving personal health rather than performance and athletic ability.

3. Recognition and awards. Providing an opportunity to recognize students for reaching personal fitness goals and physical activity behaviors is the final pillar of the Presidential Youth Fitness Program. Students who reach the Healthy Fitness Zone on at least five test items are eligible for the Presidential Youth Fitness Award. Understanding how to use recognition in a responsible manner that includes all students is a key part of the professional-development package. In addition, schools have the opportunity to be recognized for creating an environment that supports PYFP and physical activity, in general, as described through the development of comprehensive school physical activity plans (visit www.aahperd.org/cspap).

The three areas around which the program is built come together to provide a robust experience for teachers and their students.

Physical Best and the PYFP

Physical Best, including the teacher's guide and activity guides, complements PYFP's mission by providing the how and why of teaching health-related physical activity and fitness-enhancing skills and behaviors. The program's partners seek to provide a fun and beneficial experience for all youths, regardless of ability or health status.

This activity guide includes a variety of activities that can count toward a student's daily physical activity and, therefore, set him or her on a path to earning a Presidential Active Lifestyle Award (PALA+), one of the awards that make up the PYFP recognition pillar. The Physical Best Teacher's Guide provides more guidance and information on using the Presidential Youth Fitness Award.

For the latest resources and information on the Presidential Youth Fitness Program, visit www.presidentialyouthfitnessprogram.org.

Teaching Health-Related Fitness to Middle and High School Students

Chapter Contents

For foundation in teaching health-related fitness activities, we look first to national standards. Many of the national standards that have been developed for physical education, health, and dance can be applied to teaching health-related fitness activities. In the first part of this chapter, we list the national standards from these areas and emphasize the standards that are addressed most often when teaching health-related fitness.

The chapter ends with a brief summary of how Physical Best can be incorporated into a physical education curriculum at the middle and high school levels and a detailed look at the Physical Best activity template. All the activities in this book follow this template, and the explanations provided in this chapter will help you choose the right activity for a particular group of students. You can also use this template as a guide for developing your own activities.

NATIONAL STANDARDS FOR PHYSICAL EDUCATION

The national standards for physical education are based on the definition of the physically educated person as defined in *Outcomes of Quality Physical Education Programs* (NASPE, 1992). According to this document, a physically educated person

- ▶ has learned skills necessary to perform a variety of physical activities,
- ▶ is physically fit,
- ▶ participates regularly in physical activity,
- ▶ knows the implications of and the benefits from involvement in physical activities, and
- ▶ values physical activity and its contributions to a healthful lifestyle.

NASPE intended that all five parts of the definition "not be separated from each other" (NASPE, 1992, p. 6). The definition was further delineated into 20 outcome statements. The definition and outcome statements were used as the basis for the development of the national standards for physical education, originally published by NASPE in 1995 and revised in 2004. The standards define what a student should know and be able to do as a result of a quality physical education program.

NATIONAL STANDARDS FOR PHYSICAL EDUCATION

Physical activity is critical to the development and maintenance of good health. The goal of physical education is to develop physically educated people who have the knowledge, skills, and confidence to enjoy a lifetime of healthful physical activity. A physically educated person observes these standards:

- **Standard 1**: Demonstrates competency in motor skills and movement patterns needed to perform a variety of physical activities
- **Standard 2**: Demonstrates understanding of movement concepts, principles, strategies, and tactics as they apply to the learning and performance of physical activities
- **Standard 3**: Participates regularly in physical activity
- **Standard 4**: Achieves and maintains a health-enhancing level of physical fitness
- **Standard 5**: Exhibits responsible personal and social behavior that respects self and others in physical activity settings
- **Standard 6**: Values physical activity for health, enjoyment, challenge, self-expression, and/or social interaction

From *Moving into the future: National standards for physical education* (2004) from the National Association for Sport and Physical Education (NASPE), 1900 Association Drive, Reston, VA 20191-1599.

So, although all physical education standards are taught to some extent through and during health-related fitness education, two standards are most emphasized:

- ▶ **Standard 3**: Participates regularly in physical activity
- ▶ **Standard 4**: Achieves and maintains a health-enhancing level of physical fitness

Integrating the national standards in physical education, health, and dance provides an important way to promote the effects of physical activity on health and an individual's personal choice to be physically active. None of these disciplines stands alone. Few student groups are focused on just one purpose, whether in health, competition, or aesthetics. Although some students have a greater interest in or a more facile learning style for one of these areas, all youngsters benefit from learning and applying these standards. The recognition of these interdisciplinary links helps us maximize our energies for teaching and learning essential content of all three disciplines.

NATIONAL HEALTH EDUCATION STANDARDS

The national health education standards (Joint Committee on National Health Education Standards, 1995) are linked to the physical education standards. Health education affords unique knowledge about health, preventing disease,

and reducing risk factors in all situations and settings—and it helps to influence behaviors that promote these aims.

Such behaviors include not only physical activity but also other areas of personal, family, and community life. Health standards 1, 3, and 6 are most closely related to fitness education.

> ▶ **Standard 1**: Students will comprehend concepts related to health promotion and disease prevention.
> ▶ **Standard 3**: Students will demonstrate the ability to practice health-enhancing behaviors and reduce health risks.
> ▶ **Standard 6**: Students will demonstrate the ability to use goal-setting and decision-making skills to enhance health.

NATIONAL STANDARDS FOR DANCE EDUCATION

The national standards for dance education (NDA, 1996) are also linked to physical education. Dance is both a movement form (as are sports, aquatics, fitness activities, and outdoor recreational activities) and a form of physical activity that provides health and fitness benefits. Its uniqueness as a physical activity is that it is also an art form, affording opportunities to create, communicate meaning, and interpret cultural issues and historical periods. Standard 6 is of primary importance in health-related fitness education. See all of the dance standards in the sidebar on page 6.

> ▶ **Standard 6**: Makes connections between dance and healthful living

INTEGRATING PHYSICAL BEST INTO THE MIDDLE AND HIGH SCHOOL PHYSICAL EDUCATION CURRICULUM

The *Physical Best Activity Guide: Middle and High School Levels, Third Edition* is more than a compilation of activities to use with students during their physical education classes. It is designed to help physical education teachers better instruct

---

NATIONAL HEALTH EDUCATION STANDARDS

- **Standard 1**: Students will comprehend concepts related to health promotion and disease prevention.
- **Standard 2**: Students will demonstrate the ability to access valid health information and health-promoting products and services.
- **Standard 3**: Students will demonstrate the ability to practice health-enhancing behaviors and reduce health risks.
- **Standard 4**: Students will analyze the influence of culture, media, technology, and other factors on health.
- **Standard 5**: Students will demonstrate the ability to use interpersonal communication skills to enhance health.
- **Standard 6**: Students will demonstrate the ability to use goal-setting and decision-making skills to enhance health.
- **Standard 7**: Students will demonstrate the ability to advocate for personal, family, and community health.

From *Achieving health literacy: National health education standards* (1995) from the American Alliance for Health, Physical Education, Recreation and Dance (AAHPERD), 1900 Association Drive, Reston, VA 20191-1599.

NATIONAL STANDARDS FOR DANCE EDUCATION

What every young American should know and be able to do in dance:

- **Standard 1**: Identifies and demonstrates movement elements and skills in performing dance
- **Standard 2**: Understands choreographic principles, processes, and structures
- **Standard 3**: Understands dance as a way to create and communicate meaning
- **Standard 4**: Applies and demonstrates critical and creative thinking skills in dance
- **Standard 5**: Demonstrates and understands dance in various cultures and historical periods
- **Standard 6**: Makes connections between dance and healthful living
- **Standard 7**: Makes connections between dance and other disciplines

From the National Standards for Arts Education and the National Dance Association (NDA), an association of the American Alliance for Health, Physical Education, Recreation and Dance. The source of the National Dance Standards (*National Standards for Dance Education: What Every Young American Should Know and Be Able to Do in Dance*) may be purchased from the National Dance Association, 1900 Association Drive, Reston, VA 20191-1599, or 703-476-3421.

students, throughout the grade 6 through 12 physical education curriculum, about being physically fit and physically active for a lifetime. The activities build on the elementary-level book by reinforcing health-related fitness behaviors and concepts. Middle and high school students also learn skills, strategies, and behaviors to assume responsibility for their own physical fitness and to attain lifetime fitness.

Physical Best activities vary in length of time required to complete and can further vary depending on such aspects as class size and modifications that may be needed for the particular classroom environment. Because the activities vary in length, you can combine several activities to create one lesson, or you can incorporate individual activities into other lesson plans and units. Students participate in activities that are

fun, engaging, and purposeful, and at the same time they learn about the principles of training, the components of health-related fitness, and the importance of being physically active.

Providing inclusive programs requires your gaining the necessary knowledge and skills to include people with disabilities, being accountable for a positive attitude, ensuring equal treatment across all lines of diversity, and effectively communicating, both verbally and nonverbally. As the professional conducting the program, the teacher is responsible for successfully including all participants. Modifications and accommodations are often made based on students' needs and ability. Addressing the needs of all students can often be difficult. Motivating students of varying ability, enhancing skill development, and enabling all students to participate and maintain similar levels of activity is a common goal for teachers. Modifying the equipment, boundaries, rules, and instructions are things that teachers can do to help and support students with disabilities. To ensure a successful educational environment, teachers look for simple, quick solutions that can help a diverse student population. Making accommodations as well as practicing the activity ensures such success. Refer to the sidebar "Tips for Inclusion" on page 7. Reproducibles on the CD-ROM provide visual aids and extensions of the activities to help students better understand the concepts taught. Finally, students begin to develop strategies and design activities that make them healthier yet correspond to their particular needs and interests.

Practicing the Fitnessgram assessments and the Physical Best activities throughout the year helps students learn about their physical fitness levels and what it takes to become healthier. Moreover, the Physical Best program instructs teachers to involve students in physical activity outside of school.

PHYSICAL BEST ACTIVITY TEMPLATE

Activities that help students learn while doing are the most successful for teaching lifelong fitness. The *Physical Best Activity Guides* provide a wealth of activities designed specifically to help students

TIPS FOR INCLUSION

- Review the activity and determine the student's needs.
- Focus on the student's abilities, not the disability.
- Adapt the game to the individual, not the individual to the game.
- Allow all students to move freely with minimal assistance.
- Equipment—Modify equipment according to the student's abilities:
  - Vary the ball size, texture, and color according to the student's needs.
  - Attach a cord to balls and other objects so that students with mobility problems and coordination issues can retrieve these objects independently.
  - Use larger striking implements that have a broader contact surface.
  - Use lower goals, targets, platforms, and so forth.
  - Use a larger target space or larger goals.
  - Attach Velcro to an extension so that students in wheelchairs can reach independently for objects located on the floor.
  - Place objects—balls, cards, and so on—at a height so that students can reach them if they have difficulty bending over (poor balance) or if they are in wheelchairs.
  - Jump ropes—Jump ropes can be used individually or in groups of threes. Another adaptation is to cut or fold jump ropes in half for students with ambulatory concerns.
  - Scooter activities—Use long scooters for students who are not ambulatory and need to be placed on their abdomens. To create a long scooter, tie two scooters together to make a larger scooter surface. You can also use some type of trunk support attachment for students who need help using a seated position.
  - During parachute activities, attach an elastic cord from a wheelchair to a parachute so that the student in the wheelchair is attached to the activity but can move freely.
  - Attach some type of carrier (backpack or bag) to a wheelchair for students to place objects in so that their hands are free to manipulate the wheelchair for movement.
  - Hula hoops—Cut hula hoops in half so that students in wheelchairs and students using walkers can move into hula hoops when asked to do so during movement activities.
- Boundaries:
  - Mark the boundaries of the area and adjust when necessary by decreasing distance or simplifying patterns within the area.
  - Use some type of beeper to mark the boundaries for students with visual impairments so that they can move freely through space during activities.
  - Remove obstacles from the area.
- Rules—Adapt the rules so that the game or activity is challenging but still allows the student an opportunity for success:
  - Allow the ball to stay stationary.
  - Don't set time limits.
  - Provide partner assistance.
  - Adjust distance as needed.
  - Allow students extra turns to accomplish the task.
- Prompts
  - Use picture communication symbols (PCS) to set up a schedule of the class activities in the gym. This method will help students transition from one activity to another.
  - Try to avoid overloading your students with too much challenge or too much language.
  - Use picture communication symbols (PCS) to support verbal directions.
  - Demonstrate or model the activity when giving verbal directions.
  - Use visual, verbal, and physical prompts together if needed.
  - Try to use one- or two-step directions. Keep it simple!

learn through doing. These activities provide a great start to developing an excellent program, but you'll want to add more activities especially suited for your students.

Following is a step-by-step explanation of the Physical Best activity template, which can also serve as a guide for developing your own activities.

- **Level**—Carefully consider the level of the students for whom you are developing the activity. You can easily modify many activities up or down for students of varying ages and abilities.

- **Concept**—The activity teaches one or more concepts, written in language appropriate to the level of the students. Physical Best includes activities for defining the component of fitness and teaching the health benefits for that component, warm-ups and cool-downs, the FITT guidelines, and progression and overload. (Chapters 8 through 10 follow a slightly different format but still list the concept or concepts taught.)

- **Purpose**—This component of the template states the student-centered objectives, describing what you want the students to learn.

- **Relationship to National Standards**—This component explains which of the national standards in physical education, health education, and dance education the activity addresses.

- **Equipment**—This component lists everything needed to conduct the activity.

- **Reproducible**—This section lists what can be found on the accompanying CD-ROM to support the activity. These are usually charts, signs, task cards, student worksheets, and so forth. You are encouraged to print out the reproducibles that appear on the CD-ROM. They are created for letter-sized paper but can be enlarged according to your needs. Each is labeled by activity number and reproducible title to help you keep them organized.

- **Procedure**—This component lists steps to conduct the activity, including an introduc-

tion (called set-induction in the first edition), activity steps and directions, and closure.

- **Teaching Hints**—This component of the template offers ideas for variations, extensions, increases or decreases in level (for example, notes about intensity, ability groupings, and challenges), safety tips, and other ideas for effectively teaching the activity.

- **Sample Inclusion Tips**—This component offers one or more tips for adapting the activity to meet the needs of students with varying abilities and health concerns. Note that a tip for one activity may be useful for other activities. Consider modifying your environment, equipment, rules, boundaries, and instructional cues when developing a lesson plan. Refer to the sidebar "Tips for Inclusion" on page 7.

- **Variations**—Variations provide the teacher with other options when teaching this information.

- **Home Extension**—This extension of the lesson provides students with information that will help them continue the activity at home and in other nonschool environments.

- **Assessment**—This component explains how you or the students will know that they have learned the information stated in the purpose. Assessment may include teacher discussion, student feedback and review, homework assignments, and so on.

SUMMARY

When you use Physical Best, you are teaching the applicable standards through activity in an age-appropriate and sequential manner. Using the activity template will ensure that your activities are educational and easy to administer. Choose activities that fit into your lesson plans, and you will teach and reinforce important fitness concepts throughout the year. Most important, these activities have been developed by physical educators for physical educators, and so they have been tested in the real world to ensure that they not only teach the concepts but also allow your students to have fun while performing physical activity.

Introduction to Health-Related Fitness Concepts

This chapter introduces the principles of health-related fitness education. An introduction to the components of health-related fitness found at the beginning of each chapter in part II serves as a quick reference when teaching the activities in that chapter. For in-depth study and explanation of these concepts, as well as other components of total fitness, refer to *Physical Education for Lifelong Fitness: The Physical Best Teacher's Guide, Third Edition*. The new edition includes several new concepts that differ from those in the previous edition, especially in the chapter on aerobic fitness. Figure 2.1 illustrates the relationship between the health- and skill-related components of fitness as well as the various actions that can be taken to enhance each of these components. Through Physical Best activities, students will gain in-depth knowledge about the various health- and skill-related components of fitness and ways in which to enhance these areas through hands-on experiences that emphasize the use of the various fitness principles.

HEALTH-RELATED FITNESS

In teaching health-related fitness, we should not lose sight of the importance of physical activity and the development of fun activities that encourage children to be active. Physical Best has consistently emphasized the development of physical fitness as a lifelong process of having an active lifestyle rather than actually being physically fit or attaining a particular performance outcome. The focus of our lessons should be on reinforcing basic concepts and skills ideally taught at the secondary level, and emphasizing the value of physical activity so that students will be competent to participate in activities now and in the future.

Research points to three main reasons that children participate in leisure-time activity and sports (Weiss, 2000):

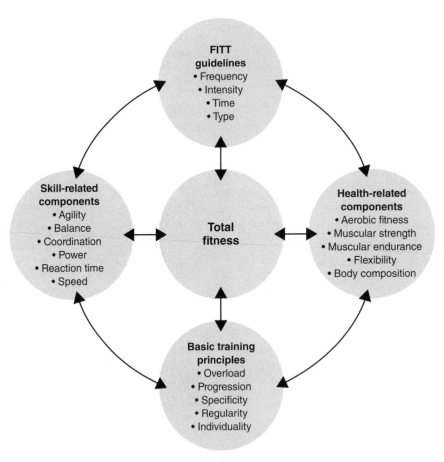

Figure 2.1 This figure shows how the components and principles of physical fitness work together. It is also available as a reproducible, Building Physical Fitness, on the CD-ROM.

▶ The development and demonstration of physical competence (athletic skills, fitness, physical appearance)

▶ Social acceptance and support from friends, peers, and significant adults

▶ Participation in fun activities that promote positive experiences

Many students with disabilities require a structured program of fitness, like Physical Best, to reduce secondary conditions so that they can maintain functional independence, to provide an opportunity for leisure and enjoyment, and to enhance the overall quality of life by reducing environmental barriers to good health. Including all your students should not be an afterthought, but an important part of your planning and teaching process. Although not every student can equally benefit from, or even participate in, every activity, including everyone in your health-related fitness program isn't just a good idea—it's the law.

As you use the Physical Best materials, keep the following definitions in mind to assist you in motivating your students to become physically active, thereby initiating the long path to lifetime fitness and associated health benefits. *Physical fitness* is defined as a set of attributes that people have or achieve relating to their ability to perform physical activity, whereas *physical activity* is defined as any bodily movement produced by muscle contraction that increases energy expenditure (USDHHS, 1996; NASPE, 2004b). Because motivation for adolescents to be physically active does not come from knowing and appreciating the health benefits of increased activity, you should impress on students that being physically active enables them to have more energy for leisure activities.

Principles of Training

The *overload principle* states that a body system must perform at a level beyond normal to adapt and improve physiological function and fitness. You can increase the overload by manipulating the frequency, intensity, or duration (time) of an activity. To explain overload to adolescents, let them experience it firsthand by keeping track of the number of minutes they can sustain an activity or how many repetitions they can perform. You can use a backpack with books or weights and monitor heart rate without the backpack and then with the backpack, explaining how the body will adapt to the heavy load and later be able to do the same load with less effort.

Progression refers to *how* a person should increase the overload. The person should gradually increase the level of exercise by manipulating the frequency, intensity, time, or a combination of all three exercise components. Students should understand that improving their level of fitness is an ongoing process.

Emphasize that all progression must be gradual to be safe. If the overload is applied too soon, the body does not have time to adapt and the benefits may be delayed or an injury may occur. Either result can discourage or prevent a child from participating. For example, a student may progress from performing a reverse curl-up, in which he or she focuses on lowering the body, and work toward performing a regular curl-up. The same strategy works well with push-ups. The student first focuses on the lowering phase. As the student progresses he or she will gain strength to perform the complete push-up. The objective is to challenge students but also create opportunity for success.

To help them understand progression and see that they are improving, give adolescents opportunities to track their progress by keeping a journal. You can also help them understand progression by using pretests and posttests.

Specificity states that explicit activities targeting a particular body system must be performed to bring about fitness changes in that area. For example, you must perform aerobic activities that stress the cardiorespiratory system if you want to improve aerobic fitness. This principle applies to all areas of health-related and skill-related fitness, and it applies within a single area of fitness. For example, performing a biceps curl will increase the strength of the biceps muscle but will have no effect on the leg muscles.

The premise behind the *regularity principle* is based on the old adage "Use it or lose it." We lose any fitness gains attained through physical activity if we do not continue to be active. Recognize that the body needs limited recovery time between bouts of exercise. Too little recovery time may lead to injury or overtraining, and too much time between activity sessions can lead to detraining, or loss of the acquired benefits of physical activity and fitness. The recommended time of recovery also varies by area of health-related fitness. For example, the American College of Sports Medicine (ACSM) recommends three alternate days per week for strength and endurance activities, whereas daily activity is best for improving flexibility. Likewise, the minimum frequency for aerobic improvement is three days per week, and for aerobic activity five to seven days per week is optimal. Try to emphasize consistency in activity. Unless you are coaching athletes, do not stress training and conditioning. Remember that recommendations for children's physical activity include daily activity, a recommendation different from that of the traditional ACSM adult model.

The *individuality principle* takes into account that each person begins at a different level of fitness, has personal goals and objectives for physical activity and fitness, and has different genetic potential for change. Although changes in children's physiological responses to training and conditioning are often difficult to measure because of confounding changes associated with normal growth and maturation, recognize that students in your classes will respond differently to the activities that you prepare for class. Some will improve, but some will not. Some will enjoy the activities, and others will not. Your job is to provide plenty of choice in your classroom, taking into account each student's initial fitness level and personal goals.

A reproducible sign of the principles are available on the CD-ROM that you can hang to remind students of these principles (see figure 2.2).

FITT Guidelines

Physical Best activities apply the FITT guidelines to improve health and fitness (see figure 2.3). The acronym *FITT* describes the frequency (how often), the intensity (how hard), the time (how long), and the type (what kind) of activity necessary for improving and maintaining fitness. The FITT guidelines also provide the recipe for safely applying the previously described principles of training. Refer to *Physical Education for Lifelong Fitness: The Physical Best Teacher's Guide, Third Edition* for detailed explanations of the FITT guidelines and new recommendations concerning their use with students.

Figure 2.2   Principles of Training.

Figure 2.3   FITT Guidelines. A reproducible version of the FITT guidelines is available on the CD-ROM.

The Activity Session

Whether you are teaching kindergarteners or high school seniors, share the purpose of the lesson and how the day's activity will help students reach class goals or personalized goals. Every activity should incorporate a systematic approach to ensure safety and prepare the body for the rigors of the workout. The main physical activity must also be developmentally appropriate for students to feel and understand, through participation, the importance of being physically active. Incorporate cool-down time and use it to review and assess learning.

SUMMARY

Give middle and high school students a variety of activities to choose from and allow them the opportunity to engage in and appreciate the value of physical activity both now and in the future. Keep in mind that fitness is a journey, not a destination, and that the goal is to progress toward self-assessment and self-delivery of health-related fitness activities. Are you and your students ready for the fun of leading a physically active life? If so, move on to the activities that follow.

PART II

Activities

Franz Pfluegl

Aerobic Fitness

Chapter Contents

The goal of any quality health and fitness education program is to present information that leads to the development of lifelong learners who appreciate and participate in physical activity, both now and in the future. If students understand why these activities are important and how they will benefit from physical activity, they are more likely to take responsibility for becoming physically educated people.

At the middle and high school levels, we begin to teach and incorporate the adult exercise prescription model in our lessons. At the same time, we do not lose sight of implementing developmentally appropriate skill development and enjoyable activities designed to provide a comprehensive instructional program that enhances the quality and productivity of every student's life through physical education.

DEFINING AEROBIC FITNESS

Aerobic fitness is the "ability to perform large muscle, dynamic, moderate to high intensity exercise for prolonged periods" (ACSM, 2000, p. 68). Many field tests are available to assess aerobic fitness. Physical Best endorses Fitnessgram (Cooper Institute, 2004). The Brockport Test (Winnick & Short, 1999) may be used with students with disabilities.

Many health benefits are associated with physical activity (USDHHS, 1996; Blair et al., 1995; Boreham et al. 1997, 2001). A recent report by Roberts et al. (2009) suggests that physically active and fit students do better academically and therefore that spending more time in physical education not only does not hurt but may help academic performance. To enhance understanding, you must connect the benefits to something that students can relate to and experience personally and immediately (such as having more energy). The following are potential health benefits of physical activity:

- Strengthens the heart (lower resting and working heart rate, faster recovery)
- Decreases blood pressure
- Strengthens muscles and bones
- Increases energy (for work or leisure activity)
- Allows performance of more work with less effort (get through the day without becoming tired)

- Reduces stress and tension (get along better with others)
- Enhances appearance and feeling of well-being; improves quality of life
- Improves ability to learn (get homework done faster)
- Promotes healthy body composition
- Increases self-confidence and self-esteem (greater social opportunities)
- Enhances sleep
- Improves lipid profile (increases HDL [good cholesterol], decreases triglycerides)
- Helps weight control

TEACHING GUIDELINES FOR AEROBIC FITNESS

Remember that we are not training and conditioning our students to be high-performing athletes; rather, we are providing the knowledge and skills necessary to participate in healthy and active lifestyles while instilling the importance of physical activity across the lifespan. Ultimately, if students increase physical activity patterns (the process), then fitness (the product) will follow. We must also remember that young people lose interest in activity if it is not fun. Xiang, McBride, Guan, and Solomon (2003) suggested, "When learning tasks are perceived as interesting, relevant, and meaningful, providing opportunities for success, and enhancing ability, students will be motivated to engage in them." Use the following guidelines to help create opportunities for your students to achieve their Physical Best.

- Teach fitness concepts through physical activity, minimizing classroom lessons in which students are inactive.
- Encourage students to use material presented in class and gained from outside readings and to make practical applications of the concepts to their personal lives.
- Circuit or station activities provide excellent opportunities to challenge students independently, refine motor skills, and develop health-related fitness. Keep your groups small, no larger than five at a station.
- Activities for middle and high school students should include challenges, decision-

making skills, and team-building skills. This approach will help them begin to develop and personalize their own fitness programs, recognizing the effect that physical activity has across the lifespan.

Unlike students at the elementary level, where the use of target heart rates is inappropriate, students at the middle and high school level should develop the skills to calculate target heart zones and incorporate them into a personalized fitness program. Expect most students in seventh grade and up to calculate target heart rate values, but avoid requiring the use of target heart rate zones for participation in physical activity in middle school or junior high. A detailed explanation of the use of target heart rate zones in children appears in chapter 5, "Aerobic Fitness," in the *Physical Education for Lifelong Fitness: Physical Best Teacher's Guide, Third Edition*. The explanation focuses on the fact that adolescents' maximal heart rates are age independent (Rowland, 1996), and the traditional target heart rate calculation will not yield the appropriate heart rate required

for training and conditioning to gain aerobic fitness.

Also note that the formula for calculating maximal heart rate has changed. Although the old formula, the heart rate max method, was simple to use, it generally overpredicted maximal heart rate (MHR) in those 20 to 40 years of age and underpredicted MHR in those over 40 years of age (Tanaka, Monahan, & Seals, 2001). Although students fall outside the age ranges of overprediction and underprediction of MHR using the old formula, the Karvonen method formula, MHR = 208 − (.7 × age), is recommended.

Table 3.1 provides information on applying the FITT guidelines for adolescents (age 11 and older) and older youth participating in athletics.

TRAINING METHODS FOR AEROBIC FITNESS

The three main training methods for developing and maintaining aerobic fitness are continuous training, interval training, and circuit training.

Table 3.1 FITT Guidelines Applied to Aerobic Fitness

	Adolescents (11 years old and older)[a]	Middle and high school youth who participate in athletics[b]
Frequency	• Daily or nearly every day • Three or more sessions per week	5 or 6 days per week
Intensity	• Moderate to vigorous activity; maintaining a target heart rate is not expected at this level • Rating of perceived exertion: 7–10 (Borg)[c], 1–3 (OMNI)[d]	• 60–90% heart rate max (HR max) or 50–85% heart rate reserve (HRR) • Rating of perceived exertion: 12–16 (Borg), 5–7 (OMNI)
Time	• 30–60 minutes daily activity • 20 minutes or more in a single session	20–60 minutes
Type	• Play, games, sports, work, transportation, recreation, physical education, or planned exercise in the context of family, school, and community activities • Brisk walking, jogging, stair climbing, basketball, racket sports, soccer, dance, lap swimming, skating, lawn mowing, and cycling	Activities that use large muscles and are used in a rhythmical fashion (e.g., brisk walking, jogging, stair climbing, basketball, racket sports, soccer, dance, lap swimming, skating, and cycling)

[a]Corbin, C.B., and Pangrazi, R.P. (2002). *Physical activity for children: How much is enough?* In G.J. Welk, R.J. Morrow, and H.B. Falls (Eds.), *FITNESSGRAM reference guide* (p. 7 Internet Resource). Dallas, TX: Cooper Institute.

[b]American College of Sports Medicine (ACSM). 2009. *ACSM's resource manual for guidelines for exercise testing and prescription*, 6th ed. Philadelphia: Lippincott, Williams, and Wilkins.

[c]Borg, G. (1998). *Borg's perceived exertion and pain scales* (Champaign, IL: Human Kinetics), 47.

[d]Robertson, R.J. (2004). *Perceived exertion for practitioners: Rating effort with the OMNI pictures system* (Champaign, IL: Human Kinetics), 141-150.

From Corbin and Pangrazi 2002; American College of Sports Medicine 2000; Borg 1998.

▶ *Continuous training* is the same activity performed over an extended period. Use caution with this type of activity, because it can become boring and deter students from physical activity rather than promote physical activity. *Fartlek,* a modification of continuous training, intersperses periods of increased intensity with continuous activity over varying natural terrain. This type of activity can be modified and used at all grade levels, but to avoid the training aspect used in coaching cross country, allow the students to vary the intensity of some segments.

▶ *Interval training* involves alternating short bursts of activity with rest periods. Use caution and build variety and skill into the intervals that you develop. Do not treat this activity as a practice session for track and field.

▶ *Circuit training* involves several different activities, allowing you to vary the intensity or type of activity as students move from station to station. It is an excellent method for creating variety and stimulating student motivation. Students at the middle and high school level may enjoy developing stations and circuit-training activities.

Youth Physical Activity Guidelines for Aerobic Fitness

Children and adolescents ages 6 to 17 should have at least 60 minutes of physical activity daily. More specifically, most of the 60 or more minutes a day should be either moderate- or vigorous-intensity aerobic physical activity and should include vigorous-intensity physical activity at least 3 days a week. The intensity of aerobic fitness activity can be defined and monitored on either an absolute or a relative scale.

▶ **Absolute intensity** is based on the rate of energy expenditure during the activity, without taking into account a person's aerobic fitness.

▶ **Relative intensity** uses a person's level of aerobic fitness to assess level of effort.

Relative intensity is a person's level of effort relative to his or her fitness. On a scale of 0 to 10, where sitting is 0 and the highest level of effort possible is 10, moderate-intensity activity is a 5 or 6. Young people doing moderate-intensity activ-

ity will notice that their hearts are beating faster than normal and that they are breathing harder than normal. Vigorous-intensity activity is at a level of 7 or 8. Youth doing vigorous-intensity activity will feel their hearts beating much faster than normal, and they will breathe much harder than normal. Table 3.2 includes examples of activities classified by absolute intensity. It shows that the same activity can be moderate or vigorous intensity, depending on factors like speed, such as bicycling slowly or fast (U.S. Department of Health and Human Services, 2008).

MOTOR-SKILL DEVELOPMENT THROUGH AEROBIC FITNESS

Teaching skill-based activities is extremely important in reaching the goal of developing lifelong physical activity habits. These skills must be incorporated into a comprehensive program that includes, for example, individual or dual sports, team sports, a variety of recreational activities designed to meet students' needs within a local community or region, dance, and activities designed simply to provide fun and enjoyment. Physical Best activities provide many opportunities to address motor-skill development during aerobic fitness activities. Motor-skill development through fitness activity is the perfect area for you to consider the abilities and limitations of all students. Some are high achievers, others are low achievers, and still others have physical or intellectual disabilities. Provide opportunities for all students to develop physical skills and be successful in your classroom. If a student is severely disabled, you may need to contact someone who specializes in adapted physical education for assistance in developing an individualized education plan.

As students become more active you will want to provide information to reduce the risk of injury that may lead to periods of inactivity. Offering this kind of instruction is especially important when students leave the structured physical education program and continue to be active after school or in the community.

Quality instructional programs should observe the following safety guidelines:

▶ Supervise the program closely and individualize the activity.

Table 3.2 Moderate- and Vigorous-Intensity Aerobic Physical Activities and Muscle- and Bone-Strengthening Activities for Children and Adolescents

Type of physical activity	Age group: Children	Age group: Adults
Moderate-intensity aerobic	• Active recreation, such as hiking, skateboarding, in-line skating • Bicycle riding • Brisk walking	• Active recreation, such as canoeing, hiking, skateboarding, in-line skating • Brisk walking • Bicycle riding (stationary or road bike) • Housework and yard work, such as sweeping or pushing a lawn mower • Games that require catching and throwing, such as baseball and softball
Vigorous-intensity aerobic	• Active games that involve running and chasing, such as tag • Bicycle riding • Jumping rope • Martial arts, such as karate • Running • Sports such as soccer, ice or field hockey, basketball, swimming, tennis • Cross-country skiing	• Active games that involve running and chasing, such as flag football • Bicycle riding • Jumping rope • Martial arts, such as karate • Running • Sports such as soccer, ice or field hockey, basketball, swimming, tennis • Vigorous dancing • Cross-country skiing
Muscle strengthening	• Games such as tug-of-war • Modified push-ups (with knees on the floor) • Resistance exercises using body weight or resistance bands • Rope or tree climbing • Curl-ups or crunches • Swinging on playground equipment/bars	• Games such as tug-of-war • Push-ups and pull-ups • Resistance exercises with exercise bands, weight machines, hand-held weights • Climbing wall • Curl-ups or crunches
Bone strengthening	• Games such as hopscotch • Hopping, skipping, jumping • Jumping rope • Running • Sports such as gymnastics, basketball, volleyball, tennis	• Hopping, skipping, jumping • Jumping rope • Running • Sports such as gymnastics, basketball, volleyball, tennis

Note: Some activities, such as bicycling, can be moderate or vigorous intensity, depending on level of effort (USDHHS, 2008).

▶ Explain rules clearly and insist that students follow them.

▶ Have students wear protective equipment and gear appropriate for the sport, including

  • proper shoes for the activity and

  • helmets for cycling and other sports that have a strong potential for head injuries.

▶ Obtain medical information concerning preexisting conditions.

▶ Minimize exposure to the sun and heat by using shaded space, by having students wear sunscreen and hats, and by encouraging students to wear light clothing in the heat.

▶ Recognize that exercise or activity on hot and humid days or cold days may increase

health risks. Young people have low tolerance to exercise under these conditions (Bar-Or & Malina, 1995) because they

  • have a large surface area per unit of mass,

  • sweat at a lower rate,

  • have high metabolic heat production, and

  • take longer to acclimate to hot environments.

▶ Recognize signs and symptoms of heat illness or cold injury and do what you can to lessen the health risk.

  • Provide plenty of cool water, shade, and rest periods, and reduce intensity of activity.

- Have students wear layered clothing and limit exposure to cold.
- When necessary, conduct class indoors to limit exposure to air pollution.

The preceding discussion of young people's environmental tolerance applies primarily to prepubescent students and to a lesser extent with pubescent and postpubescent students.

Physical Best provides you and your students with the knowledge, skills, values, and confidence to engage in physical activity now and in the future through enjoyable activities. See table 3.3 for a grid of activities in this chapter.

Table 3.3 Chapter 3 Activities Grid

Activity number	Activity title	Activity page	Concept	Middle school	High school	Reproducibles (on CD-ROM)
3.1	Clean Out Your Arteries	23	Health benefits	•		None
3.2	Aerobic Benefit Hunt	26	Health benefits	•		Aerobic Benefit Cards
						Aerobic Benefit Student Worksheet
3.3	Chart Your Heart Rate	28	Intensity		•	Chart Your Heart Rate Worksheet
3.4	Aerobic Fitness Is FITT	31	Intensity		•	Aerobic Fitness Worksheet
3.5	Fitting in Fitness	33	Frequency	•		Fitting in Fitness Sport Handouts
3.6	Heartbeat Stations	36	Intensity and time	•		Heartbeat Stations Scoresheet
3.7	Cross-Training Trio	38	Time and type	•	•	Aerobic Fitness: Cross-Training Benefits and Guidelines
						Aerobic Fitness: Cross-Training Activities Log
3.8	Continuous Relay	41	Intensity and time		•	Individual Workout Log
3.9	Mini Triathlon	44	Intensity and time	•	•	None
3.10	1,000 Reps	46	Growth and development	•	•	1,000 Reps and Seconds Chart
						Estimated Energy Expenditure for Common Activities Chart
3.11	Aerobic FITT Log	49	Progression	•	•	FITT Log
						FITT Log Worksheet

CLEAN OUT YOUR ARTERIES

MIDDLE SCHOOL

Health benefits—People can benefit in many ways from regular physical activity. Aerobic activity can help reduce the buildup of fat deposits in the arteries, promoting a healthy cardiovascular system and reducing the risk of cardiovascular disease.

Purpose

Students will develop an understanding of the relationship between physical activity and cardiovascular health.

Relationship to National Standards

▶ Physical education standard 4: Achieves and maintains a health-enhancing level of physical fitness.

▶ Health education standard 1: Students will comprehend concepts related to health promotion and disease prevention.

▶ Health education standard 3: Students will demonstrate the ability to practice health-enhancing behaviors and reduce health risks.

Equipment

▶ 4 hoops

▶ 8 cones

▶ 40 beanbags

▶ Student journals (if using second assessment tip)

Procedure

1. Divide the activity space into four quadrants. Place one hoop and two cones in each quadrant (see figure 3.1 on page 24) and place 10 beanbags in each hoop.

2. Divide the class into four teams. Students on team A compete against team B. Students on team C compete against team D. Assign each team to a quadrant and have teams play across (not diagonally) from each other.

3. Explain that each hoop represents an artery and each beanbag represents fat. The object of the game is for each team to clean the fat out of their team's artery through physical activity.

4. On the whistle, direct students to run from their positions, as shown in the diagram, to their artery (hoop) and pick up a fat (beanbag), run the fat (beanbag) to the opposing team's quadrant, and place the fat (beanbag) in the opposing team's artery (hoop). Students must run clockwise around the perimeter of the activity space (half of the gym is best if possible, for safety reasons), on the outside of the cones before they remove a new beanbag from their hoop.

5. After three to five minutes stop and count beanbags to see which team has the least amount of fat. The team that performed the most work will end up with the least amount of fat (beanbags) in their artery. Remind

Reproducible

None.

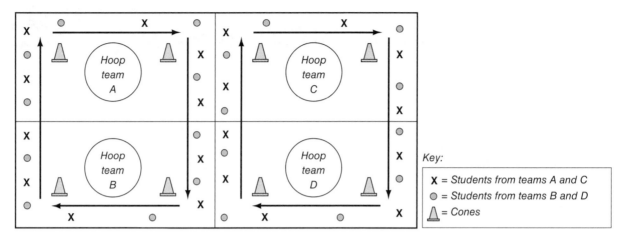

Figure 3.1 Floor setup for Clean Out Your Arteries.

students that physical activity helps keep their arteries clear of fat deposits and that the benefit may increase with increased physical activity.

6. Redivide the fat (beanbags) evenly and repeat the activity. The goal of each team is to reduce more fat than they did in the previous round. This might be a good time to alter team makeup, especially if students with disabilities are participating in the activity.

Teaching Hints

▶ Make the activity sport specific. As an alternative to using beanbags, use basketballs for fat and carts for arteries. Students dribble the balls to the opposing cart. Other options include practicing cradling for lacrosse or dribbling for soccer.

▶ Students may carry only one object at a time.

▶ Students must place, not throw, the objects into the hoop.

▶ Students must move in the same direction (clockwise) at all times to avoid collisions.

Sample Inclusion Tips

▶ Students using wheelchairs can cut across the middle of the playing area instead of having to move around the cones at the perimeter.

▶ Establish an area in the center of the playing area so that a student using a wheelchair could wheel to that alternative space.

▶ Use of a bag or carryall to carry beanbags would be helpful to promote independence.

Variations

▶ Instead of moving around the activity space students can choose favorite equipment (jump ropes, basketballs, hacky sack, and so on) and use it to be active while waiting to move to the middle and remove fat from the team artery.

▶ After a round of game play stop the students and have them meet with their teams. Ask the following questions to promote team communication.

• What were you doing that seemed to be successful?

• Identify two things that you and your team will do to be more efficient in clearing your artery.

▶ Return to the game so that students can try their new ideas for working better as a team.

Home Extension

Encourage students to teach this simple game to family and friends in the neighborhood. Instead of beanbags any combination of balls could be used. Canned goods could be substituted to add to the intensity level of the activity.

Assessment

▶ Ask the students why one artery would end up with more fat than the other artery. Help them compare this with what actually may happen in the human body.

▶ Have students journal five specific activities that would improve their cardiovascular systems.

AEROBIC BENEFIT HUNT

MIDDLE SCHOOL

Health benefits—Regular physical activity, especially aerobic fitness activities, has been shown to provide a wide array of health benefits.

Purpose

▶ Students will be able to identify the benefits of aerobic fitness.

▶ Through participation in various aerobic activities, students will be able to recognize activities that enhance aerobic fitness.

Relationship to National Standards

▶ Physical education standard 3: Participates regularly in physical activity.

▶ Physical education standard 4: Achieves and maintains a health-enhancing level of physical fitness.

▶ Health education standard 1: Student will comprehend concepts related to health promotion and disease prevention.

Equipment

▶ Aerobic steps or benches

▶ Basketballs

▶ Soccer balls

▶ Jump ropes

▶ Upbeat music and player

▶ Pencil or colored marker for each group

Procedure

1. Organize students into groups of three or four.

2. Give each group a worksheet and a pencil or marker.

3. Place the Aerobic Benefit Cards on the floor, numbered side up and scattered randomly throughout the playing area.

4. When the music starts, each group goes to any card that they wish. They must read the aerobic benefit and write the benefit on their worksheet.

5. They then turn the card over and read the aerobic

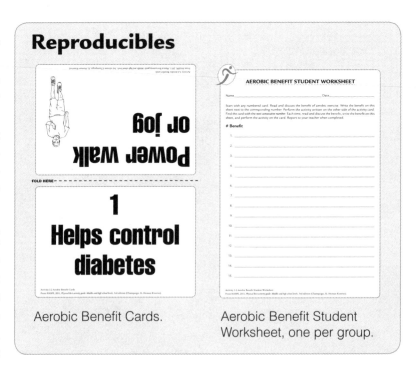

Aerobic Benefit Cards.

Aerobic Benefit Student Worksheet, one per group.

activity. All group members must perform the activity together.

6. When the group has completed the aerobic activity for a predetermined amount of time, they find the card with the next consecutive number. For example, if they started at card 8, they find card 9, write the benefit on their worksheet, and perform the aerobic activity written on the other side of the card.

7. Continue until students have completed a predetermined number of cards or continue for a certain length of time.

8. Bring students together to discuss
   - the benefits of the aerobic activity that they have written on their worksheets (point out that doing aerobic fitness activities will help them stay healthy),
   - elements that the activities have in common to identify how to determine whether an activity is aerobic, and
   - what aerobic activities students can do throughout a day.

Performing various activities and identifying their health benefits will help students understand the importance of aerobic fitness.

Teaching Hints

▶ Determine the amount of time or repetitions for each card based on the intensity of the activity as well as the age and fitness level of the students.

▶ Present aerobic activities that may be new to your students or your locale or activities that few students have participated in on their own.

Sample Inclusion Tips

▶ For students with intellectual disabilities, use both verbal and visual cues.

▶ Allow students with disabilities to attempt to perform activities before incorporating modifications.

Variations

▶ Incorporate skill development into this activity by requiring students to use a particular skill while moving to the next station. For example, as part of a rugby unit students must advance to the next station while passing the ball backward to one another (while still moving forward).

▶ Have students read the benefit rather than writing it down at every station. At the end of the activity have students write down five benefits of aerobic fitness.

Home Extensions

▶ Students can invite a friend or family member to do a favorite aerobic activity such as walking or biking.

▶ Students can tell a family member about the benefits of aerobic fitness while participating together.

Assessment

▶ Check worksheets for correct aerobic benefits.

▶ Have students turn to their neighbors and tell them three benefits of aerobic activity.

▶ Prepare a sheet of pictures that depict aerobic and nonaerobic activities. Ask students to identify the aerobic activities.

CHART YOUR HEART RATE

HIGH SCHOOL

Intensity—A warm-up increases the temperature of the body and the elasticity of the muscles, therefore reducing the risk of injury. A cool-down brings the body temperature back to normal and allows muscles to flush away wastes generated during exercise. Intensity is the level at which a person performs an activity.

Purpose

Students will learn to monitor their aerobic intensity while participating in game play.

Relationship to National Standards

▶ Physical education standard 1: Demonstrates competency in motor skills and movement patterns needed to perform a variety of physical activities.

▶ Physical education standard 4: Achieves and maintains a health-enhancing level of physical fitness.

Equipment

▶ Pencil for each student

▶ Equipment for your whole class to play multiple 3 vs. 3 Ultimate Frisbee, soccer keep-away, or any other aerobic game (for each 3 vs. 3 game, one Frisbee or soccer ball, three colored pinnies, a hoop, six Chart Your Heart Rate Worksheets, and six pencils)

▶ Upbeat music and player (optional)

Procedure

1. Set up numerous small play areas so that multiple 3 vs. 3 Ultimate Frisbee games can take place at the same time.

2. In a hoop at each playing area provide one Frisbee, three colored pinnies, six Chart Your Heart Rate Worksheets, and six pencils.

3. Have students take their 10-second resting heart rate and record this for pre-warm-up on the chart.

4. Students should then engage in a warm-up, which might include throwing and catching the Frisbee with a stationary partner and then throwing to a partner who is moving down the field. Be sure that students alternate throwing and catching. Allow time for students to stretch major muscle groups. Following the warm-up, have students take their 10-second heart rate and record for interval 1 on the chart.

5. On the start signal, play (3 vs. 3 Ultimate Frisbee) should begin. Ultimate Frisbee is played between two teams of three players on a rectangular indoor or out-

Reproducible

CHART YOUR HEART RATE WORKSHEET

Chart Your Heart Rate
Worksheet, one per student.

door space. An area marked by cones at each end creates two end zones. These are the scoring areas. A goal is scored when a team completes a pass to a player standing in the end zone they are attacking.

Players cannot run with the disc (a small foam ball can also be used instead of a disc). When a player gets the disc, he must come to a stop and try to throw it to another player. The offense passes from player to player to advance the disc toward the end zone they are attacking. If the disc hits the ground or is intercepted or knocked down by the other team, then it is a turnover and the opposing team gets the disc. The defending team attempts

By charting heart rate during games like Ultimate Frisbee, students learn how to monitor their intensity levels and set goals for future improvement.

to stop the offense from advancing the disc toward the end zone by guarding each player on the offense. This is a noncontact sport, so the defense must stay an arm's distance away and must not make contact with the offense or a penalty is called and the offensive team gets to make a free pass without a defender.

6. Twice, after 3 to 5 minutes of play, students should again take their heart rate and chart it on the worksheet for interval 2 and interval 3. Let students know that the goal is to reach their target heart rate. Let them know that they should perform aerobic activity at 60 to 85% of their maximal heart rate for at least 20 minutes on all or most days of the week.

7. At the end of game play have student cool down by walking around the activity space for 3 to 5 minutes. After students do this have them record their final 10-second heart rate for the post-cool-down section of the heart rate chart.

8. At the completion of the activity students should complete the Chart Your Heart Rate Worksheet.

Teaching Hints

▶ Students can monitor their intensity within any skill-focused lesson. The opportunity to teach skill and fitness concepts should be incorporated when possible.

▶ Graphing and interpreting graphs is part of many standardized tests; this activity offers an opportunity for students to practice this skill.

▶ Encourage students to play only in their designated areas. If their Frisbee or ball goes onto another group's field or space, have them walk to the edge of the space and say, "Ball please" or "Frisbee please." After they get the ball or Frisbee, they must carry it back to their field or court (not throw or kick it there).

Sample Inclusion Tips

▶ Students should be able to work at their own intensity level.

▶ If student fitness levels are low or students tire easily because of mobility limitations, use groups of four so that one person is always resting. This variation allows for recovery time.

▶ To include students who may be in wheelchairs, the game should be played indoors. The hard surface allows wheelchairs to roll up and down the court and provides students with the opportunity to raise their heart rates.

Variations

▶ Use the Chart Your Heart Rate Worksheet while playing any type of highly active game.

▶ Use the chart regularly and allow students to compare their previous charts to newer ones to track progress and set goals for reaching their target heart rate.

Home Extensions

▶ Once a month have students complete the chart while participating in a favorite physical activity after school.

▶ Have students complete the chart for a friend or family member who may want to see his or her heart rate graph.

Assessment

Completion of the Chart Your Heart Rate Worksheet provides evidence of students' understanding of how to monitor their intensity levels and set goals for future improvement.

HIGH SCHOOL

Intensity—Intensity describes how hard a person exercises during physical activity. Optimal intensity depends on the age and fitness goals of the participant. Heart rate has traditionally been used as a measure of training intensity to develop aerobic fitness.

Purpose

- ▶ Students will evaluate the influence of intensity on their heart rates.
- ▶ Students will determine their personal intensity level necessary to maintain their training heart rates.

Relationship to National Standards

- ▶ Physical education standard 2: Demonstrates understanding of movement concepts, principles, strategies, and tactics as they apply to the learning and performance of physical activities.
- ▶ Physical education standard 3: Participates regularly in physical activity.
- ▶ Physical education standard 5: Exhibits responsible personal and social behavior that respects self and others in physical activity settings.

Equipment

- ▶ Pencil for each student
- ▶ Standard running track or other safe activity space

Procedure

1. Review the meaning of resting heart rate, maximum heart rate, target heart rate, and the concept of frequency, intensity, time, and type (FITT).

2. Using the Aerobic Fitness Worksheet, students should record their heart rates after warm-up, after walking a lap around the track, after jogging a lap around the track, and after running one straightaway on the track.

3. After the students have that data, discuss the effect of increasing and decreasing intensity and the effect that intensity has on their heart rates.

4. Have your students, working individually, attempt to go around the track once and be in their training heart rate zone when they are done. Let them know that they can choose to walk, jog, run, or do any combination of these because the training heart rate zone will vary among students. Have them go around the track again with the same goal.

Reproducible

Aerobic Fitness Worksheet, one per student.

Teaching Hint

This activity can be done inside the gym by having the students record their heart rates after a brief warm-up, after walking three laps of the gym, after jogging three laps, and after running the length of the basketball court four times.

Sample Inclusion Tips

▶ Students with mobility difficulties can participate by taking their heart rates while doing various activities from a sitting position—passing a basketball or volleyball against a wall, tossing a light medicine ball overhead for 30 seconds, and lifting light weights for 30 seconds.

▶ Those students who are able to walk or jog but have other impairments can participate by using the buddy system, that is, by having another student assist with taking and recording their heart rates.

Monitoring their heart rates during walking, jogging, or running will help students work within their target heart rate zones.

Variation

Allow students to work with partners or small groups. They should be at similar fitness levels and be able to be productive while enjoying the social component of working out with someone.

Home Extension

Have students identify aerobic activity opportunities in the community where they could participate on a regular basis.

Assessment

Have students assess by marking the best description of the intensity necessary for them to work within their training heart rate zone.

FITTING IN FITNESS

3.5

MIDDLE SCHOOL

Frequency—Frequency describes how often a person performs a physical activity. The minimum frequency for aerobic activities is daily, but keep in mind that some aerobic activity is better than none even if doing it daily is still a challenge.

Purpose

▶ Students will understand the importance of staying active most days of the week and will be encouraged to track their activity levels.

▶ Students will recognize physical activities that are aerobic (with oxygen) and anaerobic (without oxygen).

▶ Students will identify strategies that facilitate an active lifestyle.

Relationship to National Standards

▶ Physical education standard 1: Demonstrates competency in motor skills and movement patterns needed to perform a variety of physical activities.

▶ Physical education standard 3: Participates regularly in physical activity.

▶ Physical education standard 4: Achieves and maintains a health-enhancing level of physical fitness.

▶ Health education standard 1: Students will comprehend concepts related to health promotion and disease prevention.

▶ Health education standard 3: Students will demonstrate the ability to practice health-enhancing behaviors and reduce health risks.

Reproducibles

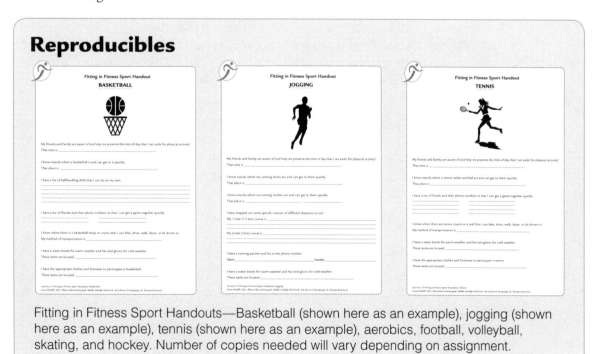

Fitting in Fitness Sport Handouts—Basketball (shown here as an example), jogging (shown here as an example), tennis (shown here as an example), aerobics, football, volleyball, skating, and hockey. Number of copies needed will vary depending on assignment.

Equipment

The activities that you choose and the space that you have will dictate the equipment needed. Following are some examples of equipment needed for some of the activities described in the procedure.

▶ One to six basketballs

▶ One to three footballs

▶ Four to six tennis rackets and balls

▶ Four to six steps (for step aerobics)

▶ Four to six hockey sticks and two hockey pucks or balls

▶ Upbeat music and player

Procedure

1. Set up seven stations indoors or outdoors that will help your students participate in seven different activities (e.g., basketball, tennis, jogging, walking, Frisbee, football, soccer, dance, hockey, or aerobic dance). Include activities that are predominantly aerobic (moderate intensity) and predominantly anaerobic (vigorous intensity) in nature. Set up stations that appeal to your students and that represent activities that they most enjoy participating in, both in physical education class and outside of class. Number the stations 1 to 7.

2. Remind the class that the surgeon general recommends that people participate in physical activity most days of the week. Remind them that the time they spend in an activity and the intensity of the workout can affect how often they exercise.

3. Explain to the class that aerobic activities are activities in which the muscles require oxygen to produce energy. Tell students that in aerobic activities, they are active for a long time and can tell that their heart and lungs are working. Walking, biking, and jogging down the soccer field are aerobic activities. Explain that aerobic activities should be done on most or all days of the week. But another type of activity is also good for them. Anaerobic activities often are done for very short periods and use muscles in a more intense way, as in sprinting or lifting a weight. Anaerobic physical activity is done in short, fast bursts in which the heart cannot supply blood and oxygen as fast as muscles use it (Corbin & Lindsey, 2005).

4. Tell the students that the seven stations that they will be moving through represent the seven days of the week. Ask the students what some of the reasons might be for taking a day off (e.g., to let the body recover after intense anaerobic activity). Inform them that in this activity they will be reviewing strategies to help them to stay active on most days of the week.

5. Describe to the class what activity they will be doing at each station. Examples:

   • Basketball—Students could play one-on-one, two-on-two, or three-on-three, depending on the number of students who are at a station. They could practice running layups, dribble in and out of cones, side shuffle as they pass, practice ball-handling drills, and so forth.

   • Jogging—Students could run in pairs on a designated path or anywhere in sight of the teacher.

6. Divide the class into pairs. Tell the pairs of students to go to a station. Each station should be limited to three pairs.

7. Start the music.

8. Allow students to participate in an activity at their stations until the music stops at a predetermined time. Students at more intense (anaerobic) stations may need to take active rests (such as marching in place).

9. When the music stops, students rotate to the next station and then stretch.

10. When the music starts again, students should begin the new activity.

Teaching Hint

By changing the activities at each station, you can reinforce the idea that there are many types of physical activities for students to choose from.

Sample Inclusion Tip

Use modifications outlined in chapter 1 of this book.

Variation

After doing this with students allow them to create their own stations to include and demonstrate to the class. Then perform the activity again using the new stations.

Home Extensions

▶ Use the Fitting in Fitness Sport Handouts (on the CD-ROM) to start your students thinking about the strategies for staying active outside of class. The handouts can be filled in for homework.

▶ Have students go to www.mypyramidtracker.gov and use the physical activity journal to track activity outside of school.

Assessment

▶ Conduct a question-and-answer session. Ask questions such as the following: What makes an activity aerobic? What activities were aerobic? What makes an activity anaerobic? What activities were anaerobic? What activities would be the easiest to participate in outside of class? What strategies for staying active were the most important to you and why?

▶ Have students track their activity levels. They can develop their own method to track their activity frequency, intensity, time, and type by creating logs on paper or by generating a graph or calendar on the computer. Students can also use the Presidential Youth Active Lifestyle Log (www.presidentschallenge.org) or other online fitness logs available to youth.

Galina Barskaya

In this activity, students learn to apply frequency in aerobic and anaerobic fitness through various sports.

HEARTBEAT STATIONS

MIDDLE SCHOOL

Intensity and time—Intensity is the level at which a person performs an activity. Intensity for aerobic activity can be correlated with heart rate and can affect the time that a person participates in an activity. Students who choose to walk, jog, or play at a high intensity level that may be above their target heart rate range will not be able to go as long as they would had they worked at a lower intensity level.

Purpose

Students will participate in a variety of activities to understand how physical activity at varying intensity levels influences their heart rate, perceived exertion, and amount of time that they will be able to maintain the activity.

Relationship to National Standards

- ▶ Physical education standard 1: Demonstrates competency in motor skills and movement patterns needed to perform a variety of physical activities.
- ▶ Physical education standard 4: Achieves and maintains a health-enhancing level of physical fitness.
- ▶ Health education standard 3: Student demonstrates the ability to practice health-enhancing behaviors and reduce health risks.

Equipment

- ▶ Heart rate monitors (if available) or a wall clock with a second hand
- ▶ Pencils, one per student
- ▶ Stopwatch

Procedure

1. Define intensity. Ask students to predict which aerobic fitness activities have greater intensity.
2. As a warm-up, have students consecutively participate in four activities—walking, power walking, jogging, and sprinting—for 60 seconds each, performing an active rest (such as marching in place) for 15 seconds between activities.
3. Set up an aerobic fitness circuit with activities that vary in intensity: walking through cones, jumping rope, jogging around the gym, dribbling a soccer ball, running an agility ladder, and so on.
4. Divide students into groups and assign each group a station.
5. After they complete each station, have students measure their heart rate, either with the heart rate monitors or by counting their pulse for six seconds and

Reproducible

Heartbeat Stations Scoresheet, one per student.

Students perform different activities at varying intensities to gauge their effect on heart rate, perceived exertion, and duration.

adding zero to the number. Have students record their heart rate on the Heartbeat Stations Scoresheet.

6. Continue to rotate students through the stations until they complete all stations.

Teaching Hints

▶ Play music to motivate students as they try each station activity.

▶ Record music in two-minute segments to accommodate the station changes.

Sample Inclusion Tip

For students with physical disabilities, supply or work with a physical education specialist to develop an alternate, adapted activity at each station.

Variation

Ask each group to develop a station and teach it to the class.

Home Extension

Have students design three to five stations using equipment they have at home or could borrow from friends with permission. Students can draw the stations and share ideas with the class.

Assessment

▶ Have each student explain which of their predictions of intensity at the start of the activity were correct and why.

▶ Ask students to identify the station at which their hearts beat the fastest and slowest and at which they had the highest and lowest perceived exertion and explain why.

▶ Ask students how their activity time might be affected at these stations.

CROSS-TRAINING TRIO

MIDDLE SCHOOL AND HIGH SCHOOL

Time and type—Time is how long a person exercises during one bout of activity. Type is the kind of exercise performed.

Purpose

▶ Students will understand and apply the time component of the FITT guidelines.

▶ Students will understand and apply the type component of the FITT guidelines.

▶ Students will learn or review safety guidelines for participation in an aerobic fitness activity.

Relationship to National Standards

▶ Physical education standard 1: Demonstrates competency in motor skills and movement patterns needed to perform a variety of physical activities.

▶ Physical education standard 3: Participates regularly in physical activity.

▶ Physical education standard 4: Achieves and maintains a health-enhancing level of physical fitness.

▶ Health education standard 1: Students will comprehend concepts related to health promotion and disease prevention.

▶ Health education standard 3: Students will demonstrate the ability to practice health-enhancing behaviors and reduce health risks.

Equipment

The activity will be done on student time, and equipment is determined by student activity.

Procedure

1. At the end of a class in which aerobic fitness was the focus, distribute one Aerobic Fitness: Cross-Training Benefits and Guidelines sheet to each student.

2. Discuss the "Cross-Training Benefits" section of the sheet. Discuss how the time component of FITT may be best addressed through varying activities. For example,

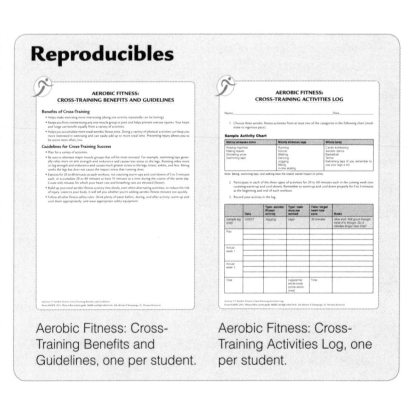

Aerobic Fitness: Cross-Training Benefits and Guidelines, one per student.

Aerobic Fitness: Cross-Training Activities Log, one per student.

Photodisc

Alternating between different exercises helps students remain interested in activities and provides a more well-rounded benefit.

people are less likely to become bored or injured when alternating activities and muscle groups or joints stressed, thus allowing them to participate for an adequate duration to receive a health benefit.

3. Discuss the "Cross-Training Guidelines" section of the sheet. Emphasize that the focus of this activity is to develop aerobic fitness, so the type component of the FITT principle will be important to address correctly.

4. Suggest the following cross-training plan for developing aerobic fitness: You jog home from school one day, you perform resistance training another day, and you in-line skate around your neighborhood a third day. Ask the following questions:

   • Does each activity help enhance aerobic fitness? (No, the resistance training won't; we also don't know how long each aerobic activity lasts.)

   • Do the two aerobic fitness activities alternate major muscles and joints that they stress? (No, they both stress mainly the legs.)

5. Suggest the following cross-training plan for developing aerobic fitness: You bike home from school one day; this trip takes you 25 minutes. On another day you swim laps for 10 minutes besides playing at the pool for 10 minutes. You walk to the mall on the third day; this trip takes you 32 minutes. Ask the same questions as in step 4. The following is a sample answer: Yes, they are performed long enough (20 or more minutes total in the same day), they are specific to aerobic fitness development (i.e., all three work the heart and lungs), and they vary in muscles and joints stressed and in joint impact.

6. Distribute one Aerobic Fitness: Cross-Training Activities Log per student. Have individuals or partners create a cross-training plan that includes three activities that enhance aerobic fitness. Allow them to record their plan on the log. Have them ask themselves the same questions as in step 4.

7. Review and approve or edit student plans.

8. Direct students to perform their plan in the coming two weeks, participating in each activity one time each week, and record their actual activity on the log.

9. Have students turn in their logs and paragraphs (see assessment ideas).

Teaching Hints

▶ Be sure to monitor students' participation through logs and discussions to emphasize safe application of all training principles.

▶ Reinforce the "Cross-Training Guidelines" as needed to ensure that students understand the concepts behind this approach.

▶ When revisiting this lesson, tie in the frequency component of FITT by having students plan one month of continued cross-training for aerobic fitness, using multiple (four or more) copies of the Aerobic Fitness: Cross-Training Activities Log. Require variations from the original plan to determine whether students know how to apply what they've learned safely.

Sample Inclusion Tip

Work individually with students who need assistance in choosing the activities for their cross-training plans, including modifications as needed.

Variation

Require students' plans to include at least 30 minutes of the activity of their choosing to be done after school.

Home Extension

This activity takes place away from school, so no home extension is needed.

Assessment

▶ Review or have partners review student logs to determine whether they understand how to apply the time and type components of the FITT guidelines to aerobic fitness development through cross-training.

▶ Require each student to write a cohesive paragraph about how they may have benefited (or will benefit) from their cross-training experience. They should mention how they did (or may) increase total time working on aerobic fitness and how they addressed the type component of the FITT guidelines.

CONTINUOUS RELAY

HIGH SCHOOL

Intensity and time—Intensity is the level at which an activity is performed, ranging from low to moderate to vigorous. To reach target heart rates during exercise, students have to raise their heart rates to 60% of their maximal heart rate. The goal of an aerobic session is to exercise in the target heart rate zone for a minimum of 20 minutes. Time is the duration of activity. An increase in time can lead to improved aerobic fitness.

Purpose

▶ Students will elevate and maintain an appropriate exercise heart rate (60 to 85% of maximum) during a continuous relay for a predetermined period.

▶ Students will be able to self-monitor their activity levels using beats per minute.

▶ Students will work to maintain or increase their fitness level as needed and have the goal of sustaining aerobic fitness activity for 20 minutes.

Relationship to National Standards

▶ Physical education standard 4: Achieves and maintains a health-enhancing level of physical fitness.

▶ Health education standard 1: Students will comprehend concepts related to health promotion and disease prevention.

▶ Health education standard 3: Students will demonstrate the ability to practice health-enhancing behaviors and reduce health risks.

Equipment

▶ Appropriate fast-paced music and player

▶ Pencils, one per student

▶ Jump ropes (optional), enough for two-thirds of the class

▶ Pedometers (optional), one per student

▶ See "Teaching Hints" for other potential equipment needs

Procedure

1. Introduce the activity by briefly discussing the importance of exercising in the appropriate target heart rate zone for developing aerobic fitness, the types of activities that elevate heart rate, and the significance of a lower resting heart rate.

2. Have students calculate their target heart rate zone (60 to 85% of maximum) or provide these numbers for the age range in the class.

3. Direct students to take their heart rates before beginning the activity. You can use the Heart Rate Based on a 10-Second Count (table 3.4 on page 42) to help students quickly compute their heart rates.

Reproducible

Individual Workout Log, one per student.

4. After an appropriate warm-up, divide students into groups of three. Student 1 is located on the end line of a basketball court. Student 2 is located on the center line. Student 3 is located on the other end line. If a lined court is not available, use another space marker such as cones.

5. Start the music.

6. End-line students perform rope-jumping skills (if no ropes are available, students can perform the skills with an imaginary rope). The middle student is the runner. The student starts running toward one of the end-line students. After the runner arrives, the jumper becomes the runner and heads toward the teammate located at the other end of the gym. Continue this activity for two to three minutes.

7. After one round of two to three minutes, stop the music and signal students to check their heart rates. Remind them to note whether they are in the appropriate zone or whether they need to increase or decrease their exercise intensity level. Have them fill in their heart rate and zone on their Individual Workout Logs.

8. Start the music and continue for another two- to three-minute round.

9. Stop the music and direct students to check their heart rates again. Have them record the information on the logs.

10. Continue for a predetermined period or number of rounds.

11. Close the activity by briefly reviewing the concepts taught in this activity.

Table 3.4   Heart Rate Based on a 10-Second Count

Beats per 10 seconds	Heart rate (bpm)	Beats per 10 seconds	Heart rate (bpm)
10	60	22	132
11	66	23	138
12	72	24	144
13	78	25	150
14	84	26	156
15	90	27	162
16	96	28	168
17	102	29	174
18	108	30	180
19	114	31	186
20	120	32	192
21	126	33	198

Teaching Hints

▶ Total time of activity should be based on the fitness level of the students. Schedule rest periods as needed.

▶ For students who are new to using their target heart rate zones, display a large poster to help them check whether their heart rate is at an appropriate level, such as a chart that offers the numbers for the age range in the class.

▶ Have students use pedometers to keep track of how many steps they were able to attain and then add all three students' steps together. Remember that students' heights will affect their number of steps, so it's best not to compare the number of steps with other teams unless students are of similar height.

Sample Inclusion Tips

▶ Students using wheelchairs may self-propel (wheel) from one end of the facility to the other and perform appropriate activities at the end line.

▶ Allow students using wheelchairs to substitute upper-body arm movements for lower-body leg movements.

Variations

▶ Give students on the center line a piece of sport equipment (e.g., a basketball) and have them perform a specific stationary ball skill (e.g., figure-eight passes at the knee) or perform muscular strength and endurance activities (e.g., variations of curl-ups or push-ups) before running to an end-line team member. Keep the number of repetitions low.

▶ Change activities at the end lines with each round. Students can identify stationary activities that will increase or maintain an appropriate exercise heart rate (e.g., line jumps, jumping jacks, or stretching, if they need to lower their heart rates).

Home Extension

Encourage students to participate in a favorite game or activity after school and record their intensity levels using the Individual Workout Log. Have a parent or guardian initial the sheet.

Assessment

▶ Have students tell their team members what their heart rate was at the beginning and end and discuss its meaning.

▶ Review the logs that students maintained during the activity. Save these for students to add to when revisiting this activity (you may want to avoid having students stop to record numbers too often because doing so defeats the purpose of keeping the heart rate elevated). Taking preexercise heart rate and postexercise heart rate is usually enough for a discussion.

▶ If using pedometers, students can record both their individual and group scores to be compared when the activity is revisited in the future.

▶ Gauge the amount of time that the class or individual students can maintain the activity when you revisit it over a period of time.

▶ Question students both orally and in writing about intensity, time, and ways to adjust their heart rate and maintain it in the target heart rate zone. For example, if a student wants to participate in an activity for a long duration, what intensity should he or she work at? (Low to moderate—toward the low end of the target heart rate zone)

In this activity and its variations, students practice tracking and adjusting intensity to reach and maintain their target heart rate zones.

MINI TRIATHLON

MIDDLE SCHOOL AND HIGH SCHOOL

Intensity and time—Intensity is the level at which an activity is performed, ranging from low to moderate to vigorous. To reach target heart rates during exercise, students have to raise their heart rates to 60% of their maximal heart rate. The goal of an aerobic session is to exercise in the target heart rate zone for a minimum of 20 minutes. Time is the duration of activity. An increase in time can lead to improved aerobic fitness.

Purpose

- Students will demonstrate the effects of exercise on the heart.
- Students will understand the importance of pacing themselves to sustain activity over a period of time.

Relationship to National Standards

- Physical education standard 2: Demonstrates understanding of movement concepts, principles, strategies, and tactics as they apply to the learning and performance of physical activities.
- Physical education standard 4: Achieves and maintains a health-enhancing level of physical fitness.

Equipment

- Cones to mark a start–finish line and turnaround point
- 10 to 15 footballs
- 10 to 15 soccer balls
- 10 to 15 lacrosse sticks, rugby balls, team handballs (or any favorite piece of equipment that could be passed)
- 10 to 15 Frisbees
- Stopwatch
- Heart rate monitors (optional)

Procedure

1. Divide the students into groups of three.
2. Discuss triathlons with the students. Explain that a triathlon is a race against other people and time. Three events are combined, and a person does one right after the other. An example is run, swim, and bike.
3. Explain that they will be doing a mini triathlon but will change some of the rules. During the mini triathlon, students should get the heart beating faster but pace themselves through the activity. This means that they shouldn't go as fast as they can right from the start because they will need to keep going throughout all the activities.

Reproducible

None.

4. On "Go," groups go to the turnaround point, return to the start–finish line, get equipment if needed, and perform the next task. First, students should jog, then dribble a soccer ball, and finally pass a football.

5. Stop the timer when participants have completed all the tasks.

Teaching Hints

▶ Discuss why pacing is important for performing over a long period.

▶ During the activity, remind students to pace themselves and keep going during the whole 10 minutes.

Sample Inclusion Tips

▶ Modify the skill sections and distance to the turnaround of the triathlon to meet the needs of included students.

▶ Use pictures and a picture schedule to promote student independence.

Variation

Repeat by having students create their own triathlon, such as a combination of football throwing, soccer dribbling, lacrosse passing, Frisbee throwing, or any other aerobic fitness exercises that they enjoy.

Home Extension

Encourage students to find and participate in a local fun run–walk or bike ride as a way to practice pacing themselves so that they can finish the race and meet a personal goal.

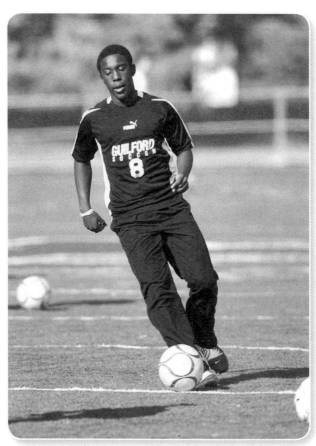

Assessment

▶ Was each student able to pace through all events?

▶ Have students check their heart rates by counting for 6 seconds and multiplying by 10.

▶ If heart rate monitors are used, have students record their resting heart rates before and at the end of the triathlon to see the effects that exercise has had on the heart.

▶ If students went too fast have them identify why they could not go for the whole period. (They went too fast, became too tired, and didn't pace themselves.)

▶ Why is pacing important when wanting to go for a long period?

A mini triathlon that involves performing various aerobic activities over a sustained period is a fun way for students to learn the importance of pacing themselves.

MIDDLE SCHOOL AND HIGH SCHOOL

Growth and development—This challenging activity for middle or high school students involves cooperation and skill development that will enhance various activity skills as well as increase student knowledge.

Purpose

▶ Students will be able to explain the relationship among diet, physical activity, and body composition.

▶ Students will be instructed on how physical activity can affect growth and development.

▶ Students will summarize how both diet and physical activity are important for maintaining optimum health.

Relationship to National Standards

▶ Physical education standard 4: Achieves and maintains a health-enhancing level of physical fitness.

▶ Health education standard 1: Student will comprehend concepts related to health promotion and disease prevention.

Equipment

▶ Pencils, one per student

▶ Other equipment will vary according to stations selected but could include the following:

• Jump ropes

• Resistance bands or dumbbells

• Basketballs and hoop

• Soccer balls and cones for goals

• Aerobic step benches

• Tennis rackets and balls

• Six mats

• TV, VCR or DVD player, and cardio kickboxing video

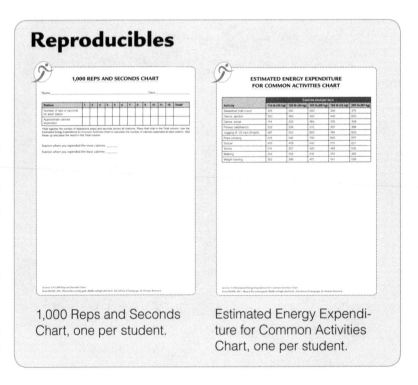

Reproducibles

1,000 Reps and Seconds Chart, one per student.

Estimated Energy Expenditure for Common Activities Chart, one per student.

Procedure

1. Set up 10 to 12 stations: Some are timed activities, and some require repetitions. The following are some suggestions:

   - Jump ropes—number of jumps in two minutes
   - Line dance—number of seconds
   - A resistance band or dumbbells for chest presses—number of presses (use weight training on energy expenditure chart)
   - Jogging—number of seconds
   - Walking—number of seconds
   - Basketballs and hoop—number of baskets attempted
   - Soccer balls and cones—number of goals attempted
   - Aerobic steps—number of seconds
   - Push-up station—number of push-ups completed (use fitness calisthenics on energy expenditure chart)
   - Curl-up station—number of curl-ups completed (use fitness calisthenics on energy expenditure chart)
   - Tennis—number of hits off a wall
   - Cardio kickboxing—number of seconds (use dance aerobics on energy expenditure chart)

2. Explain to students that physical activity (*a*) expends calories for the energy used by the activity, (*b*) requires the body to use nutrients to maintain existing muscle tissue, and (*c*) requires the body to use nutrients to build new muscle tissue, therefore contributing to the healthy growth and development of the body.

3. After a proper warm-up, distribute a 1,000 Reps and Seconds Chart and a pencil to each student. Divide students into small groups of two or three, depending on the number of students and stations, and direct students to their stations.

4. Explain that students will use the charts to record the number of repetitions or the number of seconds for the activity at each station. At skills-based stations (such as basketball shooting), ask students to count the number of attempts, not the number of successes, because the goal is activity rather than performance. For timed activities, students need to count total time. For instance, if a student jumps rope for 20 seconds and after a brief break jumps rope for 20 more seconds, she or he would record a score of 40 for that station.

The stations in this activity not only help students practice cooperation and skill development but they also reinforce important concepts, like energy expenditure, growth, and development.

5. Direct students to move clockwise to the next station every two minutes. The objective is to reach at least 1,000 at the end of the class session by adding seconds (for timed activities) and repetitions (for repeated activities).

Teaching Hints

▶ The most effective approach to this activity is to use partners (two students per station).

▶ Make and post interesting facts at each of the stations such as these: Muscle (lean tissue) weighs more than fat for equal volume. You must have a certain amount of fat to be healthy: Fat helps your body use vitamins, insulates your body, and protects your bones and body organs (Corbin & Lindsey, 2004).

▶ When revisiting this activity, change some of the stations to coordinate with the rest of your curriculum and to maintain interest. Use the second assessment idea to save time while reinforcing the learning.

Sample Inclusion Tips

▶ Supply calculators for students who will have trouble adding the numbers.

▶ Include pictures at each station to show students proper form for the skill or activity that they are to do.

▶ For the low-fit student, design the station activities to allow various levels or ways that the student could complete the activity, thus assuring a level of success. Introduce this student to an initial activity or arrange the starting place of stations from easiest to most difficult.

Variation

Have partners predict how many repetitions they will do in the two-minute period. They can record the number of repetitions completed and compare it with the prediction.

Home Extension

Ask students to research the caloric expenditure of various activities, as related to the FITT principle components of intensity, time, and type, write down their findings, and share with the class.

Assessment

▶ Distribute one copy of the Estimated Energy Expenditure for Common Activities Chart to each student. Go through an example as a class and then ask students to estimate the number of calories that they used in today's activities. Discuss the results. Insights might include that students burned different amounts of calories and that different activities expend different amounts of calories, just as different foods contain different amount of calories.

▶ When revisiting the activity, circulate among stations, asking questions to review the Estimated Energy Expenditure for Common Activities Chart and its relationship to students' activities.

▶ Ask students these questions either as a class, in small groups, or on a quiz:

• What is energy balance?

• How does the amount of physical activity that you perform affect the amount of food that you should eat?

• How does physical activity affect growth and development?

AEROBIC FITT LOG

MIDDLE SCHOOL AND HIGH SCHOOL

Progression—The overload principle states that a body system (cardiorespiratory, muscular, or skeletal) must perform at a level beyond normal to adapt and improve physiological function and fitness. Progression refers to *how* an individual should increase overload. Proper progression involves a gradual increase in the level of exercise that is manipulated by increasing frequency, intensity, time, or type, or a combination of all four components.

Purpose

Students will learn and apply the training principles of progression and overload for aerobic fitness by completing a FITT Log and FITT Log Worksheet.

Relationship to National Standards

▶ Physical education standard 3: The student participates regularly in physical activity.

▶ Physical education standard 4: The student achieves and maintains a health-enhancing level of physical fitness.

▶ Health education standard 3: The student will demonstrate the ability to practice health-enhancing behaviors and reduce health risks.

Equipment

Pencils

Procedure

1. Briefly review the two-word definitions of the aspects of FITT—frequency (how often), intensity (how hard), time (how long), and type (what kind).

2. Ask students to offer brief examples of how they have applied the FITT guidelines to aerobic fitness in previous health-related fitness lessons.

3. Share descriptions of the concepts of progression and overload.

4. Distribute one blank Aerobic FITT Log to each student. Review each category and how it relates to FITT. Outline how students can apply progression and overload as they use this form.

5. Ask the class to share aerobic activities that they enjoy and then tell them to choose one and write it on their log.

6. Have the students write their names on their logs.

7. Assign students to log the aerobic fitness activity that they perform outside class for one week.

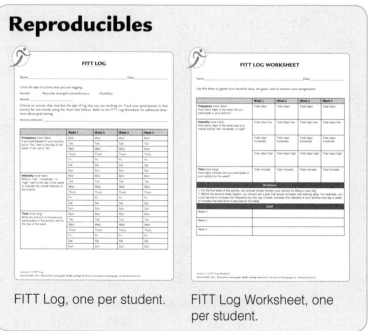

Reproducibles

FITT Log, one per student.

FITT Log Worksheet, one per student.

8. Have students fill in week 1 of the Aerobic FITT Log Worksheet.

9. Guide students in setting goals for progression and overload and writing them on the worksheet. Have them continue with the new goals for the next week.

10. At the end of each week meet with the class to discuss their progress and set new goals.

Teaching Hints

▶ Ask students at each class meeting how their logs are coming along.

▶ Require parent or guardian initials if necessary to encourage participation.

Sample Inclusion Tip

Help students with special circumstances come up with alternative activities to suit their needs and abilities. You can modify activities suggested earlier in this chapter, provide suggestions for students who must stay indoors because of safety or space constraints, or otherwise help students develop activity ideas that will work for them. See chapter 1 for modifications that enable students with disabilities to participate with their nondisabled peers.

Variations

▶ Ask the school's after-school care providers to provide space, time, and other support for students to add to their logs.

▶ Tie the Fitnessgram aerobic assessment to this activity.

▶ The activity is set up for one week and one month, but it can be changed for specific circumstances to cover one day to two weeks to a month to several months. Select the period that works best for the specific needs of the students.

Students must learn to apply what they have learned about aerobic activity outside of the classroom.

Home Extension

This activity is a home extension.

Assessment

▶ Ask the students to tell you the two word meanings for each of the FITT principles.

▶ After one week, review the logs with the students to ensure that they are participating safely and understand that maintaining the level they are working in is appropriate for a period of a week.

▶ Continue monitoring the log with the students weekly to ensure that they understand how to maintain and increase activity safely, by using the FITT principles wisely.

▶ After a certain period, perhaps a week or a month, have students review their logs with you and write about their experience by answering questions such as the following:

- Were you able to build up safely to a higher level of intensity over the course of the month, do the activities more frequently each week, or spend more time doing each activity? Which changes did you make, if any?

- If you were able to make changes, how might the changes have affected your aerobic fitness?

- If you did not make changes, what might you be able to do differently in the future?

▶ Realize that many factors, such as the child's initial level of fitness and participation (if already high, the student may not progress for that reason) and other personal factors may affect the answers to these questions. Keeping this in mind, focus on the assessment as a means to teach and reinforce the concepts of progression and overload.

Muscular Strength and Endurance

Chapter Contents

Although youth have traditionally been encouraged to participate in aerobic activities, over the past two decades a compelling body of evidence has accumulated to indicate that resistance training can be a safe, effective, and beneficial method of exercise for all youth if they follow appropriate training guidelines (Malina, 2006).

For more information concerning the principles of training for muscular strength and endurance, refer to *Physical Education for Lifelong Fitness: The Physical Best Teacher's Guide, Third Edition*.

This chapter includes several activities for developing muscular strength and endurance in middle and high school students.

DEFINING MUSCULAR STRENGTH AND ENDURANCE

Muscular strength is the ability of a muscle or muscle group to exert a maximal force against a resistance one time through the full range of motion. A student perceives this as the ability to act independently and lift and carry objects without assistance. *Muscular endurance* is the ability of a muscle or muscle group to exert a submaximal force repeatedly over a period of time.

Unlike activities conducted at the elementary level that focus on using the child's own body weight to build muscular strength and endurance, activities at the middle school and high school levels may involve lifting light weights (using machine weights and free weights) to build muscular strength and endurance. If adolescents undertake a strength training program, they should perform low-resistance exercises until they learn proper technique (American Academy of Pediatrics, 2001).

Potential benefits of resistance training include the following:

▶ Increased muscular strength (able to perform everyday activities more easily)

▶ Increased muscular endurance (able to participate in leisure activity without having sore or tired muscles)

▶ Improved aerobic fitness through muscular fitness circuit training (able to participate in leisure activities without getting tired) at a minimal level

▶ Prevention of musculoskeletal injury (will not get hurt as easily or often)

▶ Improved sport performance (become a better player)

▶ Reduced risk of fractures in adulthood (builds stronger bones)

▶ Increased bone strength and bone growth through exercise during the skeletal growth period (builds stronger bones, reduces risk of osteoporosis)

TEACHING GUIDELINES FOR MUSCULAR STRENGTH AND ENDURANCE

As with each area of health-related fitness, the principles of training (progression, overload, specificity, regularity, and individuality) should be incorporated into the activity. Manipulate the FITT guidelines based on the age of each student. Keep in mind that chronological age may not match physiological maturation. The guidelines in table 4.1 are merely guidelines for the development of muscular strength and endurance.

TRAINING METHODS FOR MUSCULAR STRENGTH AND ENDURANCE

A student with no resistance training experience should begin at the previous level, regardless of age, and move to the next level as he or she develops exercise tolerance, skill, and understanding of the lifting techniques.

Several recommendations or position stands exist for resistance training (not weightlifting; see chapter 6 in *Physical Education for Lifelong Fitness: The Physical Best Teacher's Guide, Third Edition*), providing guidance in developing adolescents' resistance training programs (ACSM, 2000; AAP, 2001; Hass et al., 2001; NSCS, 1985). Save resistance training using machine weights or barbells for postpubescent students. Use the guidelines in table 4.1 to help you develop a safe and developmentally appropriate unit on muscular strength and endurance.

Table 4.1 FITT Guidelines Applied to Muscular Fitness

Ages	9-11 years[a,b]	12-14 years[a,b]	15-16 years[a,b]	17+ years[c]
Frequency	2 or 3 days/week	2 or 3 days/week	2 or 3 days/week	2 days/week
Intensity	Very light weight	Light weight	Moderate weight	Light to heavy weight (based on type selected)
Time	At least 1 set (may do 2 sets), at least 20 minutes	At least 1 set (may do 3 sets), 6–15 reps, at least 20 minutes	At least 1 set (may do 3 or 4 sets), 6–15 reps, at least 20 minutes	Minimum 1 set, 8–12 reps
Type	Major muscle groups, 1 exercise per muscle or muscle group	Major muscle groups, 1 exercise per muscle or muscle group	Major muscle groups, 2 exercises per muscle or muscle group	Major muscle groups, 8–10 exercises; select muscular strength, power, or endurance

[a]Modified from AAP 2001.
[b]Modified from Faigenbaum and Micheli 2002.
[c]Modified from American College of Sports Medicine 2000.

MOTOR-SKILL DEVELOPMENT THROUGH MUSCULAR STRENGTH AND ENDURANCE ACTIVITIES

It is not always necessary, or appropriate, to use the weight room to develop muscular strength and endurance. Students may engage in a variety of skill development activities as well as individual, dual, team, and dance activities to increase muscular strength and endurance. For example, older students may enjoy team-building activities that require arm strength for success. Encourage middle school and high school students to select activities that they enjoy now and will continue to participate in after graduation.

Motor-skill development through fitness activity is the perfect area for you to consider the abilities and disabilities of all students. Some are high achievers, others are low achievers, and still others have physical or intellectual disabilities. Provide opportunities for all students to develop physical skills and be successful in your classroom. If a student has severe disabilities, you may need to contact someone who specializes in adapted physical education for assistance in developing an individualized education plan (IEP). Many of the Physical Best activities either incorporate a variety of motor skills or allow you to create modifications to the activity to address the motor development needs of your students. See table 4.2 on page 54 for a grid of activities in this chapter.

Table 4.2 Chapter 4 Activities Grid

Activity number	Activity title	Activity page	Concept	Middle school	High school	Reproducibles (on CD-ROM)
4.1	Go for the Team Gold	55	Health benefits	•		Go for the Team Gold Task Cards
						Go for the Team Gold Handout
4.2	Safely Finding the 8- to 12-Rep Range	57	Intensity		•	Weight Training Chart
4.3	Warm Up With Weights	60	Warm-up and cool-down		•	Weight Training Chart
4.4	Muscle FITT Bingo	62	Specificity	•	•	Muscle FITT Bingo Cards
4.5	Muscles in Action	64	Specificity	•		Muscle Cards
						Labeled Muscle Diagram
						Muscles in Action Plan Worksheet
4.6	Mission Push-Up Possible	67	Intensity and progression	•		Mission Push-Up Possible Card
						Mission Push-Up Possible Chart
						Individual Push-Up Progress Sheet
4.7	Get Fit	70	Specificity	•		Get Fit Worksheet
						Get Fit Exercise Signs
4.8	Muscle Up	72	Specificity		•	Muscle Groups Diagram
						Muscle Up Classification Chart
4.9	Muscular Fitness Scavenger Hunt	75	Specificity	•	•	Muscular Fitness Scavenger Hunt Handout
						Muscular Fitness Scavenger Hunt Puzzle
						Muscular Fitness Scavenger Hunt Station Cards
4.10	Know Your Way Around the Weight Room	78	Type		•	Know Your Way Around the Weight Room: Peer Teaching Exercise Descriptions
						Know Your Way Around the Weight Room Peer Assessment
						Know Your Way Around the Weight Room Exercises
						Common Weight Room Errors
4.11	Muscular Strength and Endurance FITT Log	80	Progression	•	•	FITT Log
						FITT Log Worksheet

MIDDLE SCHOOL

Health benefits—Muscular strength and endurance activities are important in the musculoskeletal function of the body. When done properly, they improve body composition, bone density, and posture; prevent injuries; and help a person perform tasks of daily living and work.

Purpose

- ▶ Students will describe the benefits of muscular strength and endurance.
- ▶ Students will correctly perform the strength and endurance exercises.

Relationship to National Standards

- ▶ Physical education standard 4: Achieves and maintains a health-enhancing level of physical fitness.
- ▶ Physical education standard 5: Exhibits responsible personal and social behavior that respects self and others in physical activity settings.
- ▶ Health education standard 1: Students will comprehend concepts related to health promotion and disease prevention.

Equipment

- ▶ Mats for floor work
- ▶ Curl-up strips
- ▶ Aerobic steps or benches
- ▶ Stretch bands
- ▶ Dumbbells (optional)

Procedure

1. Review the role of strength training in not only building strong muscles but also assisting in correct posture, reducing low-back pain, promoting healthy body composition, and advancing other benefits listed in the chapter introduction.

2. Divide the class into small groups of three students each. Give each group one strength task from the Go for the Team Gold Task Cards and two to three minutes to discuss their exercise. Each group will describe how to perform the exercise, explain the health benefits of the exercise, and lead the group in a 30-second set of the exercise. Assign each member a responsibility or role such as the following:

Go for the Team Gold Task Cards.

Go for the Team Gold Handout, one per student.

- Strength trainer describes the exercise to the class.
- Medical expert explains the exercise benefits.
- Olympic athlete uses correct form and performs the exercise during the discussion.

3. Have each group in turn lead the entire class in a 30-second set of the exercises, allowing students to complete a 1-1 or 1-2 tempo cycle during the 30 seconds for 10 to 15 repetitions. (Tempo is just as important for muscular strength and endurance development as performance technique is. The 1-1 tempo cycle is 1-second concentric and 1-second eccentric movement. The 1-2 tempo cycle is 1-second concentric and 2-second eccentric movement.)

Students learn first by performing skills and then by teaching their classmates that muscular strength and endurance activities do more than just build muscle; they can improve body composition and posture as well.

Teaching Hints

▶ Review the safety tips for strength training exercises including proper form and exhaling upon exertion.

▶ The second time you teach this lesson, complete a continuous exercise routine, with students taking turns leading the exercise that they led during the previous meeting.

▶ Use the Go for the Team Gold Handout to extend this lesson into the community while reinforcing the concepts and literacy development.

▶ Familiarize students with the task card activities through a previous lesson; circulate the room to assist as needed during the groups' two- to three-minute planning time.

Sample Inclusion Tips

▶ Develop task cards specific to students with physical disabilities. The cards should have muscular strength tasks that students with physical disabilities can do (e.g., biceps curls for a student who is in a wheelchair but has use of his or her arms).

▶ Include pictures on task cards so that students with intellectual disabilities can easily interpret how to perform the exercise correctly.

Variation

Have students make their own task cards by using digital pictures to show proper technique and cues as well as safety tips for each lift.

Home Extension

Have students make a video of their Go for the Team Gold presentation and share it with a friend, family member, or local Boys and Girls Club.

Assessment

▶ Have students explain how the benefits obtained from strength training extend beyond muscle development.

▶ Have each student identify at least one health-related benefit from engaging in regular strength training activity.

▶ Have each student gather three pictures from newspapers, magazines, or the Internet that show how strength training assists health-related fitness (e.g., a teenager throwing a ball far, a construction worker lifting a concrete block, an older person looking healthy and happy).

HIGH SCHOOL

Intensity—How hard a person exercises during a physical activity session. When developing muscular strength and endurance, intensity is increased or decreased by adjusting the amount of resistance (weight) or number of repetitions.

Purpose

Students will learn how to determine a safe 8- to 12-rep range for each of at least two weight training exercises (one upper-body exercise and one lower-body exercise).

Relationship to National Standards

▶ Physical education standard 4: Achieves and maintains a health-enhancing level of physical fitness.

▶ Physical education standard 5: Exhibits responsible personal and social behavior that respects self and others in physical activity settings.

▶ Health education standard 1: Students will comprehend concepts related to health promotion and disease prevention.

Equipment

Variety of free weights or weight machines

Procedure

1. Gather students and briefly introduce the rationale for the lesson—why we find the 8- to 12-rep set: It's an ideal range of repetitions for a muscular strength and endurance program. It provides an intensity that provides benefits to both muscular strength and muscular endurance while minimizing risk of injury.

2. Demonstrate or have a student (whose abilities you're sure of) demonstrate as follows:

    • Simulate that you're on the 7th rep and you're having trouble. Ask, "What should I do?" (Rest for a minute and go to a lighter weight.)

    • Simulate that you're on the 13th rep and things are easy. Ask, "What should I do?" (Go to a heavier weight.)

3. Remind students of the need for proper form and other safety rules. Make it clear that a rep with proper form is the only type of rep that counts toward the 8- to 12-rep range. If they cannot maintain proper form, they are lifting too heavy a weight.

4. Explain the procedure for the day:

    • In groups of two to three at each station, warm up with light weights for 30 seconds, using only enough to get the motion for 8 to 12 reps (e.g.,

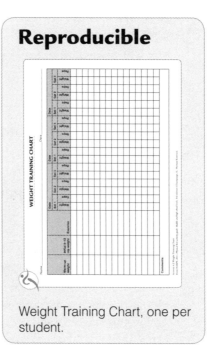

Reproducible

Weight Training Chart, one per student.

empty bar with a free weight or only one, two, or three pegs [plates] down on a weight machine). Use this warm-up weight to help you guess when you might reach fatigue in the 8- to 12-rep range.

- If you cannot lift at least 8 reps with proper form, rest one minute and try again at a lower weight. If you can lift more than 12, rest one minute and then try a heavier weight. Your part-ner can lift while you rest, and you can spot each other. Help each other use proper form. You have a limit of three sets per exercise to find your 8- to 12-rep range. If you do not, adjust your weight 5 to 10 pounds (2.5 to 5 kg) up or down and write it down on your Weight Training Chart for the next time.

5. Have students perform a general body warm-up for three to five minutes. Then release students to the weight stations or machines to do their weight-specific warm-up and range finding.

Students use free weights or machine weights to discover their 8- to 12-rep range.

6. End class with an appropriate cool-down such as stretches specific to the exercises that they've been performing.

Teaching Hints

▶ Although finding the weight at which a person can perform exactly 10 reps of an exercise is considered ideal (Baechle & Earle, 2008), the 8- to 12-rep range is used in this lesson to increase safety through the following means:

- Providing flexibility for students of varying abilities
- Reducing the chance of fatigue by reducing the total number of sets that a person must lift to find the range
- Making it easier to judge a safe weight at which to start, thus limiting the likelihood that a person will lift a weight that is too heavy to be safe for him or her

▶ Emphasize safety at all times:

- Use only exercises for which students have previously learned proper form. Then closely monitor—and have peers monitor—proper form during the lesson.
- Strongly discourage competition for the highest 8- to 12-rep ranges. Explain that the purpose of this lesson is to be able to use safe *lower* or *higher* weights in subsequent lessons to develop individual muscular endurance and strength (respectively), not to determine athletic prowess.
- After students are familiar with their 8- to 12-rep ranges and are achieving adequate fitness levels, you may opt to explain and supervise students in gaining more strength at 6 to 10 reps or more endurance at 10 to 15 reps, depending on their needs and interests. Remember that the 8- to 12-rep range strikes a balance between strength and endurance.

• Remember that you should never ask or allow students to find their 1RM (one-repetition maximum) during class time. Use common sense and always err on the side of safety when adapting this lesson to your students' abilities.

Sample Inclusion Tips

▶ Strength training machines, seats, and benches serve as natural supports and boundaries for students with visual and physical impairments. As appropriate, allow a peer to provide physical assistance to position the student on bench press, leg press, wide-grip pull-down or row, shoulder press machines, and so on before beginning any lifting.

▶ Pictures placed on equipment or a picture schedule will help students work independently.

Variation

After a day of rest, have students identify an additional upper-body and lower-body exercise that they could add to their workouts.

Home Extension

Have students identify exercises that they could do at home and still safely find the 8- to 12-repetition range for one upper-body and one lower-body resistance exercise.

Assessment

▶ Check students' use of the charts against the weights and reps that they recorded on the Weight Training Charts.

▶ After you are sure that each student has successfully determined the 8- to 12-rep range for each of the two exercises through this lesson, have them apply the knowledge by repeating the activity with another exercise or two.

▶ Determine students' ease of connecting the information in this lesson to finding safe warm-up weights by using the activity Warm Up With Weights (pages 60-61); this process may help you determine each student's understanding of the current lesson.

HIGH SCHOOL

Warm-up and cool-down—Increases the temperature of the body and the elasticity of the muscles. A warm-up improves the ability of the muscles to perform work and reduces the risk of injury. A cool-down is the reverse process of the warm-up. A proper cool-down may reduce muscle soreness, help bring body temperature back to normal, and allow muscles to flush wastes generated by exercise.

Note that students need to know their 8- to 12-rep weights per exercise to calculate the weight for each exercise at which they can safely perform a warm-up. The activity Safely Finding the 8- to 12-Rep Range (pages 57-59) contains an activity with guidelines for doing so.

Purpose

▶ Students will understand the importance, benefits, and procedure of warming up before and cooling down after muscular strength and endurance activities, in this case weight training.

▶ Students will figure out an individualized level of resistance for warm-ups and cool-downs.

Relationship to National Standards

▶ Physical education standard 4: Achieves and maintains a health-enhancing level of physical fitness.

▶ Physical education standard 5: Exhibits responsible personal and social behavior that respects self and others in physical activity settings.

▶ Health education standard 1: Students will comprehend concepts related to health promotion and disease prevention.

Equipment

▶ Variety of free weights or weight machines

▶ Pencils, one per student

Procedure

1. Discuss or review with students the importance and benefits of a properly conducted warm-up, especially with the higher resistance of weight training.

2. Divide students into pairs or small groups. Instruct groups to monitor each other's form and performance while encouraging each other to get the most out of the activity.

3. Have students perform multiple-joint strength exercises for warming up. Appropriate exercises include bench presses; leg presses, lunges, or squats; wide-grip pull-downs or rows; and shoulder presses, because these each involve several muscle groups.

4. For each of the exercises selected, students should have previously determined the amount of weight they can properly handle for 8 to 12 repetitions (activity 4.2).

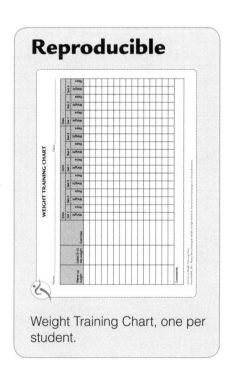

Reproducible

Weight Training Chart, one per student.

5. Direct them to reduce that amount of weight by half for their warm-up weight. For example, if a student can do 10 reps with 60 pounds (25 kg), the student's warm-up weight would be 30 pounds (12.5 kg).

6. Direct students to record their individual warm-up weights for each exercise on their Weight-Training Charts. Have them refer to these weights each time they warm up before a strength training workout.

7. For a cool-down, have students use the same amount of weight as was calculated for the warm-up.

Teaching Hints

▶ Be sure that students warm up and cool down each time they work out so that they develop the habit.

▶ Alternate and modify the exercises you choose for warm-ups and cool-downs based on your equipment and student needs.

▶ Caution students against lifting free weights without a spotter if they plan to strength-train outside of class.

Sample Inclusion Tips

▶ Have students trade charts with each other to check that they calculated their warm-up weights correctly before performing the warm-up.

▶ Pictures placed on equipment or a picture schedule will help students work independently.

Weights can be used to warm up and cool down muscles.

Variations

▶ Incorporate flexibility exercises in the cool-down that are specific to the muscle groups being used in each exercise.

▶ Allow students to work with a partner and discuss benefits of working out with others.

Home Extension

Have students identify proper warm-up resistance exercises that they could use for the at-home exercises they created in activity 4.2.

Assessment

▶ At the conclusion of the lesson, ask students to list the importance, benefits, and procedures of properly warming up and cooling down.

▶ Review students' weight charts for their warm-up information. Make sure that they have calculated reasonably low weights to prevent injury.

▶ Have students choose a favorite physical activity and write a proper warm-up and cool-down routine for the activity, based on the principles learned.

▶ Include questions on the importance, benefits, and procedures of warming up and cooling down on a strength training unit assessment.

▶ Ask students how having a partner or small group might help them work on strength training outside of class time (e.g., motivation, encouragement, proper form). Ask this during a class discussion or when monitoring groups, or have students record their thoughts in a journal.

MUSCLE FITT BINGO

MIDDLE SCHOOL AND HIGH SCHOOL

Specificity—The principle of specificity states that to bring out changes in a particular body system, muscle, or skill, a person must perform activities that target that particular body system, muscle, or skill.

Purpose

Students will match exercises and the muscles that they are working out when completing fitness exercises.

Relationship to National Standards

- ▶ Physical education standard 2: Demonstrates understanding of movement concepts, principles, strategies, and tactics as they apply to the learning and performance of physical activities.
- ▶ Physical education standard 3: Participates regularly in physical activity.
- ▶ Physical education standard 4: Achieves and maintains a health-enhancing level of physical fitness.

Equipment

- ▶ Pencils, one per student or group
- ▶ Resistance bands of various levels of resistance, one per student (allow students to choose one that meets their fitness level)
- ▶ Mats for floor work

Procedure

1. Each student or group of students gets a Muscle FITT Bingo Card.
2. A muscle name is drawn out of a hat, and students try to find the exercise on the bingo card that will work out the muscle.
3. After a match is found, students mark the spot on their card and complete the activity listed on the card for 30 seconds.
4. Continue pulling muscle names until bingo (FITT) is called (or until all squares on the bingo card are marked [covered]).

Teaching Hint

Make sure that students know how to complete all the listed exercises safely before they perform them.

Sample Inclusion Tips

- ▶ Students are allowed to work with partners or supplemental materials.

Reproducible

Muscle FITT Bingo Card

F	I	T	T
Shoulder presses	Flys	Crunches	Curls
Lateral shoulder raises	Upright rows	Overhead extensions	Press-ups
Rows	Shrugs	Push-ups	Side crunches
Squats	Lying leg curls	Standing calf raises	★

Activity 4.4 Muscle FITT Bingo Card
From NASPE, 2011, Physical best activity guide: Middle and high school levels, 3rd edition (Champaign, IL: Human Kinetics).

Muscle FITT Bingo Cards, one per student or group.

- ▶ Students can brainstorm exercises and muscles before playing to help prepare for the activity.
- ▶ Use pictures of body parts beside written task cards to help body part recognition.

Variation

Use the blank bingo card to create your own version of the game by adding new exercises as you teach them.

Home Extension

Have students create their own Muscle FITT Bingo Cards that include exercises they can do at home.

Assessment

1. Instead of giving students a Muscle FITT Bingo Card that is already completed with the exercises, have the sheets be filled out with the muscle names. When a muscle is called, they have to write the exercise down in the box that would exercise that muscle.

The familiar game of bingo helps students apply the concept of specificity by matching activities with the muscles being worked during those activities.

2. After the students have all the activities and muscles matched, have them develop a program to follow.

MUSCLES IN ACTION

MIDDLE SCHOOL

Specificity—The principle of specificity states that to bring about changes in a particular body system, muscle, or skill, a person must perform activities that target that particular body system, muscle, or skill.

Purpose

▶ Students will identify the location of the following muscles and muscle groups: trapezius, deltoid, pectorals, latissimus dorsi, obliques, gluteus maximus, rectus abdominis, quadriceps, hamstrings, gastrocnemius, triceps, and biceps, and select exercises for those muscles.

▶ Students will be able to name the muscle when shown its location on the body.

Relationship to National Standards

▶ Physical education standard 4: Achieves and maintains a health-enhancing level of physical fitness.

▶ Physical education standard 5: Exhibits responsible personal and social behavior that respects self and others in physical activity settings.

▶ Health education standard 1: Students will comprehend concepts related to health promotion and disease prevention.

▶ Health education standard 3: Students will demonstrate the ability to practice health-enhancing behaviors and reduce health risks.

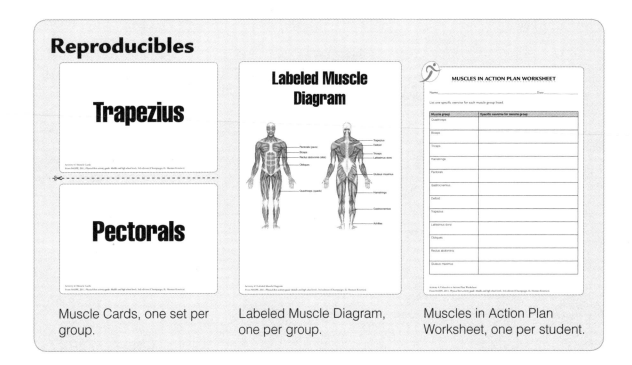

Muscle Cards, one set per group.

Labeled Muscle Diagram, one per group.

Muscles in Action Plan Worksheet, one per student.

Equipment

- ▶ Masking tape for each group
- ▶ Folders, each of which contains a Labeled Muscle Diagram; one folder for every three students

Procedure

1. Before class, tape a Labeled Muscle Diagram on one wall of the activity area, spacing them evenly. Explain that today the students will be putting their muscles into action by creating a muscle model and a plan for exercising those muscles.

2. Divide students into groups of three. Give each group a set of laminated Muscle Cards. Direct each group to select one person to model the Muscle Cards, that is, to become the muscle model. The other two group members alternate taping the laminated cards to the correct muscle location on their muscle model.

3. When all 12 Muscle Cards have been placed on the model, one group member asks the teacher for the folder with the Labeled Muscle Diagram. The group uses the diagram to check the accuracy of the muscle cards that they taped to their muscle model. Any incorrectly placed Muscle Cards must be corrected.

4. When a group feels confident that each member can identify the location of all 12 muscles, they return the Muscle Cards and diagram folder to the teacher, who gives each student a Muscles in Action Plan Worksheet.

5. After reviewing the labeled Muscles in Action Exercise Posters posted on the wall, each student designs a personal Muscles in Action Plan by selecting one exercise for each muscle or muscle group listed on the plan.

6. When all members of the group have completed their Muscles in Action Plan Worksheet, students in the group alternate leading their group in the selected exercises.

7. Students need to keep their plans in their fitness portfolios.

8. In a large group discuss (1) which muscle locations and names are most difficult to remember; (2) which exercises are their favorites; and (3) how best to use the Muscle in Action Plan Worksheets.

Students practice muscular fitness activities to determine which muscle groups are affected.

Teaching Hints

▶ Laminate the exercise pictures and muscle diagrams.

▶ Encourage students to be respectful when placing the Muscle Cards on the models.

▶ If students' touching each other creates a management problem, form same-sex groups and ask models to attach cards themselves, based on peer instructions.

Sample Inclusion Tip

This activity introduces the identification of specific anatomical body parts. All students must begin to develop the initial concepts of personal body image. Students with cognitive or learning disabilities may have a peer buddy assist them in identifying a general locale to a specific muscle group, such as by touching the body part and giving a generally acceptable muscle name or anatomical site for the more specific name (e.g., pectorals as pecs or chest muscles; deltoids as shoulder muscles; obliques as abdominals).

Variations

▶ When students think that they know the muscles, they can all label the muscle diagram sheet on their own and turn it in to the teacher.

▶ If students are not already familiar with the muscle groups and exercises, select a few to focus on at each class and complete the activity over two or three class periods.

Home Extension

Ask students to create a full-body workout that they could do at home over the summer or semester break to maintain their muscular fitness level.

Assessment

▶ Point to a specific exercise picture and ask students to identify the muscle group worked.

▶ Name a muscle group and ask students to demonstrate one exercise designed to affect that muscle group.

MIDDLE SCHOOL

Intensity and progression—Intensity refers to how hard a person exercises during a physical activity session. The appropriate intensity for an activity session depends on the age and fitness goals of the participant. When developing muscular strength and endurance, intensity is increased or decreased by adjusting the amount of resistance (weight) or number of repetitions. Progression refers to how a person increases the overload, thereby placing greater than normal demands on the musculature of the body. The level of exercise should be gradually increased and may be manipulated by increasing the frequency, intensity, time, or a combination of all three components. In muscular strength and endurance training, progression involves a systematic approach to increasing the resistance and intensity of the activity.

Purpose

▶ Students will identify and perform push-ups that are appropriate for their individual fitness level.

▶ Students will explain how the principles of intensity and progression apply to this activity.

Relationship to National Standards

▶ Physical education standard 3: Participates regularly in physical activity.

▶ Physical education standard 4: Achieves and maintains a health-enhancing level of physical fitness.

▶ Physical education standard 5: Exhibits responsible personal and social behavior that respects self and others in physical activity settings.

Reproducibles

Mission Push-Up Possible Card, one per group.

Mission Push-Up Possible Chart, one per group.

Individual Push-Up Progress Sheet, one per student.

▶ Physical education standard 6: Values physical activity for health, enjoyment, challenge, self-expression, and/or social interaction.

▶ Health education standard 1: Students will comprehend concepts related to health promotion and disease prevention.

▶ Health education standard 3: Students will demonstrate the ability to practice health-enhancing behaviors and reduce health risks.

Equipment

▶ Large envelopes with "Mission Push-Up Possible" written on the outside in large letters; one envelope for every three to four students

▶ Two colored markers in each envelope

▶ Chairs, one for every three or four students

▶ Benches, one for every three or four students

▶ Mats, one for every three or four students

▶ Chart paper, one sheet for every three or four students

▶ Wall tape (to secure chart paper to wall)

▶ Optional: *Mission Impossible* music and player

Procedure

1. Review the concepts of intensity and progression, providing several examples.

2. Divide students into groups of three or four. Give each group a Mission Push-Up Possible envelope. Review the Mission Push-Up Possible Card that is in each group's envelope. Each group will design five different push-ups that range in difficulty from least difficult to most difficult. Encourage all students to experiment with different types of push-ups. Emphasize that students are determining their baseline for push-ups, that the activity is not a competition, and that all students are capable of progressing to higher-level push-ups if they carefully apply the fitness principles of intensity and progression.

3. Post a large version of the Mission Push-Up Possible Chart for all to see.

4. Allow groups time to create their Push-Up Progression Charts, illustrating the five push-ups that they have designed (see the instructions on the Mission Push-Up Possible Cards).

5. Ask students to post their group's chart of push-up illustrations on the wall, leaving about 6 feet (2 m) between each chart. If wall space is not available, secure charts by other means, such as to the back of a chair or in slotted cones.

6. After a group's chart is posted, ask each student in the group to select the push-up level that best matches his or her fitness level. Each student attempts to perform at least 10 repetitions of the selected push-up, while maintaining proper form.

7. When a student can perform more than 10 push-ups at a given level, the student may move to the next level. If a student cannot perform 10 push-ups at a given level, the student should stay at that level until she or he can perform 10 push-ups.

8. Give each student an Individual Push-Up Possible Progress Sheet to document progress over a period of several weeks. Have students keep their sheets in a fitness portfolio or other organizer for future use.

9. Ask each group to share their most creative push-ups with the class. Discuss the principles of progression and intensity as they relate to this activity.

Teaching Hints

▶ Provide a list of push-ups such as high-five push-up, wall push-up, clap in between push-up, hands close together push-up; hands far apart push-up; crossed-leg push-up; knee push-up; incline push-up.

▶ Ask students to review all groups' Mission Push-Up Possible Charts and collectively select seven or eight progressively difficult push-ups that can become the Class Push-Up Chart.

Sample Inclusion Tips

A student with a disability can perform push-ups in a variety of ways.

▶ Allow a student who uses a wheelchair to remain in the chair and perform wheelchair push-ups (release chair seatbelt and allow the student to position him- or herself as needed; the student places the hands on the arm rests, pushes self up and lowers self down with control, and performs as many as possible).

▶ Students who cannot support their weight with their arms might do variations of biceps curls, arm circles, or triceps extensions.

▶ Allow students with limited upper-body strength to perform bent leg push-ups or standing push-ups in an inclined position against the wall.

▶ Use a wedge or bolster to support the chest area of students who have poor strength and mobility.

Variations

Allow time for students to create a push-up variation routine alone, with a partner, or with a small group (emphasize that not everyone has to do the same exercises at the same time or do the same number).

Home Extension

Encourage students to help a friend or family member find a push-up variation that is appropriate for her or his fitness level by teaching the person several push-up variations.

Assessment

Review the students' Individual Push-Up Progress Sheets:

▶ Is each student recording progress on the sheet?

▶ Is each student making progress?

▶ Have students pair up and share with each other how the push-up activity relates to the principles of intensity and progression. Randomly call on pairs to share their thoughts with the entire class.

It is important for students to learn how to adjust their intensity levels so that they can get the most effective workout. In Mission Push-Up Possible, they experiment with various kinds of push-ups to discover varying intensities.

GET FIT

MIDDLE SCHOOL

Specificity—To bring about changes in a particular body system, muscle, or skill, a person must perform activities that target that particular body system, muscle, or skill.

Purpose

Students will work to improve their muscular fitness by trying a variety of exercises and making choices about how best to work at their own intensity level.

Relationship to National Standards:

▶ Physical education standard 4: Achieves and maintains a health-enhancing level of fitness. (The exercises completed in this lesson can easily be performed in any environment to enable the student to participate outside of class).

▶ Physical education standard 5: Exhibits responsible personal and social behavior that respects self and others in physical activity settings. (Group members will take turns leading their group through the task, assisting those who need guidance.)

▶ Physical education standard 6: Values physical activity for health, enjoyment, challenge, self-expression, and/or social interaction.

Equipment

▶ Four cones

▶ Four poly spots

▶ Mats for floor work

▶ Aerobic steps or benches (optional)

▶ Chairs or weight benches

▶ Floor tape

Procedure

1. Set up the activity space using the four cones as boundaries. Place a poly spot to the inside of each cone (inside the space) and place the index cards on each poly spot separated by muscle group (upper, lower, abdominal, and full body). (See figure 4.1 for setup.)

2. Allow students to choose a partner with whom they can work well and instruct them to go to one of the four cones.

Reproducibles

Get Fit Worksheet, one per student.

Lower Body

Wall Sits

Position your back against the wall, your feet flat on the floor, and your knees at 45 or 90 degrees. Count 15, 45, or 60 seconds.

Get Fit Exercise Signs, one per pair.

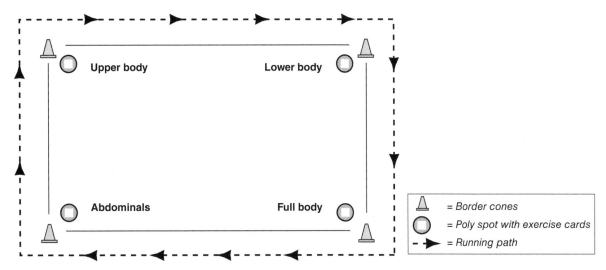

Figure 4.1 Get Fit floor diagram.

3. On the whistle, one partner draws a card from the stack and reads the instructions. The other partner begins running three laps around the coned area only after his or her partner reads, understands, and begins the exercise.

4. The partner performing the exercise continues until his or her partner completes three laps.

5. The partners then switch tasks and repeat. Before rotating to the next station, they return the card to the bottom of the pile.

6. Then both partners rotate clockwise to the next station.

7. Partners repeat steps 4 through 6 until they complete their assessment sheet.

Teaching Hints

▶ Students can take their target heart rate and record their results on the assessment page.

▶ Students can use pedometers and keep track of their steps throughout the activity.

▶ Instruct students to select a partner with whom they can work productively by staying on task even when they think that the teacher can't see them.

Sample Inclusion Tips

▶ Exercise task cards that offer choices can help accommodate various abilities (i.e., modified push-ups on knees or various numbers of repetitions: 8 low, 12 medium, 15 high).

▶ Instruct students to work according to their skill level, allowing for a break between sets of repetitions while their partners are completing their laps.

▶ Using pictures for task cards and numbers at each station can promote student independence.

Variations

▶ Allow students to do a set and rest briefly as needed while their partners complete their three laps.

▶ Students doing laps could also dribble a soccer ball or basketball or jump rope at the go signal.

Home Extension

Encourage students to go to a local workout club and ask to interview a fitness trainer about the principle of specificity and creating full-body workouts.

Assessment

Teachers can use the Get Fit Worksheet to help students keep track of heart rate as well as steps (if pedometers are used).

MUSCLE UP

HIGH SCHOOL

Specificity—To bring about changes in a particular body system, muscle, or skill, a person must perform activities that target that particular body system, muscle, or skill.

Purpose

▶ Students will identify muscles used to improve specific skills.

▶ Students will describe the principle of specificity.

Relationship to National Standards

▶ Physical education standard 4: Achieves and maintains a health-enhancing level of physical fitness.

▶ Physical education standard 5: Exhibits responsible personal and social behavior that respects self and others in physical activity settings.

▶ Health education standard 1: Students will comprehend concepts related to health promotion and disease prevention.

Equipment

▶ Pencils, one per student

▶ Items specific to the sample stations described in the procedures, with substitutes used as needed:

• Medicine ball
• Hand weights
• Resistance bands or resistance tubing
• Floor tape
• Cones
• Balance boards
• Volleyballs or basketballs

Procedure

1. Before class, set up 10 stations around the perimeter of the activity area. As an example, refer to the sidebar "Activity Station Suggestions for Basketball"

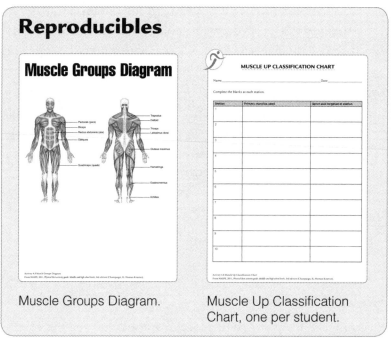

Muscle Groups Diagram.

Muscle Up Classification Chart, one per student.

Students learn to use various muscle groups by performing activities to discover which muscle groups are emphasized.

on page 74. Leave the center area open for aerobic activity. Briefly review the major muscle groups using the Muscle Groups Diagram and the principle of specificity.

2. Distribute a Muscle Up Classification Chart and a pencil to each student. Explain that the charts will be completed as the students progress through the stations.

3. Divide students into 10 small groups and assign each group to a different station. Explain that students will rotate clockwise to the next station every two minutes.

4. After groups have completed two or three stations, signal them to move to the aerobic area and perform a selected aerobic activity for two to three minutes.

5. Have students return to the stations and continue progressing through them, rotating to an aerobic activity after they complete every two or three stations.

6. Ask students to share and discuss their Muscle Up Classification Charts within their groups.

Teaching Hint

Play music in two-minute segments to accommodate the station changes and increase motivation.

Sample Inclusion Tips

▶ Decrease time or intensity of certain activities. For example, use lighter weights or no weights or substitute various sizes of beanbags as hand weights.

▶ Activity stations designed to self-challenge and self-test students with behavioral and emotional disorders are considered developmentally appropriate activities for this population.

Variation

You can use this activity as a springboard for any sport. The key is for the stations to emphasize the primary muscles used in the sport.

Home Extension

Allow students to create their own resistance exercise plan for a favorite activity of their own.

Assessment

▶ Monitor the small group discussions of the Muscle Up Classification Charts.

▶ In a large group, discuss students' work on the classification chart and respond to questions or errors.

▶ Ask students to write a definition of specificity and an example of specificity on a separate sheet of paper or in their fitness portfolios.

ACTIVITY STATION SUGGESTIONS FOR BASKETBALL

The following stations can be used to develop muscular strength, muscular endurance, and motor skills specific to basketball.

Medicine Ball Pass
Students chest-pass a medicine ball to each other.

Lateral Slides and Vertical Jumps
Set up four or five obstacles for students to slide around. After they have completed slides, have students move to the closest wall, where you have placed six 4-inch (10 cm) pieces of tape on the wall at varying heights. Students progress through the tape area, jumping six times, each time attempting to better the height of their previous jump.

Wrist Curls
Using hand weights or resistance bands, students perform sets of 10 wrist curls and 10 reverse wrist curls.

Wall Sit
Students maintain a wall-sit position for as long as possible.

Rebound
Students chest-pass a ball against the wall and continually rebound their tosses.

Squat Jumps
Students perform as many squat jumps as possible for two minutes.

Agility Drill
Use gym tape to outline a ladder on the floor. Ask students to jump with both feet together "up and down" the ladder without stepping on the tape. Have them perform both laterally and straight forward and backward.

Dot Drill
Ask students to perform the dot drill pattern as quickly and accurately as possible. Dot drills are used for agility and leg strength and muscle endurance. The student stands on two dots that are spread about 2 feet (60 cm) apart, jumps back with both feet together, and then jumps back again with the legs spread. The student jumps forward again with feet together and then jumps forward with legs apart again. Students perform this activity going forward and backward as quickly and accurately as possible.

Balance Drill
Use balance boards or ask students to hold the following poses: stork stand with eyes open and then with eyes closed; one leg up at 90 degrees with eyes open and then with eyes closed; rise up on toes and hold.

Deltoid Drill
Have students perform a series of lifts that strengthen the deltoids (e.g., shoulder presses, lateral raises, front raises, rear raises). They can use either hand weights or resistance bands.

MUSCULAR FITNESS SCAVENGER HUNT

MIDDLE SCHOOL AND HIGH SCHOOL

Specificity—The principle of specificity states that to bring about changes in a particular body system, muscle, or skill, a person must perform activities that target that particular body system, muscle, or skill.

Purpose

▶ Students will be able to define specificity (type) with respect to muscular fitness.

▶ Students will choose muscular fitness exercises to develop specific muscle groups.

Relationship to National Standards

Physical education standard 4: Achieves and maintains a health-enhancing level of physical fitness.

Equipment

▶ 12 hula hoops

▶ Resistance bands

▶ Upbeat music and player (optional)

▶ Storage bags (sandwich baggies) to hold puzzle pieces, one per station

Reproducibles

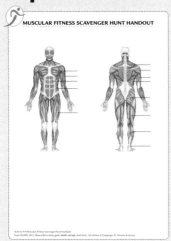

Muscular Fitness Scavenger Hunt Handout, one per student.

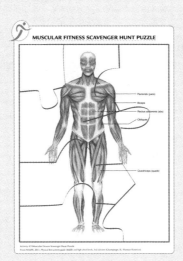

Muscular Fitness Scavenger Hunt Puzzle. Cut into pieces along the dashed lines and place one puzzle in a numbered baggie for each group of two or three students. Place numbered baggies in the center of the activity space.

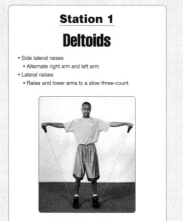

Muscular Fitness Scavenger Hunt Station Cards. Set up stations around the outside of the activity space.

▶ Mats for floor work
▶ Medicine balls
▶ Aerobic steps or benches

Procedure

Set up the activity before students enter the activity space.

1. Set up 12 muscular fitness stations around the outer edges of the gym. At each station place the necessary equipment in a hoop.

2. Place one Muscular Fitness Scavenger Hunt Puzzle for each group in a numbered plastic storage bag in the middle of the gym or activity space. If you are using a basketball court, place station cards around on the side and end-line areas and baggies with a puzzle in the middle of the court. Because there are 12 stations, it is best to have 12 numbered baggies. You will tell students that the station number where they are standing is their group number and puzzle number.

After students arrive, the activity proceeds as follows:

1. Divide students into groups of two or three. Send each group to one of the 12 stations.

2. Give each student a Muscular Fitness Scavenger Hunt Handout and ask them to work together to label their muscle diagram. Students will work together, but each completes her or his own muscle diagram sheet.

3. After a group thinks that they have labeled their diagrams correctly, they should place their papers face down.

4. Let students know that they will check their answers by putting together their Muscle Man Puzzle, which they will find in a baggie in the middle of the activity space. Tell students to look at the station number where they are starting to know their group number and the number on the baggie that contains their puzzle. Each team works together to retrieve all puzzle pieces.

5. One at a time, students run to their puzzle in the middle of the floor to retrieve one puzzle piece and run back to the group. Each member of the group runs to retrieve a piece until they have collected all the puzzle pieces.

6. All other group members must walk, jog, or jump rope in place when they are not the one going to get a puzzle piece from the middle of the floor. This aerobic activity acts as a warm-up for the students before they perform the muscular fitness activities at the stations.

7. After the group puts together all the puzzle pieces, they will see the answers to the Muscular Fitness Scavenger Hunt Handout that they tried to complete on their own. Have students check and correct their answers using the answers revealed on the puzzle.

8. Say the following: "I will know your group's puzzle is complete and everyone in the group has the correct answers when everyone in a group sits down and shouts together, 'PE IS GREAT, YES, INDEED, PE IS GREAT!' "

9. Groups now rotate to all stations. Rotate about every three minutes. Music can be used to signal rotations to new stations.

10. At each station students choose muscular fitness exercises that they want to perform for a specific muscle and attempt to do one or two sets of 10 to 12 repetitions. Let students know that they can choose to perform more than one exercise at each station. This option allows them the freedom to choose and explore different activities.

11. Have students record the name of the exercises and the number of repetitions that they completed on their muscle diagram next to the correct muscle label.

Teaching Hints

▶ If you do not have resistance bands, hand weights can be used at the stations.

▶ The concept of specificity can be introduced after students label the muscle diagram and are ready to choose exercises to perform at each station.

Sample Inclusion Tips

▶ Students should be able to work at their own intensity level if they can choose among the following things:

  • several different resistance bands,

  • the number of reps and sets that they perform, and

  • the type of exercise that they perform at each station.

▶ Change the type of exercise and intensity level as needed for students to be appropriately challenged at various stations.

▶ Have students work with a partner in the group to help them identify and label muscles.

Variation

Station cards can be used without the puzzle or student handout sheet.

Home Extension

Remind students to complete upper- and lower-body muscular fitness exercises at home two or three days a week.

Assessment

▶ Students can turn in their labeled muscle diagrams.

▶ Create an exit slip asking students to define and provide an example of specificity.

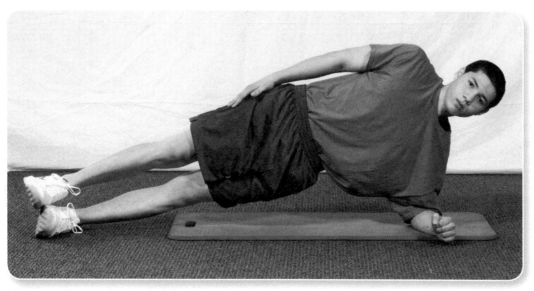

Muscular Fitness Scavenger Hunt allows students to explore specificity when they choose from a variety of exercise options.

KNOW YOUR WAY AROUND THE WEIGHT ROOM

HIGH SCHOOL

Type—The kind of exercise that the person engages in.

Purpose

- ▶ Students will understand and apply the type component of the FITT guidelines.
- ▶ Students will understand the principle of specificity as it applies to weight training.
- ▶ Students will understand the importance of incorporating a variety of exercises into a personal fitness plan.

Relationship to National Standards

- ▶ Physical education standard 1: Demonstrates competency in motor skills and movement patterns needed to perform a variety of physical activities.
- ▶ Physical education standard 3: Participates regularly in physical activity.
- ▶ Physical education standard 4: Achieves and maintains a health-enhancing level of physical fitness.
- ▶ Physical education standard 5: Exhibits responsible personal and social behavior that respects self and others in physical activity settings.
- ▶ Physical education standard 6: Values physical activity for health, enjoyment, challenge, self-expression, and/or social interaction.

Equipment

Weight room, a variety of weights and weight machines

Reproducibles

Know Your Way Around the Weight Room: Peer Teaching Exercise Descriptions, one per group.

Know Your Way Around the Weight Room Peer Assessment, one per student.

Know Your Way Around the Weight Room Exercises, one per group.

Common Weight Room Errors, one per group.

Procedure

1. Divide the class into groups of two to four students. Explain to the groups that each will be responsible for researching a particular exercise to teach to the class in a peer teaching scenario.

2. Before the peer teaching experience, model the teaching of an exercise so that the students are familiar with the expectations of the assignment.

3. Provide the students with the Know Your Way Around the Weight Room Exercises and Common Weight Room Errors handouts and any additional resources that will assist them in planning their exercise (i.e., books, Web sites). Emphasize to the students the importance of being critical consumers of information.

4. Allow the groups class time to research their exercise and practice their teaching before the actual peer teaching experience.

5. Allow two or three groups five to eight minutes to present their exercise to the class each day (presentations may take several days depending on how many exercises are assigned). Groups not presenting will complete a peer assessment that examines three things that they learned because of the teaching of an exercise. All presentations are done in the first several minutes of class, and students may then proceed to their scheduled workouts.

Teaching Hints

Include insights that make this activity easy to understand and execute.

▶ Be sure to monitor the progress of each group and answer any questions that students may have about their assigned exercise. Emphasize correct form and safety at all times.

▶ Reinforce the FITT guideline of type as it applies to weight training through group discussion and written assessments.

▶ Emphasize the concept of specificity as it applies to weight training and the ways in which weight training can positively benefit muscular strength and endurance.

Sample Inclusion Tips

▶ Work individually with students who need assistance in modifying equipment.

▶ Consult the special education teacher concerning techniques that will allow all students to have an active role in the peer teaching experience.

Variation

Do this activity for exercises that all focus on a specific muscle group (all upper body, for example).

Home Extension

Have students go to a local workout club to interview certified personal trainers on proper weight training technique related to their assignment.

Assessment

▶ Written assessment may be used to check for understanding of the various exercises demonstrated.

▶ Class discussion may focus on strategies to incorporate the various exercises into a personal fitness plan.

▶ Require students to incorporate the various exercises into a personal fitness plan.

Students learn about exercise type by teaching their peers muscular strength and endurance exercises.

MUSCULAR STRENGTH AND ENDURANCE FITT LOG

MIDDLE SCHOOL AND HIGH SCHOOL

Progression—How a person should increase overload. Proper progression involves a gradual increase in the level of exercise that is manipulated by increasing frequency, intensity, or time, or a combination of all three components.

Purpose

▶ Students will learn and apply the training principles of progression and overload.

▶ Students will learn and apply the training principles of progression and overload for muscular strength and endurance by completing a FITT log and worksheet.

Relationship to National Standards

▶ Physical education standard 3: Participates regularly in physical activity.

▶ Physical education standard 4: Achieves and maintains a health-enhancing level of physical fitness.

▶ Health education standard 3: The student will demonstrate the ability to practice health-enhancing behaviors and reduce health risks.

Equipment

Pencil for each student

Procedure

1. Briefly review the two-word definitions of the aspects of FITT—frequency (how often), intensity (how hard), time (how long), and type (what kind).

2. Ask students to offer brief examples of how they applied the FITT guidelines to muscular strength and endurance in previous health-related fitness activities.

3. Share descriptions of the concepts of progression and overload.

4. Distribute one blank FITT Log to each student. Review each category and how it relates to each aspect of FITT.

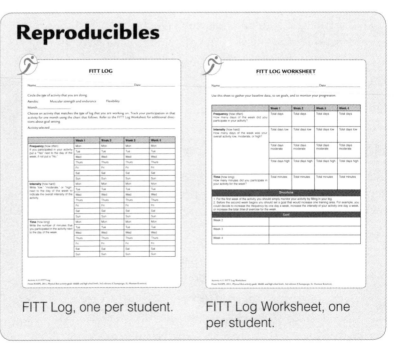

FITT Log, one per student.

FITT Log Worksheet, one per student.

5. Ask the class to share muscular activities that they enjoy and tell them to choose one and write it in their log.

6. Ask each child to circle "muscular strength and endurance" on the FITT Log to indicate the type of activity that they are tracking. Have them also write their name on the log.

7. Assign students to log their muscular strength and endurance physical activity performed outside class one week.

8. Have students complete week 1 of the FITT Log and FITT Log Worksheet.

9. Guide students in setting goals for progression and overload and writing them on the worksheet.

10. At the end of each week, meet with the class to discuss their progress and set new goals.

Teaching Hints

▶ Ask students at each class meeting how their logs are coming along.

▶ Require parent or guardian initials if necessary to encourage participation.

▶ Have students demonstrate the home-based activity ideas at an open house.

▶ Ask the school's after-school care providers to provide space, time, and other support for students to add to their logs.

The Muscular Strength and Endurance FITT Log will help students become aware of how their activities outside of school help them to use and build their muscles.

▶ Tie in the Fitnessgram muscular strength and endurance assessments with this activity.

Sample Inclusion Tip

Help students with special circumstances come up with alternative activities to suit their needs and abilities. You can modify activities suggested earlier in this chapter, provide suggestions for students who must stay indoors because of safety or space constraints, or otherwise help students develop activity ideas that will work for them.

Variations

▶ Ask the school's after-school care providers to provide space, time, and other support for students to add to their logs.

▶ Tie the Fitnessgram muscular strength and endurance assessments to this activity.

▶ The activity is set up for one week and one month, but it can be changed for specific circumstances to cover one day to two weeks to a month to several months. Select the period that works best for the specific needs of the students.

Home Extension

This activity is a home extension.

Assessment

After the month, have students review their logs with you and write about their experience by answering questions such as the following:

▶ Were you able to build up safely to a higher level of intensity over the course of the month, do the activities more frequently each week, or spend more time doing each activity? Which changes did you make, if any?

▶ If you were able to make changes, how might the changes have affected your muscular fitness?

▶ If you did not make changes, what might you be able to do differently in the future?

Realize that many factors, such as the child's initial level of fitness and participation (if already high, the student may not progress for that reason), and other personal factors may affect the answers to these question. Keeping this in mind, focus on the assessment as a means to teach and reinforce the concepts of progression and overload.

Flexibility

Chapter Contents

Forgiss

Flexibility is the ability to move a joint through its complete range of motion. The goal is to develop and maintain normal joint range of motion. Keep in mind that having too much flexibility predisposes people to injury and therefore can be as potentially detrimental as having too little flexibility (ACSM, 2009).

Flexibility can bring about many benefits:

▸ Decreased muscle tension and increased relaxation—I can sleep better.

▸ Greater ease of movement—I can move easier.

▸ Improved coordination—I can perform better in sport or dance.

▸ Increased range of motion—I can bend, stretch, and twist into many positions.

▸ Reduced risk of injury—I can move safely.

▸ Better body awareness and postural alignment—I have good posture.

▸ Improved circulation and air exchange—I can breathe easier.

▸ Smoother and easier contractions—My muscles work better.

▸ Decreased muscle soreness—I am less sore after leisure activities.

▸ Possible prevention of low-back pain and other spinal problems—I can sit through my day at school without my back feeling sore.

▸ Improved personal appearance and self-image—I feel good about myself.

▸ Facilitates the development and maintenance of motor skills—I can participate in a variety of activities.

DEFINING FLEXIBILITY

Two types of flexibility (static and dynamic) and four types of stretches (static, active, PNF, and passive) foster the development of flexibility and improved range of motion.

▸ Static flexibility is defined as the range of motion at a joint or group of joints.

▸ Dynamic (ballistic) flexibility is the rate of increase in tension in a relaxed muscle as it is stretched (Knudson, Magnusson, & McHugh, 2000).

▸ A static stretch is a slow, sustained stretch of the muscle held for 10 to 30 seconds. The person stretches the muscle–tendon unit to the point of mild discomfort and then backs off slightly (holding the stretch at a point just before discomfort occurs).

▸ In an active stretch, the person stretching provides the force of the stretch (for example, in the sit-and-reach, the person leans forward and reaches as far as possible).

▸ In a passive stretch, a partner provides the force of the stretch.

▸ Proprioceptive neuromuscular facilitation (PNF) is a static stretch that uses combinations of the active and passive stretching techniques. Pubescent and postpubescent students as well as those who have developed a solid base of training and are undergoing formal athletic conditioning can perform this type of stretch (Bompa & Carrera, 2005). Safety, proper instruction, and responsibility are key issues in performing the PNF stretch. Injury may result when students are not responsible or fail to listen to the cues of their partners, thereby forcing a stretch or incorrectly performing a stretch.

TEACHING GUIDELINES FOR FLEXIBILITY

As in all areas of health-related fitness, the principles of training (progression, overload, specificity, regularity, and individuality) must be applied. The FITT guidelines (table 5.1) also play a key role in improving flexibility.

In applying the principles of training and the FITT guidelines, be aware of the factors that affect flexibility (see *Physical Education for Lifelong Fitness: The Physical Best Teacher's Guide, Third Edition*) and therefore the improvement that you may or may not observe.

TRAINING METHODS FOR FLEXIBILITY

Choose a variety of flexibility exercises and a variety of teaching methods to incorporate flexibility concepts and to prevent boredom and the drudgery of performing the same stretches in your daily lesson plans. This is also the time to explain the relationship between flexibility exercises performed in class

Table 5.1 FITT Guidelines Applied to Flexibility

Frequency	Three times per week, preferably daily and after a warm-up to raise muscle temperature.
Intensity	Slow elongation of the muscle to the point of mild discomfort and back off slightly.
Time	Up to 5 stretches per muscle or muscle group. Hold each stretch 10–30 sec. Always warm up properly before stretching.
Type	The preferred stretch for the classroom is slow static stretching for all muscles or muscle groups.

Note: Although 10–30 seconds is recommended as the length of time to hold a stretch, an advanced student may hold a stretch up to 60 seconds.

Modified from Knudson, Magnusson, and McHugh 2000; modified from American College of Sports Medicine 2009.

with the back-saver sit-and-reach test and shoulder stretch test (Fitnessgram) performed during the fitness assessment portion of your program. When teaching flexibility concepts, stress safety and proper technique. Students should use slow, controlled movements when stretching, holding each stretch to the point of mild discomfort (and perhaps backing off slightly) for 10 to 30 seconds. Holding the stretch at the point of discomfort and backing off slightly ensures application of the overload principle.

Other safety precautions include the following:

▶ Avoid locking any joint (soft knees, soft joints).

▶ Do not overstretch a joint (pay attention to the tightness felt during the stretch).

▶ Never stretch the neck or spine too far.

▶ Do not perform ballistic stretches (reserved for controlled, sport-specific training of secondary students and adults).

▶ A trained health care professional should check a student who has excessive mobility.

Along with observing these safety precautions, be aware of questionable exercises or contraindicated exercises as presented in *Physical Education for Lifelong Fitness: The Physical Best Teacher's Guide, Third Edition.*

Flexibility is an important component of health-related fitness, so resist the temptation to relegate it to warm-ups and cool-downs. The activities that follow provide several opportunities to use flexibility as the focus of your lesson or to add variety to your warm-ups and cool-downs.

MOTOR-SKILL DEVELOPMENT THROUGH FLEXIBILITY ACTIVITIES

Being flexible through a full range of motion (ROM) is essential to performing motor skills successfully, and a student with limited ROM will have greater difficulty performing a motor skill that a classmate with greater flexibility will learn easily. The specificity principle applies here. For example, if a student wants to be able to punt a football or perform a high kick in a soccer game, he or she must have good leg and hip flexibility. Good flexibility, then, enhances the ability to perform the motor skill.

Motor-skill development through fitness activity is the perfect area for you to integrate activities while considering the abilities of all students. Some are high achievers, others are low achievers, and still others have physical or intellectual disabilities. Provide opportunities for all students to develop physical skills and be successful in your classroom. If a student has a severe disability, you may need to contact a person who specializes in adapted physical education for assistance in developing an individualized education plan.

When students see the connections between flexibility and physical activities that they are engaging in, they are more likely to continue working on enhancing flexibility as part of their health and fitness plan. In short, you create a deeper awareness of the need for flexibility. See table 5.2 on page 86 for a grid of activities in this chapter.

Table 5.2 Chapter 5 Activities Grid

Activity number	Activity title	Activity page	Concept	Middle school	High school	Reproducibles (on CD-Rom)
5.1	Stretch Marks the Spot	87	Specificity	•		Stretch Marks the Spot Handout
						Flexibility Task and Benefit Cards
5.2	All-Star Stretches	89	Health benefits	•	•	Flexibility Task and Benefit Cards
						Guidelines for Safe Stretching Poster
						Benefits of Good Flexibility Poster
5.3	Flexibility Puzzles	92	Flexibility benefits	•	•	Benefits of Good Flexibility Poster
						Flexibility Puzzle
						Flexibility Word Search Answer Key
						Flexibility Word Search Worksheet
						Stretch Station Cards
5.4	Type Cast	95	Specificity	•	•	Flexibility Task and Benefit Cards
						Benefits of Good Flexibility Poster
5.5	Sport Spectacular	98	Specificity		•	Sport Stretch Pages
5.6	Introduction to Yoga	100	Frequency and time	•	•	Yoga Signs
						Yoga Pose Cards
						Yoga Log
5.7	Flexibility FITT Log	103	Progression	•	•	FITT Log
						FITT Log Worksheet

STRETCH MARKS THE SPOT

MIDDLE SCHOOL

Specificity—To increase flexibility of a particular area, a person must perform exercises for a specific muscle or group and must do it on a regular basis (can be done daily).

Purpose

▶ Students will be able to define flexibility and identify specific flexibility exercises for various body parts and muscle groups.

▶ Students will understand the importance of stretching exercises as a means of injury prevention and muscle and joint health.

Relationship to National Standards

▶ Physical education standard 2: Demonstrates understanding of movement concepts, principles, strategies, and tactics as they apply to the learning and performance of physical activities.

▶ Physical education standard 3: Participates regularly in physical activity.

Equipment

▶ Mats for floor work

▶ Pencil or marker, one per student

Procedure

1. Explain to students the definition of flexibility and importance of flexibility exercises and their role in maintaining normal joint range of motion. To stretch a muscle properly, exercises should be performed slowly and carefully. The performer is stretching a muscle properly if she or he feels a slight pulling sensation in the belly of the muscle.

2. For this activity the Flexibility Task and Benefit Cards should be posted around the room.

3. Put students in groups of two to four at the various stations.

4. Upon the command to begin, students perform the flexibility exercise as pictured and hold for 10 seconds.

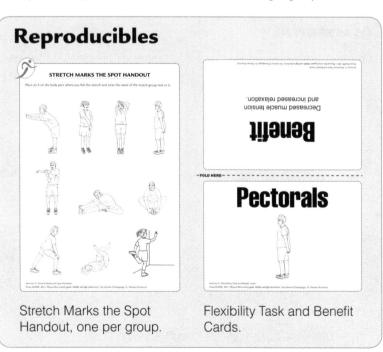

Stretch Marks the Spot Handout, one per group.

Flexibility Task and Benefit Cards.

5. Upon completion, the group should discuss what muscle group was being targeted and place an X on the worksheet.

6. After a few moments the group should rotate to the next station.

Teaching Hints

▶ Remember to have students complete a full warm-up and cool-down before performing stretches.

▶ Students should rotate in one direction to avoid collision.

Sample Inclusion Tip

Students with limited attention may require the assistance of an aide.

Variation

Teachers can cut the cards instead of folding so that the anatomical name *isn't* included on the station cards, making it more difficult for students to fill in their worksheets.

Flexibility exercises can help students learn about the musculature of their bodies.

Home Extension

Have students identify a friend or family member whom they want to teach about flexibility. Tell the students to demonstrate a stretch and name the muscle for each major muscle group. Allow students to practice this activity in class. They should ask the friend or family member to write a short note indicating that the student has completed the task.

Assessment

Upon completion review the worksheets for proper identification of targeted muscle areas.

MIDDLE SCHOOL AND HIGH SCHOOL

Health benefits—Keeping the joints flexible is important in promoting overall health and safe participation in physical activity. Benefits of stretching include a maintained or increased range of motion; decreased risk of injury in sport, daily chores, and tasks; increased blood supply and nutrients to the joints; reduced muscular soreness after activity; and improved balance, mobility, and posture.

Purpose

▶ Students will understand the benefits of good flexibility.

▶ Students will identify unsafe versus safe stretches and stretching practices.

Relationship to National Standards

▶ Physical education standard 4: Achieves and maintains a health-enhancing level of physical fitness.

▶ Physical education standard 5: Exhibits responsible personal and social behavior that respects self and others in physical activity settings.

▶ Health education standard 1: Students will comprehend concepts related to health promotion and disease prevention.

Equipment

Mats for floor work

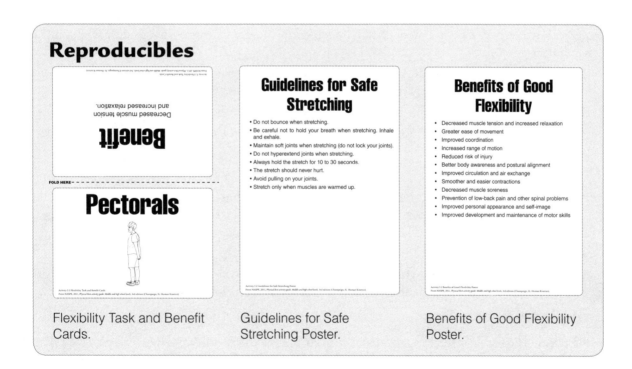

Flexibility Task and Benefit Cards.

Guidelines for Safe Stretching Poster.

Benefits of Good Flexibility Poster.

All-Star Stretches help students understand the health benefits of good flexibility while they sort out which stretches are safe and unsafe.

Procedure

1. Explain that good flexibility can be achieved only through practicing safe stretching techniques. Students who injure themselves stretching incorrectly will not benefit. Review the Guidelines for Safe Stretching Poster. Mention that certain types of stretches that students may have heard of or used, such as PNF and dynamic (ballistic) stretches, are only for specific situations, such as sport training, and can be done safely only under carefully guided conditions. In this lesson, the focus will be on static and active stretching, as described on the poster.

2. Lead or have student leaders lead the class through a whole-body warm-up lasting three to five minutes (e.g., walking and then jogging in place or a fast-paced review of dance steps).

3. Shuffle the Flexibility Task and Benefit Cards. Lead or have student leaders lead the class through each of the 16 cards. Leaders will read the benefit and demonstrate how to perform the stretch.

Teaching Hints

▶ To increase time on task for experienced students, eliminate step 1 under "Procedure" and simply hang the safety poster at each group's area to remind students of the safety guidelines.

▶ Connect the safety guidelines and benefits to the back-saver sit-and-reach test and shoulder stretch test in Fitnessgram.

▶ You may wish to point out that stretching to the point of mild discomfort and backing off slightly (but still feeling the stretch) applies the overload principle of training to flexibility.

Sample Inclusion Tips

▶ Provide yoga-style stretching straps or similar aids to assist students who have limited flexibility or find it difficult to get into the correct positions. You can use towels, belts, neckties, lengths of clothesline, rope, or resistance bands as stretching straps.

▶ Some students with Down syndrome will be prone to hyperflexibility (because of laxity in joint ligaments). Observe and assign a peer buddy to observe the posture and alignment of the student with a disability during flexibility movements. Provide verbal and physical cues to produce correct movement.

Variation

Place all task cards face down on the floor in the middle of the gym. Group students in pairs or groups of three. Have student groups positioned around the outer edges of the gym. On the "Go" signal, groups send one group member to the middle to draw a card and take it back to the group. The group member reads the card and leads the exercise. Another group member takes the card back to the middle and picks up another one. Groups repeat this until the teacher signals "Stop."

Home Extension

Have students create a stretching routine that they perform at home several days a week.

Assessment

▶ Have students name one or more benefits of good flexibility and relate those benefits to their everyday activities or sport activities in which they participate.

▶ Offer a worksheet that shows three safe stretches and one unsafe practice. Ask students to identify the unsafe practice and to write or tell why it is unsafe.

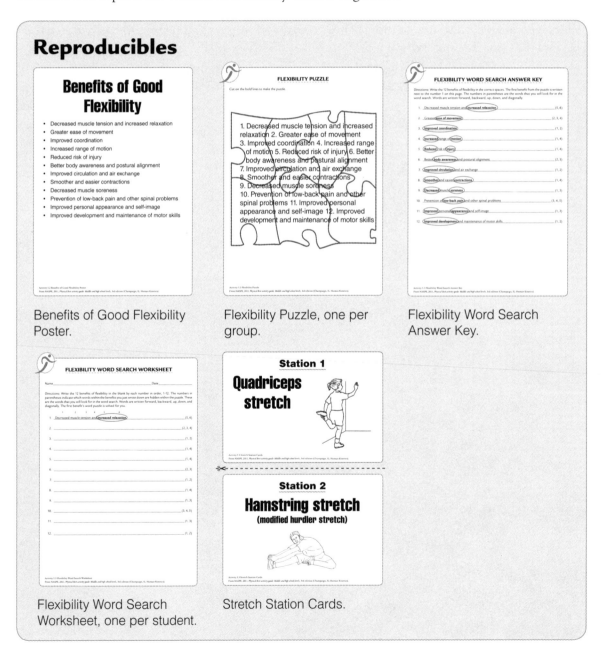

5.3

FLEXIBILITY PUZZLES

MIDDLE SCHOOL AND HIGH SCHOOL

Flexibility benefits—Flexibility is the ability to move a joint through a full range of motion. Some benefits of flexibility include a decreased risk of injury in sports; being able to perform daily chores and tasks; increased blood supply and nutrients to the joints; reduced muscular soreness after activity; and improved balance, mobility, and posture.

Purpose

Students will explore the benefits of flexibility while being active.

Reproducibles

Benefits of Good Flexibility Poster.

Flexibility Puzzle, one per group.

Flexibility Word Search Answer Key.

Flexibility Word Search Worksheet, one per student.

Stretch Station Cards.

Relationship to National Standards

▶ Physical education standard 1: Demonstrates competency in motor skills and movement patterns needed to perform a variety of physical activities.

▶ Physical education standard 2: Demonstrates understanding of movement concepts, principles, strategies, and tactics as they apply to the learning and performance of physical activities.

▶ Physical education standard 4: Achieves and maintains a health-enhancing level of physical fitness.

Equipment

▶ Mats for floor work

▶ Writing implements

Procedure

1. Students perform a five-minute warm-up session to make sure that muscles are warm, loose, and ready to be stretched. The warm-up can be related to skills that students may have recently learned such as dribbling a soccer ball in self-space, rallying with a partner across a line or net with short-handled paddles or badminton rackets, a 3 vs. 3 half-court basketball game, or a favorite tag game.

2. Place the 12 stretch stations around the gym with pictures of the stretches as well as words that explain the stretches.

3. Students visit each station for one minute. They read the card or look at the picture and complete the stretch. After they are done with the stretch, they pick up a puzzle piece for that station and carry it with them to all stations. Students may work in partners or small groups, depending on class size.

4. After students have visited all stations, they put the puzzle together. Listed on the puzzle are the 12 flexibility benefits.

5. Students write the benefits down on the word search card. The word search card tells the students which words to look for in the puzzle.

6. When the puzzle is completed, the students then work individually to complete a word search based on the puzzle, trying to find the 12 benefits. The benefits are paraphrased, and the students are given the list of what to look for exactly in the word search.

Teaching Hints

▶ All students can improve their flexibility with time and specificity. Encourage students to stretch on their own at home as well as during physical education class.

▶ Make sure that students know how to do these stretches properly before sending them out to participate. Also, make sure that the students are stretching statically (not bouncing).

Sample Inclusion Tips

▶ Be sure that pictures of stretches are easy to see for those who may have trouble reading or understanding English.

▶ Modify stretches so that students who use wheelchairs can stretch each major muscle group in a sitting position. Stretches can also be modified so that they can be performed standing up if students have trouble getting to or from the floor.

▶ An adult partner can help students hold stretches.

Variations

▶ To make this activity more difficult, take some of the key words out of the puzzle pieces and have the students fill them in as they learn about flexibility benefits.

▶ To make the activity easier, do only one puzzle or the other.

Home Extension

Have students teach one stretch for each major muscle group to a friend or family member.

Assessment

▶ Before beginning a stretching focus, have the students take angle measurements for the various stretches. At the end,

Students collect puzzle pieces and gain the benefits of flexibility training in Flexibility Puzzles.

have them take the same measurements again to see whether they have improved. Numerous calculations can be made with the numbers, such as percent improvement or decline.

▶ Have each student learn one stretch and benefit. Then have the students form groups that have one student for each stretch and benefit. The students teach the stretches and benefits to their classmates.

MIDDLE SCHOOL AND HIGH SCHOOL

Specificity—To increase flexibility of a particular area, a person must perform exercises for a specific muscle or group and must do it on a regular basis (can be done daily).

Purpose

▶ Students will learn how to apply the principle of specificity in the area of flexibility.

▶ Students will identify specific muscle groups used in particular sports or activities.

Relationship to National Standards

▶ Physical education standard 2: Demonstrates understanding of movement concepts, principles, strategies, and tactics as they apply to the learning and performance of physical activities.

▶ Physical education standard 4: Achieves and maintains a health-enhancing level of physical fitness.

▶ Physical education standard 5: Exhibits responsible personal and social behavior that respects self and others in physical activity settings.

Equipment

▶ Blank index cards, enough for one per group at each station

▶ Pencils, one per group

▶ Mats for floor work

▶ Relaxing background music and music player (optional)

Procedure

1. Place flexibility stations around the activity area, each with one Flexibility Task and Benefit Card and several index cards.

2. After the class participates in a simple warm-up such as a brisk walk around the activity area, define and discuss flexibility. You may want to include the following points:

   • Flexibility is the ability to move a joint through its complete range of motion.

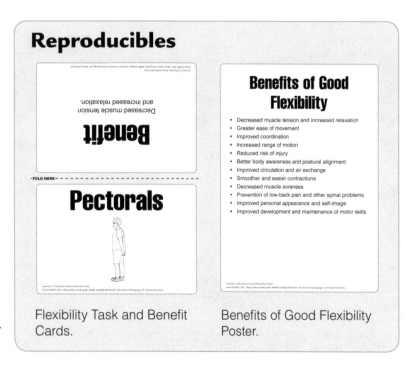

Flexibility Task and Benefit Cards.

Benefits of Good Flexibility Poster.

- A safe way to improve flexibility is to use static stretching. A static stretch is a slow, sustained stretch of the muscle.
- Stretch to the point of mild discomfort, back off slightly, and hold the stretch for 10 to 30 seconds. (Or hold the stretch at the point just before it becomes uncomfortable.)
- Identify the relationship between flexibility exercises and the ability to participate safely in physical activities.
- Explain that flexibility exercises are used after a warm-up to prepare the body for physical activity and after cool-down to develop flexibility further.
- Review with students the difference between warm-up and stretching. Warm-up is a low-level, nonstressful activity that uses the whole body to stimulate blood flow throughout the body. The warm-up is different from stretching. Stretching comes after warm-up and after cool-down. This point is important because students may think that stretching is a warm-up and cool-down. Too often students begin group stretching without any warm-up. This procedure is not conducive to obtaining a good stretch and can lead to injury.

3. Remind students that flexibility is specific to the muscle group worked. That is, to gain flexible leg muscles, they have to perform stretches that stretch the leg joints and muscles; to gain flexible shoulders, they have to stretch the shoulder joint muscles. Point out that different activities—such as soccer, dance, and swimming—require flexibility in different parts of the body.

4. Divide students into groups of three or four, give each group a pencil, and send each group to a station.

5. Instruct students to
   - perform the static stretch that appears on the Flexibility Task and Benefit Card for 10 to 30 seconds,
   - determine an activity that would benefit from this stretch (e.g., guarding in soccer, leaping in dance, using arm strokes in swimming, and so on),
   - write that activity on a blank index card, and
   - leave both the index card (face down) and the Flexibility Task and Benefit Card at the station.

6. Rotate groups to new stations every couple of minutes, based on the amount of time available and the number of stations. Stopping and starting music may help make the transition easier.

Teaching Hints

▶ If needed, before starting the activity, review the location and function of each muscle group that students are stretching as well as correct stretching form.

▶ Set up enough stations to keep each group at four or fewer students. Make second copies of some of the cards if needed.

▶ Use flexibility stations after a warm-up or cool-down.

Different activities and sports require the use of different muscles, often in different ways. In Type Cast, students start thinking "outside the gym" about what other activities might be enhanced through specific flexibility exercises.

Sample Inclusion Tips

▶ Use peer assistants to demonstrate the proper technique for each stretch.

▶ Before incorporating modifications, allow students with disabilities to attempt to perform activities.

▶ Tape arrows on the wall or floor to direct students to the next station.

Variation

Rather than just asking students to list any activity that would benefit from the stretch, have them write down activities that they would like to do or learn about in physical education.

Home Extension

Have students write down everyday chores and tasks that each stretch may help them to do with ease even as they get older.

Assessment

▶ Collect all index cards with students' activity suggestions written on them. As a class, review and evaluate students' selection of activities for several flexibility stations.

▶ Have students as a whole class name the muscle group or groups stretched at each station.

SPORT SPECTACULAR

HIGH SCHOOL

Specificity—To increase flexibility of a particular area, a person must perform exercises for a specific muscle or group and must do it on a regular basis (can be done daily).

Purpose

▸ Students will explore specific stretches for a physical activity or sport in which they are interested.

▸ Students will enhance their flexibility through participating in sport- or activity-specific stretches over time and connect the principle of type (specificity) to the benefits of injury prevention and enhanced performance.

Relationship to National Standards

▸ Physical education standard 3: Participates regularly in physical activity.

▸ Physical education standard 4: Achieves and maintains a health-enhancing level of physical fitness.

▸ Health education standard 1: Students will comprehend concepts related to health promotion and disease prevention.

Equipment

▸ Mats for floor work

▸ Blank sheets of paper for self-designed specific flexibility workout pages

▸ One sign per sport or activity to mark stations where related reproducible can be found

▸ Pencils

Procedure

1. Review or teach students the principle of specificity. Briefly discuss how it applies to flexibility training.

2. Give an overview of the sports and activities for which you have flexibility training workout sheets to offer. Ask students to select one sport or activity to work on with flexibility today. Lead or have student leaders lead a whole-body warm-up for a minimum of five minutes (an aerobic fitness activity is best).

3. Divide the class into four groups and send each group to one of the activity areas to practice the stretches shown on the related sheet. Require students to repeat the stretches according to safety guidelines as time allows. Have students fill in the "Muscles and body parts stretched" section individually or as a group.

4. Gather students back into the main group to discuss briefly how they predict that the specific stretches might enhance their sport performance, if performed

Reproducible

Sport Stretch Pages, one per student.

frequently enough with appropriate intensity.

Teaching Hints

▸ If possible, have students follow their sport- or activity-specific stretching with the sport or activity itself, both in and outside of class, and end it with a cool-down that includes some or all of the sport- or activity-specific stretches.

▸ Over multiple class sessions, have students switch to different activity areas until they complete all four Sport Stretch Pages.

Sample Inclusion Tips

▸ Before incorporating modifications, allow students with disabilities to attempt to perform activities.

▸ The buddy system allows all students the opportunity to work with others. Use verbal and visual aids (picture cues) as well as physical cues or demonstrations and allow students with disabilities to mirror peers.

Students learn how to use flexibility specificity to their advantage when engaging in various sports and activities.

Variation

If a student is not interested in any of the sports or activities offered in the reproducibles, help that student choose appropriate stretches from other sources, for another sport or activity. In other words, choose wisely to create a specific flexibility training workout that will enhance performance in the preferred sport or activity.

Home Extension

Encourage students to lead their friends or teammates in a stretching routine after a brief warm-up but before intense movement begins.

Assessment

▸ Discuss the "Muscles and body parts stretched" section for each sport and stretch.

▸ Require students to log their sport- or activity-specific flexibility training over the course of one to four weeks. Ask students to write comments about how specificity in flexibility training may enhance their performance in the sport or activity.

MIDDLE SCHOOL AND HIGH SCHOOL

Frequency and time—The recommended frequency for flexibility training is daily to attain the maximum benefits. Time refers to how long the stretch is held, and recommendations vary widely from 10 seconds to 1 minute. A person should always begin holding a stretch for a short time and gradually progress to 30 seconds.

Purpose

▶ Students will learn to apply the frequency and time components of the FITT guidelines to flexibility through an introduction to yoga.

▶ Students will learn a flexibility activity that can reduce stress and increase relaxation.

Relationship to National Standards

▶ Physical education standard 6: Values physical activity for health, enjoyment, challenge, self-expression, and/or social interaction.

▶ Health education standard 3: Students will demonstrate the ability to practice health-enhancing behaviors and reduce health risks.

Equipment

▶ Mats for floor work

▶ Relaxing music and player

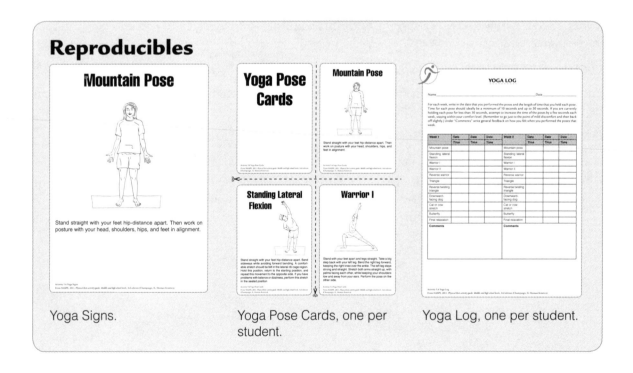

Reproducibles

Yoga Signs.

Yoga Pose Cards, one per student.

Yoga Log, one per student.

Procedure

1. Place mats and Yoga Signs at stations throughout the activity area (or use your own cards if you prefer). Lights should be dim, and relaxing music should be playing as students enter.

2. To introduce the activity, explain the procedure to students during the preceding class period. Ask them to remember to enter the class setting quietly. You might briefly discuss yoga, its benefits, its history, and so on. In addition, mention how yoga can reduce stress and increase feelings of relaxation.

3. Have students perform a light warm-up, such as walking for a few minutes.

Yoga offers a flexibility activity that helps students work on the mind and the body.

4. After brief instructions, have students remove their shoes and choose a station. Remind students to be quiet. Have students face you and lead them in the mountain pose as a group. Although this pose is not a stretch, it is an opportunity to set the tone for the activity. Following that, have the students read the card and look at the picture, and then attempt the yoga position.

5. Allow about two minutes for reading and practicing. Then turn the music down as a signal to move to the next station.

6. Allow students to go through as many stations as you desire or as time permits. Finish with the final relaxation pose as a group.

7. Pass out the Yoga Pose Cards and Yoga Logs and ask students to practice the poses three times per week when their muscles are warmed up. Discuss time in relation to flexibility and ask them to log their frequency and time on their log for the next two to four weeks.

Teaching Hints

▶ Familiarize yourself and the students with yoga poses and related safety information before teaching this activity.

▶ Before the lesson, design a bulletin board display of yoga pictures and basic information, including its relationship to athletic performance (and overall wellness).

▶ Note that some poses will need to be performed on both sides of the body.

Sample Inclusion Tips

▶ For students with a cognitive or learning disability or those with a behavioral or emotional disorder, use the peer buddy system.

▶ You can move around the room providing assistance as needed.

Variations

▶ Use available yoga videos that students can easily follow after they have practiced. Some videos even combine yoga with power and endurance moves for challenging workouts. We recommend Beth Shaw's *YogaFit* (2001) book and video as references for this activity. For more information on *YogaFit*, visit www.yogafit.com or call Human Kinetics at 800-747-4457 to order copies. The video is about 30 minutes long, which is a good length for school classes.

▶ Have students design their own yoga routine, using the poses—starting with the mountain pose and finishing with the final relaxation pose.

Home Extension

Have students find a friend or family member to perform a yoga routine with at least two days a week.

Assessment

After the two- to four-week period, collect logs and lead a class discussion on the logs. Here are additional discussion suggestions:

▶ What do the students think was the most challenging aspect of this activity?

▶ Have the students describe why yoga can reduce stress.

▶ How might the students incorporate yoga into an overall fitness plan?

FLEXIBILITY FITT LOG

MIDDLE SCHOOL AND HIGH SCHOOL

Progression—How a person should increase overload. Proper progression involves a gradual increase in the level of exercise that is manipulated by increasing frequency, intensity, or time, or a combination of all three components. The overload principle states that a body system (cardiorespiratory, muscular, or skeletal) must perform at a level beyond normal for it to adapt and improve physiological function and fitness.

Purpose

Students will learn and apply the training principles of progression and overload to flexibility by completing a FITT Log and Worksheet.

Relationship to National Standards

▶ Physical education standard 3: Participates regularly in physical activity.

▶ Physical education standard 4: Achieves and maintains a health-enhancing level of physical fitness.

▶ Health education standard 3: Students will demonstrate the ability to practice health-enhancing behaviors and reduce health risks.

Equipment

▶ Pencils

▶ Any equipment required by the assessment selected

Procedure

1. Briefly review the two-word definitions of the aspects of FITT—frequency (how often), intensity (how hard), time (how long), and type (what kind).

2. Ask students to offer brief examples of how they have applied the FITT guidelines to flexibility in previous health-related fitness activities.

3. Share descriptions of the concepts of progression and overload.

4. Distribute one blank FITT Log to each student. Review each category and how it relates to FITT. Outline how students can apply progression as they use the form.

5. Ask the class to share flexibility activities, to choose two or three stretches for various body parts

Reproducibles

FITT Log, one per student.

FITT Log Worksheet, one per student.

and to write them on the "Activity selected" line of their logs.

6. Have each student write her or his name on the log.

7. Assign students to log their flexibility physical activity performed outside class for one week.

8. Have students fill in one week of the FITT Log.

9. Guide students in setting goals for progression and overload and have them write their goals on the FITT Log Worksheet.

10. At the end of each week, meet and discuss their progress and set new goals.

Teaching Hints

▶ Ask students at each class meeting how their logs are coming along.

▶ Require parent or guardian initials if necessary to encourage participation.

Sample Inclusion Tips

▶ Help students with special needs develop alternative activities based on their level of ability.

To see true progression in flexibility health, students should continue to practice their stretching exercises outside of the classroom.

▶ You can modify activities suggested and keep a basic log as required by other students.

▶ Students with special needs also need to set a personal goal under the guidance of an adult.

Variations

▶ Ask the school's after-school care providers to provide space, time, and other support for students to add to their logs.

▶ Tie in the Fitnessgram flexibility assessments.

Home Extension

The lesson and the variations give the extension of the activity outside of class.

Assessment

After the month, have students review their logs with you and write about their experience by answering questions such as the following:

▶ Were you able to safely build up to a higher level of intensity over the course of the month, do the activities more frequently each week, or spend more time doing each activity? Which changes did you make, if any?

▶ If you were able to make changes, how might the changes have affected your flexibility fitness?

▶ If you did not make changes, what might you be able to do differently in the future?

Realize that many factors, such as the child's initial level of fitness and participation (if already high, the student may not progress for that reason) and other personal factors may affect the answers to these questions. Keeping this in mind, focus on the assessment as a means to teach and reinforce the concepts of progression and overload.

Body Composition

Chapter Contents

© Elke Dennis - Fotolia.com

Activities in this chapter provide a means to present the concepts of body composition and basic nutrition in relationship to the development of appropriate levels of health-related fitness. At the middle and high school levels, students should understand the major concepts regarding body composition:

▶ Energy intake and expenditure

▶ Guidelines for healthy eating such as the Food Guide Pyramid

▶ Factors that affect body composition such as genetics, diet, and physical activity

When participating in these activities, students should understand how their actions affect their body composition. The following information introduces the subject of body composition at the middle and high school levels. For more information on this topic, refer to *Physical Education for Lifelong Fitness: The Physical Best Teacher's Guide, Third Edition,* chapters 4 and 8, which focus on nutrition and body composition.

BODY COMPOSITION, PHYSICAL ACTIVITY, AND NUTRITION

Body composition is the amount of lean body mass (all tissues other than fat, such as bone, muscle, organs, and body fluids) compared with the amount of body fat, usually expressed in terms of percent body fat. Among the common ways to assess whether body composition is appropriate are BMI-for-age tables, skinfold caliper testing, height–weight tables, and waist-to-hip ratio.

As with any other component of health-related fitness, a person's body composition does not develop in isolation from the other components. Indeed, you should show students the connections among all health-related fitness components so that they can see how their personal choices affect this area of health-related fitness. Although genetics, environment, and culture play significant roles, body composition results largely from physical activity levels in the other components of health-related fitness:

▶ Aerobic fitness—Aerobic activities expend calories.

▶ Muscular strength and endurance—Muscle cells expend (metabolize) more calories at rest than fat cells do. To increase the likelihood that students will maintain appropriate body composition, emphasize physical activity that follows the principles of training.

▶ Flexibility—A flexible body can better tolerate aerobic activities and muscular strength and endurance activities.

Nutrition also plays an important role in body composition. In addition to reviewing the Food Guide Pyramid (see reproducible on the CD-ROM for activity 6.6, "Health Quest"), lessons should also present an opportunity to discuss appropriate portion sizes. In the United States, portion sizes have been increasing for the last three decades. The Western diet includes many highly processed, high-fat, high-sugar, and high-salt foods. The human body was designed to work best with whole grains, vegetables, and fruits.

Nutrients fall into six classes: carbohydrate, protein, fat, vitamins, minerals, and water. Because all nutrients are essential for good health, the diet must contain all six.

▶ Carbohydrate provides most of the energy for people across the world and represents the major source of energy for the body. People obtain carbohydrate from whole grains, cereals, vegetables, and fruits. Refined grains and sugars can also provide carbohydrate.

▶ Protein serves as the structural component for vital body parts. Every cell in the body contains protein. In the United States, meat is the primary source of protein.

▶ Fat serves as a concentrated form of energy, and the human body stores excess calories as fat.

▶ Vitamins and minerals contain no calories, but small amounts are essential for good health.

▶ Many students do not realize that water is an essential nutrient. Students need to drink at least six to eight cups of water daily.

TEACHING GUIDELINES FOR BODY COMPOSITION

Approach discussions about body composition objectively and with sensitivity. Strive to point out connections among physical activity, nutrition, and body composition related to daily life, recreational activities, and physical education activities. Never use a student as a positive or negative example regarding body composition. Emphasize that a person who is "overfat" because of genetics can still greatly reduce health risks by being physically active. Remember that students will follow your lead with their peers. If you're comfortable with the topic, they will be, too.

Society places a great deal of emphasis on physical appearance, and this attention to appearance becomes important during puberty. As a physical educator, you must help students find satisfaction with their appearance rather than try to measure up to cultural expectations. When presenting this topic, you may encounter students who are below or above normal ranges for body composition or who have diagnosed or undiagnosed eating disorders, such as the following:

▶ Anorexia nervosa—characterized by extremely low caloric intake with a distorted body image.

▶ Bulimia nervosa—characterized by large food binges followed by purging with vomiting, laxatives, or overexercising.

▶ Binge-eating disorder—characterized by large food binges with no compensatory behavior. This results, of course, in periods of rapid weight gain.

Be on the lookout for warning signs of eating disorders. If you suspect an eating disorder, be sure to discuss this with the school nurse, school dietitian, and principal before deciding how to proceed.

Although approaching body composition in the physical education setting can be a delicate matter, it's an important component of fitness that should be addressed. Handle body composition instruction professionally by concentrating on how a healthy diet and active lifestyle can positively affect it. Encourage a positive self-image and emphasize that normal bodies come in all sizes. See table 6.1 on page 108 for a grid of activities in this chapter.

Table 6.1 Chapter 6 Activities Grid

Activity number	Activity title	Activity page	Concept	Middle school	High school	Reproducibles (on CD-Rom)
6.1	All-Sport Body Composition Quizzo	109	Body composition	•		Body Composition Quizzo Chart
						Body Composition Quizzo Term Cards
						All-Sport Body Composition Activity List
6.2	Body Composition Survivor	112	Health benefits	•	•	Body Composition Survivor Challenges
						Benefits of Developing and Maintaining Ideal Body Composition Puzzle
						Risks of Having a High Percentage of Body Fat Puzzle
						Body Composition Facts Puzzle
						Super Survivor Questions
6.3	Frisbee Calorie Blaster	116	Health benefits	•		None
6.4	Nutrition Memory	118	Food and portion size	•		Food and Portion Memory Cards
						Food and Portion Memory Card Key
6.5	Cross-Training Triumph	120	Growth and development		•	Cross-Training Triumph Tasks
6.6	Health Quest	123	Nutrition	•	•	Checkpoint Signs
						Health Quest Answer Sheet
						Food Guide Pyramid
6.7	Fast-Food Frenzy	126	Nutrition	•		Fast-Food Frenzy Discovery Worksheet
						Calorie Chart
						Fast-Food Frenzy Station Signs
						Lunch Menu Suggestion Cards
						Health Behavior Contract
6.8	Calorie Balancing Act	131	Energy expenditure and weight management		•	Activity and Calorie Information Sheet
						Eat the Food, Do the Time Worksheet
6.9	Jump Rope Digestion	134	Nutrition and digestion	•		Digestive System Component Chart
						Food Guide Pyramid

MIDDLE SCHOOL

Body composition—While participating in a variety of skill development activities, students enhance their knowledge of body composition and the ways in which it affects personal health.

Purpose

▶ Students will review a variety of body composition terms while engaging in physical activity.

▶ Students will match the body composition term to its corresponding definition.

Relationship to National Standards

▶ Physical education standard 4: Achieves and maintains a health-enhancing level of physical fitness.

▶ Health education standard 1: Students will comprehend concepts related to health promotion and disease prevention.

Equipment

▶ Basketballs, one per group

▶ Volleyballs, one per group

▶ Jump ropes, one per group

▶ Tennis rackets and Koosh balls, one per group

▶ Soccer balls, one per group

▶ Dot Drill Mat (or dots taped to the floor)

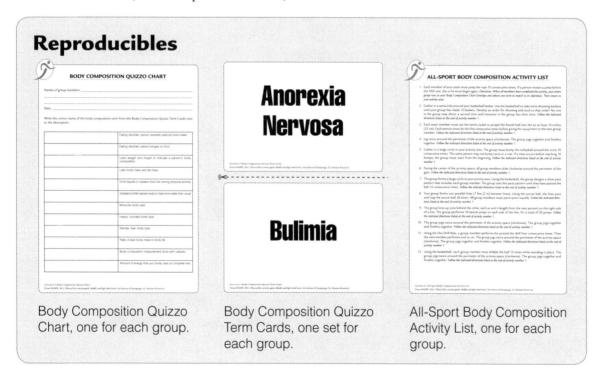

Reproducibles

Body Composition Quizzo Chart, one for each group.

Body Composition Quizzo Term Cards, one set for each group.

All-Sport Body Composition Activity List, one for each group.

▶ Laminated envelope

▶ Pencils

Procedure

1. Before class begins, post each group's Body Composition Quizzo Chart in a separate area of the activity space; evenly space these charts.

2. Next to each chart, post an envelope that contains all the Body Composition Quizzo Term Cards.

3. Ask students to explain the relationship between body composition and physical activity.

4. Explain that today's lesson will combine physical activity with a review of body composition terms.

5. Ask students to name a few body composition terms (metabolism and so on).

6. Discuss the activity guidelines:

   • Each group works cooperatively as a team to accomplish specific tasks and earn term cards. After a team has earned a term card, they must report it on their Body Composition Quizzo Chart by writing the term next to the correct description.

   • After they have matched a term correctly, the team may begin the next activity on their list. After completing each separate activity (in order) on the list, the team may select one more term from the envelope to match to its definition on their Body Composition Quizzo Chart.

   • The ultimate goal is for each group to match all the term cards to the correct definitions on their Body Composition Quizzo Chart. But remind them that a group can earn only one term card for each completed activity. To earn another term card, the group must complete the next activity.

   • Divide students into groups of four to six students.

   • Give each group an All-Sport Body Composition Activity List. Then assign each group to a specific area of the gymnasium where they will find the equipment necessary to complete the activities.

   • When a group has completed all activities and thereby matched all terms to their appropriate definitions, ask the group to double-check their answers.

Teaching Hints

▶ Modify the All-Sport Body Composition Activity List to meet the interests of your students or your equipment inventory.

▶ To use the activity repeatedly or with other classes, laminate each of the reproducible items and place Velcro on the backs of the Body Composition Quizzo Term Cards and on the blanks on the Body Composition Quizzo Chart.

▶ The Body Composition Quizzo Term Cards are in the correct order (reading from top to bottom) to match the Body Composition Quizzo Chart. You will want to shuffle the cards for the students' use, but you can refer to the original printout of the cards as an answer key.

Sample Inclusion Tips

▶ For classes that have students with cognitive or learning disabilities, assign a group leader to read aloud, interpret the activities, and guide the group in performing the activities.

▶ For students with physical impairments, modify the activities as needed. For example, split jump ropes, lower the basketball hoop, and so on.

Variation

Ask each group to take one food group and list all the benefits that those foods have on physical activity. After all groups have made their list ask group members to share and discuss how eating a balanced diet can help improve physical performance.

Home Extension

Have students keep a dietary journal for three days. In their journals they write how many servings from each food group they ate during meals or snacks. At the end of each day they compare their diet to the Food Guide Pyramid and note variations. At the conclusion of the three days ask students to summarize their diets in relation to the Food Guide Pyramid and list any adjustments that they should make.

Assessment

When all groups finish, ask students to assemble in front of one group's Body Composition Chart. Ask the following questions:

- ▶ Which term was the easiest to match? Why?
- ▶ Which term was the most challenging to match? Why?
- ▶ How can the activities that you completed today affect your individual body composition?
- ▶ How would you explain body composition to an elementary-aged student?

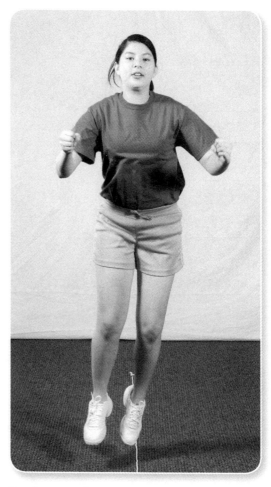

Students perform activities to match body composition terms with their proper definitions.

BODY COMPOSITION SURVIVOR

MIDDLE SCHOOL AND HIGH SCHOOL

Health benefits—Through active participation, middle and high school students will gain knowledge related to the benefits of achieving and maintaining healthy body composition.

Purpose

Students will participate in an activity that teaches the benefits of healthy body composition, risks associated with a high percentage of body fat, and many other facts related to body composition.

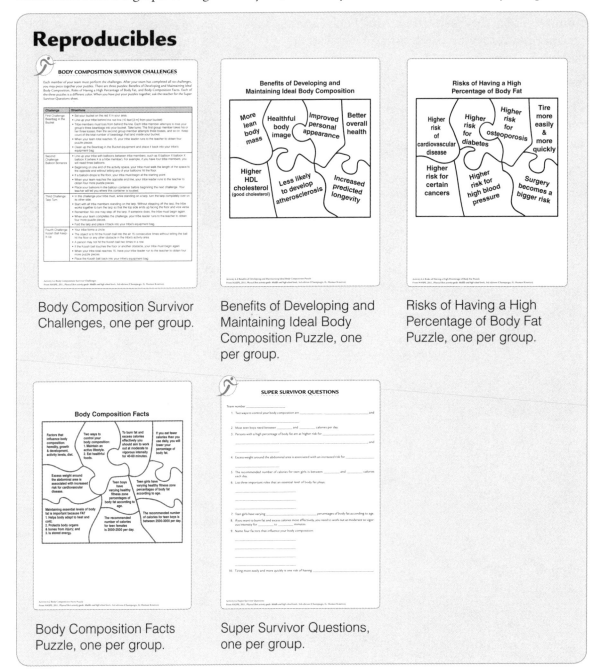

Body Composition Survivor Challenges, one per group.

Benefits of Developing and Maintaining Ideal Body Composition Puzzle, one per group.

Risks of Having a High Percentage of Body Fat Puzzle, one per group.

Body Composition Facts Puzzle, one per group.

Super Survivor Questions, one per group.

Relationship to National Standards

▶ Physical education standard 4: Achieves and maintains a health-enhancing level of physical fitness.

▶ Physical education standard 5: Exhibits responsible personal and social behavior that respects self and others in physical activity settings.

▶ Health education standard 1: Students will comprehend concepts related to health promotion and disease prevention.

Equipment

▶ Red, blue, and yellow cardstock

▶ Quart-sized (liter-sized) plastic bags, one for each group, containing all of that group's puzzle pieces

▶ Pencils

▶ Koosh balls, one per team

▶ Inflated balloons, three per four-person team

▶ 4-inch-by-4-inch (10 cm by 10 cm) tarps, one per team

▶ 12-inch-by-12-inch (30 by 30 cm) carpet square

▶ Three beanbags per team

▶ One small bucket per team

▶ Red floor tape (to mark spot for each tribe's bucket and the line 10 feet [3 m] from the bucket)

▶ Two poly spots per group

Procedure

Advance preparations:

1. Print the Benefits of Developing and Maintaining Ideal Body Composition Puzzle sheet onto 8 1/2-by-11 inch (21.6 by 27.9 cm) red cardstock. Print the Risk of Having a High Percentage of Body Fat Puzzles sheet onto blue cardstock. Print the Body Composition Facts Puzzle sheet onto yellow cardstock. Print a copy of each sheet for every four students (number of students per tribe) in your class.

2. Cut each sheet of cardstock into individual puzzle pieces. Place puzzle pieces for each group in a quart-size (liter-size) plastic bag. Use a permanent marker to number each of the bags (1 through 6, if you have six bags.)

3. Give a copy of the Body Composition Survivor Challenges to each group of four. Make the same number of copies of the Super Survivor Questions to pass out later.

4. To accommodate the Beanbag in the Bucket Challenge, tape a red X on the floor and tape a red line 10 feet (3 m) from the X, using the red floor tape. Do this in each group's designated area.

5. Place each group's equipment in a giant trash bag. Each group needs one Koosh ball, four balloons, one tarp, three beanbags, one small bucket, and three poly spots. Put this bag in each tribe's designated area.

During class do the following:

1. Explain that the class will be competing in a new game show: Body Composition Survivor, a.k.a. BC Survivor. The class will be divided into tribes of four, which will compete in challenges to earn pieces of the three different puzzles. Each tribe will have a tribe number, which is the number printed on that tribe's plastic bag of puzzle pieces. (The teacher keeps these

bags.) The completed puzzles will outline important body composition information that the tribes will need so that they can complete the Super Survivor Questions. The ultimate challenge is to be the first tribe to put together all three of the puzzles and correctly answer the Super Survivor Questions. That team will win the coveted Super Survivor Champs Award.

2. Designate a specific spot of the activity area for each tribe. Each tribe's equipment bag should be placed in this area. (Note to teacher: Be certain you that have taped on the floor the red X and red line for each tribe's Beanbag in the Bucket Challenge.)

3. Emphasize that the tribe members must work cooperatively to accomplish their challenges. After a tribe has completed a challenge, the tribe leader must report to the teacher, who will give the leader four puzzle pieces from that tribe's plastic bag. (The tribe leader must state his or her tribe's number before receiving puzzle pieces from the teacher.) This process will be repeated after a tribe successfully completes each challenge (on the Body Composition Survivor Challenges).

4. When a tribe has accumulated all puzzle pieces, they piece together each puzzle. When a tribe has put together all three puzzles, the leader reports to the teacher, who will provide the Super Survivor Questions and a pencil. Note: The only way that a tribe can have all puzzle pieces is if they have finished all six Survivor Challenges.

5. The first tribe to answer all the questions on the Super Survivor Question Sheet correctly wins the title of Super Survivor Champs.

Teaching Hints

▶ During the introduction to the activity, play a recording of the theme music from the *Survivor* television show.

▶ Divide tribes into heterogeneous groups.

Students keep active while learning about the benefits of developing and maintaining ideal body composition and the risks of not doing so.

▶ Laminate the puzzle pieces to preserve them.

▶ Design an outrageously fun award for the winning team, perhaps a small trophy with plastic flower decorations or Mardi Gras beads for each winner with a big laminated cardstock medal that states "Body Composition Survivor Champ."

Sample Inclusion Tip

For classes that have students with cognitive or learning disabilities, assign a group leader to read aloud, interpret the activities, and guide the group in performing the activities.

Variation

To extend the activity, have each tribe design a poster or write a paragraph that summarizes the body composition concepts learned during the BC Survivor game.

Home Extension

Have students review the various benefits of maintaining an appropriate percentage of body fat. Have them find photo examples of people exhibiting a balanced level of body composition. They can cut out the photos and paste them on poster board. Ask the student to write a brief comment under each photo about how appropriate body composition can help physical performance.

Assessment

▶ At the conclusion of the activity, gather all tribes in a central location to process the body composition information:

• What fact surprised you the most? Why?

• What fact would you most want to share with your parent or guardian? Why?

• Which fact do you believe teenagers most need to know? Why?

• What are the benefits of maintaining ideal body composition?

FRISBEE CALORIE BLASTER

MIDDLE SCHOOL

Health benefits—Using physical activity and tossing skills, students develop a sense of relationship between physical activity and calorie expenditure.

Purpose

▶ Students will learn that reducing or expending 500 more calories a day than one needs to maintain weight will result in a 1-pound (.45 kg) weight loss over a week.

▶ Students will see that physical activity can be fun and that physical activity helps expend calories, leading to healthy body composition.

Relationship to National Standards

▶ Physical education standard 4: Achieves and maintains a health-enhancing level of physical fitness.

▶ Health education standard 1: Students will comprehend concepts related to health promotion and disease prevention.

Equipment

▶ Small Frisbees, two per student

▶ 14 plastic bowling pins

▶ Floor tape or poly spots (optional) to mark the playing zones

Procedure

1. Set up seven pins at each end of the activity space, 5 to 10 feet (1.5 to 3 m) from the wall (see figure 6.1). Spread the pins evenly across the width of the space. Establish an area of 4 to 6 feet (1.2 to 1.8 m) in front of the pins as the neutral zone, where no one may enter for the purpose of defense (guarding the pins). Mark a midcourt, or center, line. Floor tape or poly spots can be used if lines on the floor are not available.

2. Discuss with the class that for those who wish or need to improve body composition, moderate and consistent changes in diet and activity level will result in positive changes in body composition. Having a healthy body composition can lead to many health benefits, including a healthier cardiovascular system, lower risk of diabetes, increased self-esteem, less strain on joints, and more energy.

3. Teach the rules of the game. Explain that the objective is to knock down the opposing team's pins by sliding the Frisbees across the floor before they eliminate your pins. In today's activity, each pin represents 500 calories. By knocking down, or eliminating, all seven pins, students will eliminate 1 pound (.45 kg) of body weight (3,500 calories). Students cannot cross the midcourt line at any time. Students must play offense, defend their pins, and retrieve Frisbees to be successful.

4. Have students practice the Frisbee slide by sliding their Frisbees skillfully and safely.

Reproducible

None.

5. Divide the students into two teams. Have students scatter randomly in their half of the playing area. Evenly distribute Frisbees to each team. Have team members decide who will slide the Frisbees toward the other team's pins and who will guard their pins. Defenders may retrieve Frisbees but may not enter the neutral zone.

6. On your signal, students begin the game (and expend those calories!).

7. This activity requires quite a bit of movement. You can play until one team has eliminated the other team's pins or for a set period. Teams set up the pins and switch sides for additional rounds.

8. Play as many rounds as desired.

Teaching Hints

▶ After students learn the game, play upbeat music in the background.

▶ In large classes split teams into three groups—throwers (along the midcourt), defenders (in front of the neutral zone), and retrievers (behind the pins along each end wall; they must pass the Frisbees up to the throwers). Have each group wear different color pinnies and rotate each round. Although this procedure minimizes overall movement, it may prove safer for large groups and it emphasizes the strategies necessary for success.

Figure 6.1 Floor diagram for Frisbee Calorie Blaster.

Sample Inclusion Tips

▶ A student with a disability can be provided with other types of objects that are safe to roll or toss and may be easier to grip and manipulate.

▶ Incorporating appropriate safety techniques can allow students with disabilities to move closer for more opportunity to throw and knock down pins.

Variation

To enhance soccer skills, have four students dribble soccer balls around the cone area. On a signal they kick the balls and attempt to hit a pin. Rotate kickers after each series of kicks.

Home Extension

Have students keep journals of physical activity. For each 15 minutes of continuous activity they achieve 500 points. Their goal is to accumulate 5,000 points in a three-day period.

Assessment

▶ Ask students to name some activities they enjoy doing that they think expend calories and promote healthy body composition. Ask how they could realistically reduce the amount of calories consumed on a daily basis if they needed to improve their body composition. (Point out that not everyone should reduce the number of calories consumed. A person of below-normal body composition should not try to lose weight.)

▶ Have students design a one-week plan that reduces 3,500 calories through a combination of reduced calorie intake and increased activity level. (They should use calorie charts or food labels and determine calorie expenditure for chosen activities.) Consider having students who should maintain or gain weight design a one-week plan to maintain their weight or add calories through healthy eating while participating in regular physical activity.

NUTRITION MEMORY

MIDDLE SCHOOL

Food and portion size—This movement-focused activity provides middle school students with the opportunity to participate in a variety of physical activities while enhancing their knowledge of the components of a healthy diet.

Purpose

▶ Students will identify what counts as one serving for many different types of foods.

▶ Students will identify how many servings are recommended for each food group.

Relationship to National Standards

▶ Physical education standard 4: Achieves and maintains a health-enhancing level of physical fitness.

▶ Physical education standard 5: Exhibits responsible personal and social behavior that respects self and others in physical activity settings.

Equipment

▶ Ziploc bags (one for each set of memory cards)

▶ Various equipment for skill-related movement, such as hula hoops, basketballs, jump ropes, and tennis balls and rackets

Procedure

1. Each group gets their set of cards and lays them out facedown on the floor or a table.

2. The students can turn over two cards at a time. Students go one at a time; after one student has turned two cards over, another student may go.

3. The goal is to match a Food Guide Pyramid category with the appropriate suggested number of servings. For example, a picture of grains would be a match with the card with "6 to 7 ounces (175 to 200 g)" written on it.

4. When the students find a matching pair, they set them side by side and away from the other cards.

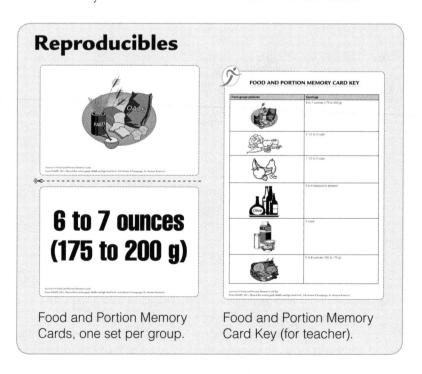

Food and Portion Memory Cards, one set per group.

Food and Portion Memory Card Key (for teacher).

A challenge to anyone wishing to eat healthy is knowing proper food portion sizes. Nutrition Memory puts students to the test by having them perform exercises while they match food types to portion sizes.

5. If students do not make a match, they turn both cards back over so that they are lying face-down. Repeat until all matches have been made.

6. After students think that they have matched all the cards correctly, the teacher has a key to check them. If any matches are wrong, the students can just switch them and try to get them into correct pairs. The teacher tells students the number of correct pairs.

7. Set cards away from the students and require students to power walk, jump rope, dribble a ball, bounce a ball with a racket, or use any other skill-related movement as a means to pick up and return cards to the group. A hula hoop with a variety of equipment placed inside it could be made available for students to choose how and what they want to use to travel to the cards.

Teaching Hint

Use a different color for each set of cards to ensure they do not get mixed up. Also, placing each set in a Ziploc bag will help keep them organized.

Inclusion Tips

▶ The cards could all be placed faceup and rearranged into pairs. This modification would allow students just to make the pairs without having to remember which card was where as in the regular game.

▶ You can make finding the pairs easier for the students by placing a mark or symbol on the pairs. For example, matching pairs could have a star marked in the upper left-hand corner. Each pair would have a different symbol.

Assessment

▶ Have the students plan a meal with appropriately sized portions that fulfills the Food Guide Pyramid.

▶ Use the activity as a pretest and posttest. The students could work as a group during the pretest and then individually during the posttest.

CROSS-TRAINING TRIUMPH

HIGH SCHOOL

Growth and development—Using a cross-training approach, high school students will develop knowledge of the relationship between body composition and various forms of physical training.

Purpose

▶ Students will be able to explain the significance to body composition of combining strength training (promoting metabolically active lean tissue) and aerobic fitness (expending more calories).

▶ Students will design a fitness plan that includes both strength training and aerobic fitness training.

Relationship to National Standards

▶ Physical education standard 4: Achieves and maintains a health-enhancing level of physical fitness.

▶ Health education standard 1: Students will comprehend concepts related to health promotion and disease prevention.

Equipment

▶ Three markers (one color per group)

▶ Jump ropes (several for groups A and C)

▶ Aerobic step boxes (several for group A)

▶ Basketballs (several for groups A and C)

▶ Hand weights (several sets of varying weight for groups B and C)

▶ Resistance tubing or elastic bands (several for groups B and C)

Procedure

1. Before class begins, place the required equipment in three distinctly separate areas of the activity space: the jump ropes, aerobic steps, and basketballs in one area for group A; the hand weights and resistance tubing in another area for group B; and more hand weights and basketballs in a third area for group C.

2. Create a master point chart and post it at the front of the room and place three markers near the chart.

3. Divide students into three groups—A, B, and C—each of which will perform a different set of activities. Activities are listed on each group's Cross-Training Triumph Task.

4. Read the following scenario to the class. Encourage students to think about the question during the

Reproducible

Group A

Cross-Training Triumph Tasks

Every group member must perform each task before the task name and points can be recorded on the master point chart.

Task 1: Jump rope 50 times = 70 points

Task 2: Jog three laps while dribbling a basketball = 50 points

Task 3: Do step aerobics, basic step for three minutes = 50 points

Task 4: Slide sideways around the perimeter of the activity area two times = 70 points

Activity 6.5 Cross-Training Triumph Tasks - Group A
From NASPE, 2011, *Physical Best activity guide: Middle and high school level*, 3rd edition (Champaign, IL: Human Kinetics).

Cross-Training Triumph Tasks, one per group.

lesson. Tell students that this question will be repeated and discussed at the conclusion of the lesson:

June is trying to lose weight and maintain her weight loss. She has been doing step aerobics three times a week, increasing her intensity each week. She lost weight for the first two months, but then her progress stopped. What does June need to do differently with her workout?

5. Give each of the three groups a different Cross-Training Triumph Task. As a group finishes each task on their card, have them use their marker to record the name of the activity performed and the number of points earned on their section of the master point chart.

6. Have groups continue this for each task listed. Allow students 10 to 15 minutes to complete all the tasks listed for their group. Group C—who did the combined aerobic fitness and muscular strength and endurance training—will end up with the largest point total.

Teaching Hints

▶ If you do not have some of the equipment listed, substitute a different aerobic fitness activity or another muscular strength activity. Group A must have all aerobic activities, group B must have all muscular strength activities, and group C must have two of each. Be certain that you change the task cards to reflect the substitutions. Possible substitutions include using stationary bicycles (aerobic fitness) and push-ups (muscular strength).

▶ Students who have experienced the activity Cross-Training Trio in chapter 3 may need you to clarify that there are many ways to define and apply cross-training principles. In the aerobic fitness activity, the focus was on cross-training among various muscle groups and joints while focusing solely on aerobic fitness development. In this activity, the focus is on cross-training among the various health-related fitness components to enhance body composition.

Sample Inclusion Tips

General inclusion tip suggestions for each group activity:

▶ Aerobic step boxes: Allow a student with a disability to walk or run with a partner. Or, if the student is using a wheelchair, allow her or him to wheel for a designated time.

▶ Basketballs: Substitute smaller, lighter balls for the activity.

▶ Basketball hoops: Substitute basketball hoops that can be lowered to ensure success. Pair the student with a disability with a peer buddy during activity to rebound balls in an expedient fashion.

▶ Stationary bicycles: This activity is highly effective for most students with disabilities, particularly those with visual impairments. Allow the student with a disability to use the bicycle through the duration of the activity. At the completion of spinning on the bicycle, time or distance can be recorded.

In general, recognize that even with accommodations for strength, endurance, and power, for some students with disabilities time may need to be decreased, rest periods may need to be increased, and in game situations, frequent rotation in and out of the game may be necessary.

Variation

Ask students to tell what they have learned about how various forms of physical training relate to the FITT principle and how each component is addressed.

Home Extension

Have students research the long-term effects of various forms of physical training on body composition. They can compare and contrast healthy levels of body composition to those that may be considered unhealthy and examine the effects of physical training.

Assessment

When all three groups have completed the activities listed on their task cards, ask the groups to gather around the master point chart. Process the activity by asking the following questions:

▶ How many activities did each group complete? (Four)

▶ Examine the master point chart and identify the difference in the tasks completed by each group. How do they differ? (Aerobic only, muscular only, and combination. The combination group received the most points.)

▶ What conclusion can you draw from this activity? (A combination of aerobic fitness and muscular strength and endurance conditioning has the greatest value to body composition by both expending calories through aerobic activity and promoting healthy lean body weight through muscle conditioning. This combination of activities has a positive effect on metabolism.)

▶ Present again the situation read at the beginning of class:

June is trying to lose weight and maintain her weight loss. She has been doing step aerobics three times a week, increasing her intensity each week. She lost weight for the first two months, but then her progress stopped. What does June need to do differently with her workout? Using the information you gained in class today, design a new workout plan for June.

Maintaining a good body composition requires more than just eating healthy or performing just one type of exercise. It requires cross-training with aerobic, muscular strength and endurance, and flexibility activities. Cross-Training Triumph gives students practice in considering how these different activities help influence healthy body composition.

HEALTH QUEST

MIDDLE SCHOOL AND HIGH SCHOOL

Nutrition—Using the orienteering format, middle and high school students enhance their knowledge related to planning healthy diets using the Food Guide Pyramid or MyPlate (ChooseMyPlate.gov).

Purpose

Students will learn through discovery and discussion that eating a diet that provides all six categories of nutrients in sufficient amounts through a variety of foods will help them achieve their Physical Best.

Relationship to National Standards

▶ Physical education standard 5: Exhibits responsible personal and social behavior that respects self and others in physical activity settings.

▶ Health education standard 1: Students will comprehend concepts related to health promotion and disease prevention.

Equipment

▶ 7 to 10 compasses (one per group, with groups of two to four students at most)

▶ Flags, poly spots, hoops, or other objects that can serve as checkpoints

▶ Pencils, one per student

▶ *Teaching Orienteering* (optional; available from www.HumanKinetics.com)

Reproducibles

Checkpoint 1
Water

When health is absent,
(Write this phrase on line 1 on your Health Quest Answer Sheet, Part A.)

List five ways to get water into your diet and stay well hydrated on your Health Quest Answer Sheet, Part B, checkpoint 1.

Set your compass to this degree: _____

Go the following distance: _____

Checkpoint Signs.

HEALTH QUEST ANSWER SHEET

Part A
Copy the line listed at each checkpoint.

Line 1 _____
Line 2 _____
Line 3 _____
Line 4 _____
Line 5 _____
Line 6 _____

Who is credited with this statement? _____

When is he believed to have written this? _____

Part B
List the five items requested at each checkpoint.

Checkpoint 1: Water
_____
_____
_____
_____
_____

Checkpoint 2: Carbohydrate
_____
_____
_____
_____
_____

Health Quest Answer Sheet, one per student.

Food Guide Pyramid

Food Guide Pyramid or MyPlate, one per student.

Procedure

1. Set up an orienteering course that has six checkpoints using the six checkpoint signs. Each sign contains blanks where you need to fill in the compass bearings and distances specific to your orienteering course.

2. Set up six incorrect checkpoints, so that not all points on the course are correct. Students will then have to follow the compass and distance directions to get to the correct points.

3. Discuss the six categories of nutrients with the class. Pass out a copy of the Food Guide Pyramid or MyPlate to each student. Tell them that today they are going to participate in an activity that will explore the categories of nutrients. Tell students that people throughout history have recognized the importance of good health, and that today they'll follow an orienteering course to discover one early scientist and philosopher's belief about good health. In the process, they'll also recall what they know about the six categories of nutrients.

4. Divide the class into as many teams as there are compasses and review compass basics:

   • Tell students to hold the compass level on the palm of a hand so that the needle can float freely in the fluid to give a correct reading.

   • Make sure that students know how to turn the azimuth ring to the correct reading (the degree that they want to travel in should be lined up with the direction-of-travel arrow, also known as the orienteering arrow). For example, to go east, you would need to turn the azimuth ring so that 90 degrees is lined up with the direction-of-travel arrow.

   • Tell the students that they have to make sure that the red part of the arrow is pointing north. (The red arrow should be placed in the north alignment arrow outline that is located in the base of the compass housing. This is important because all bearings represent degrees from north. The teacher or students could come up with a slogan to remind students that before they travel in the direction that the travel arrow is pointing, they must have the red magnetic north arrow placed in the direction-of-travel arrow, also known as the orienteering arrow).

   • When the red arrow is pointing north and the azimuth ring has the correct reading, students can head off following the directional arrow on the base unit of the compass.

   • Distance is important and can make the difference between checking in at the right or wrong checkpoint. Remind your students that they need to follow the distance directions carefully to locate the correct checkpoint.

5. Each group starts the course in two-minute intervals or more as time allows. Team members must try to find the correct checkpoints, copy the line of the saying, and answer the question about nutrition at each point.

Teaching Hints

▸ Students need to be able to calculate the distance that they are traveling, whether it is in steps or precise units of measure.

▸ It is helpful to set up the course so that it leads all the teams back to the starting point.

▸ Finding some permanent checkpoints on your school grounds will make it easier to set up a course. (For example, you might use the corner of the school to the softball backstop to the field hockey goal to the corner of the blacktop to the baseball backstop to the basketball hoop and back to the corner of the school.)

▸ Setting up a duplicate course with some slightly different checkpoints will force your students to follow the directions carefully.

▸ The poem used for this activity is credited to Herophiles, a Greek scientist, philosopher, and physician, and he was believed to have written this around 300 BC.

Sample Inclusion Tips

▶ Pair students with visual impairments with buddies to guide them through the course or place directions on a portable sound player, giving directions of which way to face and how many steps to walk. Place a student with a cognitive or learning disability in the center of team members to engage him or her in the activity.

▶ If you have students with ambulatory difficulties (crutches, braces, wheelchairs), make sure that the course follows a smooth, wide path. Consider creating a short course for these students.

Variation

Include a different physical activity at each checkpoint. When coming to the checkpoint students must perform that activity before proceeding to the next checkpoint.

Students explore nutrient categories while navigating an orienteering course.

Home Extension

Using the same student groups have each group create their own course, including compass headings and activities to complete at each checkpoint.

Assessment

▶ Students should turn in their completed Health Quest Answer Sheets to you for review.

▶ Ask the class these questions: What are the categories of nutrients? What were some of their answers for each checkpoint?

▶ Ask students to log everything that they eat for two days and categorize the foods and number of servings according to the Food Guide Pyramid or MyPlate.

Note: Recently the USDA created a new graphic, MyPlate, to provide a better illustration of food portions. Both the MyPyramid and MyPlate graphics have educational value and can be used with Physical Best activities.

FAST-FOOD FRENZY

MIDDLE SCHOOL

Note: This activity requires that students have had several previous experiences using resistance bands, because they will be creating their own routines. See chapter 4 for resistance band activities.

Nutrition—Food habits developed in adolescence are the ones most likely to carry into adult life. Adolescents make many choices for themselves about what they eat. Social or peer pressures may push them to make both good and bad choices. Students acquire information, and sometimes misinformation, about nutrition from personal, immediate experiences. They are concerned with how food choices can improve their lives and looks now, so they may engage in crash dieting or the latest fad in weight gain or loss. Conversely, it is also common to see increased calorie consumption, especially of fat and carbohydrate, among adolescents.

Reproducibles

Fast-Food Frenzy Discovery Worksheet, one per student.

Calorie Chart.

Fast-Food Frenzy Station Signs.

Lunch Menu Suggestion Cards, two cards per student.

Health Behavior Contract, one per student.

Purpose

▶ Students will be able to select the healthiest sandwiches and salads available at given fast-food restaurants.

▶ Students will name more healthful alternatives to high-calorie or high-fat foods.

▶ Students will design a nutrition health behavior contract.

Relationship to National Standards

▶ Physical education standard 4: Achieves and maintains a health-enhancing level of physical fitness.

▶ Physical education standard 5: Exhibits responsible personal and social behavior that respects self and others in physical activity settings.

▶ Health education standard 1: Students will comprehend concepts related to health promotion and disease prevention.

▶ Health education standard 6: Students will demonstrate the ability to advocate for personal, family, and community health.

Equipment

This comprehensive station activity spans a two-day period. You may set up all the stations or incorporate a few of these nutrition stations into your circuit training activities.

▶ "Ghostbusters" song and music player (*Ghostbusters: Original Soundtrack*; various artists; 1984, Elmer Bernstein. Release date: October 25, 1990. Label: Arista.)

▶ Resistance bands, one per student

▶ Bell, train whistle, or bicycle horn (to serve as the fat-buster signal)

▶ Large sheets of chart paper, one per group (same as number of stations)

▶ Wide-tip markers, one per group (same as number of stations)

▶ Masking tape

▶ Pencils, one per student

All other materials are listed by station:

Station 1

▶ 60 individually wrapped straws

▶ 60 pieces of notebook paper

▶ Cone

▶ 60 pieces of construction paper

▶ Trash can

▶ Station 1 Instruction Poster: Unclog Those Arteries

Station 2

▶ Four empty cans of different types of soda with the number of teaspoons of sugar that each contains written on bottom of each can

▶ Measuring spoons: one teaspoon and one tablespoon

▶ Four cups (one in front of each of the four sugary drinks)

▶ Large bowl

▶ 2 pounds (1 kg) of sand (to represent sugar)

▶ Numbers to label each can or container (1, 2, 3, 4)

▶ Station 2 Instruction Poster: Sugar Time

Station 3

▶ Seven yellow index cards. Each card lists one of the following food items: one chocolate brownie; one piece of devil's food cake; one cup of ice cream; one cup of soda pop; 1 ounce (30 g) of macadamia nuts; 12 potato chips; one teaspoon of mayonnaise.

▶ Seven pink index cards. Each card lists one of the following food items: one apple, one piece of angel food cake, one cup of grape juice; 1 ounce (30 g) of almonds; one cup of pretzels; one teaspoon of yellow mustard.

▶ Station 3 Instruction Poster: Instead of . . . Why Not Try

▶ Four copies of Calorie Charts, in folders

Station 4

▶ 60 Lunch Menu Suggestion Cards

▶ Four school lunch menus (listing five days of lunch menus for your school)

▶ Station 4 Instruction Poster: Lunch Menu Suggestions

▶ Suggestion box (shoebox marked "Suggestion Card Deposit Box")

Station 5

▶ Five small empty bags of snacks with nutritional information (corn chips, potato chips, mini cookies, pretzels, popcorn, and so on)

▶ Station 5 Instruction Poster: Snack Attack

▶ Pencils

Station 6

▶ Poster listing five different fast-food sandwiches (could use empty sandwich containers or pictures of each sandwich to illustrate)

▶ Copy of the nutritional information for each of the five sandwiches (find the nutritional information for each of the sandwiches by logging on to the Web sites of specific fast-food restaurants, such as www.mcdonalds.com; www.burgerking.com; www.hardees.com; www. pizzahut.com; www.tacobell.com)

▶ Folder labeled "Nutritional Info for Sandwich Choices"

▶ Station 6 Instruction Poster: Healthy Meal Deal: Sandwich

Station 7

▶ Poster listing salads from five different fast-food restaurants (could use pictures of each salad to illustrate)

▶ Copy of nutritional information for each of the salads (find nutritional information for each salad by logging on to the Web sites of specific fast-food restaurants; don't forget salad dressing nutrition information)

▶ Folder labeled "Nutritional Info for Salad Choices"

▶ Station 7 Instruction Poster: Healthy Meal Deal: Salads

Procedure

1. Before class, set up all nutrition stations around the perimeter of the activity area. Place the resistance bands randomly throughout the middle of the activity area.

2. At the beginning of the activity, ask the following questions:

   • What is fast food?

   • How can eating fast food frequently affect a person's diet?

   • Why do people choose to eat fast foods?

   • What are some fast foods that are nutritious?

3. Explain that this activity will help students discover some interesting facts about fast foods and snacks.

4. Briefly outline the purpose of each station.

5. Distribute a Fast-Food Frenzy Discovery Worksheet to each student.

6. Divide students into seven groups (or the number of stations that you have) and assign each group to a station. Emphasize the importance of following the directions posted at each station and staying on task.

7. Explain that when the fat-buster signal sounds, they move to the next station.

8. Tell students that when the "Ghostbusters" song plays, they need to move to the center area, select a resistance band, and perform a resistance band exercise of their choice until the music stops. Instruct them to leave their worksheets and pencils neatly at their station before coming to the center. Play the music after students complete every other station, not after each station.

9. If students can handle this appropriately, ask them to substitute the words "fat busters" for the word "ghostbusters" in the song. In other words, when the song says "ghostbusters," the students shout "fat busters" instead.

10. When the music stops, have students carefully lay down their resistance bands in the center, pick up their pencils and sheets at the station, and move to the next nutrition station.

11. At the end of the station activity, give each group a large sheet of paper and a marker. Ask students to use the chart paper to answer the following questions in their group:

    - What was the most shocking fact that you learned at the nutrition stations?
    - What specific diet change do you recommend that teens make to maintain a healthy diet?
    - What other areas of nutrition would you like to explore?
    - What questions do you have about the nutrition stations?

12. Ask each group to post their chart paper in the room.

Teaching Hints

▶ If using the first assessment idea, before this lesson teach students the process for developing a health behavior contract.

▶ Use only one or two stations at a time as part of an activity circuit (e.g., muscular strength and endurance), until you've covered all seven stations with all students.

▶ At first glance, this activity may seem like a lot of work to prepare. Use these tips to minimize your preparation time:

The choices made at fast-food restaurants can have extreme influences on overall health. Fast-Food Frenzy keeps students active while they learn about options in fast food.

- Well ahead of time, ask students to gather and prepare as many of the materials needed as possible, one or a pair of students per station. Simply review and refine their work before using it in class. Reimburse for small items, such as straws, if receipts are presented. If appropriate, offer extra credit for this help.

- Cut your future preparation time for revisiting this activity. Laminate cards and posters and then place small items for each station in a zip-type bag. Clip large items to the bag and place materials for all seven stations in a large bin. Simply pull out the bin when you repeat the activity.

▶ For safety's sake, remind students to stay in their own space when using resistance bands.

▶ To reduce time spent writing, have groups designate a recorder to complete one worksheet per group, and have a spokesperson present the answers for one station from the worksheet instead of creating a large chart.

Sample Inclusion Tips

▶ Use the designated recorder teaching tip to assist students who have difficulty transferring their thoughts to written word.

▶ Encourage students who have only upper-body capability to use bands to develop their upper-body strength further.

Variations

▶ Use alternative physical activities instead of resistance band exercises in the center area.

▶ Have students design additional nutrition stations that could be used at a later date.

Home Extension

Have students in groups of four develop two stations, including posters and activities, that could be used when this lesson is presented again.

Assessment

▶ Ask students individually or as a group to fill out a Health Behavior Contract.

▶ Have each group choose a spokesperson to present their contract to the entire class. (See step 11 under "Procedure.")

CALORIE BALANCING ACT

6.8

HIGH SCHOOL

Energy expenditure and weight management—High school students participate in a meaningful activity directly related to exploring caloric intake and its relationship with caloric expenditure through physical activity.

Purpose

▸ Students will have a general understanding of energy expenditure as it relates to weight management.

▸ Students will know the procedure for calculating the energy cost of basic physical activities for the purpose of weight control and energy expenditure.

Relationship to National Standards

▸ Physical education standard 5: Exhibits responsible personal and social behavior that respects self and others in physical activity settings.

▸ Health education standard 1: Students will comprehend concepts related to health promotion and disease prevention.

▸ Health education standard 6: Students will demonstrate the ability to use goal-setting and decision-making skills to enhance health.

Equipment

▸ Plastic foods or pictures of food items with the number of calories marked on it

▸ Large plastic bag or container for the food items

▸ Calculator, one per group

▸ Pencil or marker, one per group

Procedure

1. Explain to students that all foods provide energy in the form of calories. A calorie is a unit of energy that is used for physical activity. The more intense the physical activity is, the more energy the body requires to meet the needs of the activity. This concept, called energy expenditure, is affected by several

Reproducibles

Activity and Calorie Information Sheet, one per group.

Eat the Food, Do the Time Worksheet, one per group.

131

variables, among them age, gender, and body weight. Generally, the body at rest requires approximately .45 kcal per pound per hour (.99 kcal per kg per hour) or .0075 kcal per pound per minute (.016 kcal per kg per minute). To approximate the energy cost for physical activity for less than one hour, simply divide kcal per pound (or per kilogram) per hour by 60 minutes to get kcal (calories) burned per minute.

2. Listed here is the energy cost for general exercises:
   - Sitting around = 0.45 kcal per pound per hour (.99 kcal per kg per hour) or .0075 kcal per pound per minute (.016 kcal per kg per minute).
   - Walking leisurely = 1.5 kcal per pound per hour (3.3 kcal per kg per hour) or .025 kcal per pound minute (.055 kcal per kg per minute).
   - Low- or moderate-intensity exercise such as jogging in place = 3.6 kcal per pound per hour (7.9 kcal per kg per hour) or .06 kcal per pound minute (.132 kcal per kg per minute).
   - Moderate-intensity exercise such as mountain climbers or curl-ups = 4.5 kcal per pound per hour (9.9 kcal per kg per hour) or .075 kcal per pound minute (.165 kcal per kg per minute).
   - Vigorous exercise such as jumping jacks = 5.6 kcal per pound per hour (12.3 kcal per kg per hour) or .093 kcal per pound minute (.205 kcal per kg per minute). Example: A 150-pound (68 kg) person sitting around for 1 hour would use 67.5 kcal (calories).

     150 × .45 kcal per pound per hour × 1 hr = 67.5 kcal or 1.12 kcal per minute (68 × .99 kcal per kg per hour × 1 hr = 67.3 kcal).

3. The energy cost of specific exercises can be used to approximate the time required to burn the number of calories equivalent to specific foods.

   For example, a large order of french fries is approximately 500 calories and therefore will take 445 minutes, or 7.4 hours, of sitting around for a 150-pound (68 kg) person to burn.

   500 calories = 7.4 hours at 67.5 kcal per hour.

   But if a 150-pound person were to exercise vigorously, only 35 minutes would be required to burn 500 calories.

   500 calories = 35 minutes of vigorous exercise at 14 kcal per minute.

4. Note that this lesson does not include information about resting energy metabolism. For the purpose of this activity, caloric values of foods items selected should be low, ranging from 2 to 50 calories per food item to avoid requiring extended exercise times.

5. For this activity students should be place into groups of three or four with a worksheet, a calculator, and a chart of weight conversions.

6. Each student reaches into a large bag located in the center of the gymnasium and pulls out a plastic food. The plastic food should be marked with an approximate caloric value.

7. Students write down the value of all the foods selected within the group on the worksheet.

8. The group discusses the type of exercise routine that is most appropriate using all levels of intensity (with the exception of sitting around) and the time required to burn the calories for each of the food items selected. They write it on their worksheet.

9. After the group has discussed the type of exercise that would be most appropriate, the entire group performs that activity for 30 seconds.

10. After the group performs the activity they return the "food" to the bag and take another.

11. The rotation continues until each group has chosen six different foods.

Teaching Hint

Exposing students' actual body weight should be avoided. For the purpose of this activity a standard 125- or 150-pound (57 or 68 kg) person should be used for the entire class, regardless of gender.

Sample Inclusion Tip

For students with physical disabilities, provide a buddy system by having a peer work with a partner with a disability to assist in the physical activity and help with involvement in discussions.

Variation

In addition to the foods found in the bag, add cards that list various physical activities. Have the students list the positive effects of those activities on balancing the diet.

Home Extension

Have students keep a journal of caloric intake versus expenditure through physical activities.

Assessment

▶ Check the worksheet for accuracy of calculations.

▶ Students can be given a separate worksheet for personal use and calculations of realistic food items.

Stephen Coburn - Fotolia

Healthy weight management, though difficult for some to achieve, can be simplified when students consider energy expenditure: calories in, calories out. Calorie Balancing Act helps students learn how much activity is necessary for burning off calories.

JUMP ROPE DIGESTION

MIDDLE SCHOOL

Nutrition and digestion—Digestion allows the body to get the nutrients and energy it needs from the food consumed.

Purpose

▶ Students will learn all the parts of the digestive system.

▶ By actually traveling through the digestive system, students will learn how it functions.

▶ Students will have fun while learning how the digestive system works.

▶ Students will improve their knowledge of the Food Guide Pyramid by using food examples from each section of the pyramid while traveling through the digestive system.

Relationship to National Standards

▶ Physical education standard 3: Participates regularly in physical activity.

▶ Physical education standard 4: Achieves and maintains a health-enhancing level of physical fitness.

▶ Physical education standard 5: Exhibits responsible personal and social behavior that respects self and others in physical activity settings.

▶ Physical education standard 6: Values physical activity for health, enjoyment, challenge, self-expression, and/or social interaction.

Equipment

You will set up six digestive systems. The following is a list of equipment needed for one station (you will need to multiply it by six).

▶ Two regular and two long jump ropes

▶ Pictures of food from each section of the Food Guide Pyramid such as grains (brown rice), milk (yogurt), oils (nuts).

▶ One hula hoop at the end of each digestive system and four additional hula hoops (the number will vary depending on class size and how many systems are needed)

▶ One towel

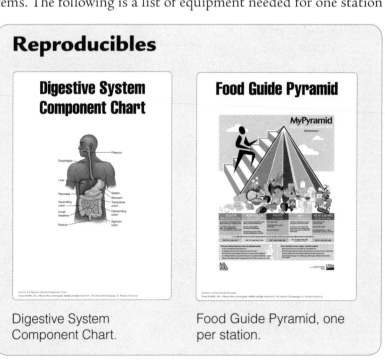

Digestive System Component Chart.

Food Guide Pyramid, one per station.

Procedure

1. Before class starts set up six digestive systems, one system for each of the food groups from the food pyramid, including oils. See figure 6.2 to set up equipment for each digestive system. Put students into groups of three or four. If you have a very large class you can have 12 stations set up with two digestive systems representing one section of the pyramid.

2. Start class by asking the students to name the parts of the digestive system. See the Digestive System Component Chart for details.

3. Have pictures of the Food Guide Pyramid set up at each digestive system and review the pyramid with the students before starting.

4. Tell the class that each group will go one at a time and pick up one picture of the food from that section of the Food Guide Pyramid. They will then move their piece of food through the digestive system by doing the following:

   • Jump rope 10 times to simulate chewing.

   • Get on your hands and knees and crawl through the hula hoops on hoop holders to simulate going through the esophagus.

   • Pick up the towel and wave it up and down twice to simulate the stomach breaking down the food.

   • Walk on the large jump rope to simulate going through the large intestine.

   • Walk on the large longer jump rope to simulate going through the small intestine.

   • Then place the fruit or vegetable in the last hula hoop.

   • Clap your hands together four times to simulate washing your hands.

   • The next person in the group then goes through the entire system.

5. Jump Rope Digestion is finished when the group has six to nine fruits or vegetables in the end hula hoop.

Teaching Hints

▶ Review the digestive system before the students start so that everyone is clear on all the parts and functions.

▶ Make it clear that there are no winners or losers and that every team needs to have six to nine fruits and vegetables in their hula hoop to be finished.

▶ This is a fun way to learn the digestive system, so make sure that all students are enjoying themselves.

▶ Select music that has the same theme as the activity.

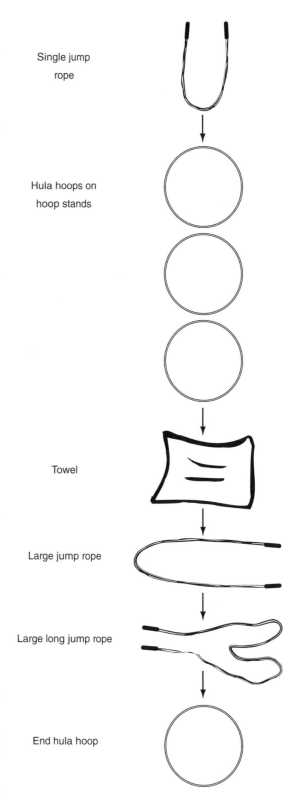

Single jump rope

Hula hoops on hoop stands

Towel

Large jump rope

Large long jump rope

End hula hoop

Figure 6.2 Floor diagram for Jump Rope Digestion.

Sample Inclusion Tips

▶ Students with disabilities can be given a fruit or vegetable, go along outside the digestive system, and then place the fruit or vegetable in the hula hoop at the end.

▶ A student with a disability can be paired with another student who goes along with him or her and names each part of the digestive system as they pass it.

Variation

Allow students to create their own obstacle course to simulate digestion.

Home Extension

Have students create an obstacle system using equipment available at home. They should use it to explain the digestive system to a friend or family member.

Assessment

▶ For the next class, place all the equipment in a pile and have the students construct the digestive system.

▶ You can stand at each part of the digestive system and ask students for the name and function of each part.

▶ A paper and pencil assessment can follow this activity. Prepare a sheet with a blank digestive system and have each team fill it out.

Combined-Component Training

Chapter Contents

This chapter focuses on activities designed to provide adolescents with the opportunity to engage in activities that combine multiple components of health-related fitness. In addition, activities can be adapted up or down so that at the middle school level, students participate in activities that build on those introduced at the elementary level. At the high school level, students apply their knowledge in a way that involves decision making, goal setting, and individual choice.

TEACHING GUIDELINES FOR COMBINED-COMPONENT TRAINING

Activities in this chapter are designed to teach and reinforce the following concepts:

- ▶ Definition and identification of health-related and skill-related fitness components
- ▶ Benefits of health-related fitness to students in designing personal health and fitness plans
- ▶ Exploring options and making choices in health-related fitness and other lifestyle activities

To maximize the benefits from these activities, students should have a basic knowledge of the individual components of fitness. If they have not been exposed to these principles, the previous chapters will be useful in teaching those concepts. For students already familiar with the health-related fitness concepts and activities, the previous chapters can be used to reinforce important knowledge. In presenting activities in this chapter, you should provide students with individual choices so that they can challenge themselves at a personal level and participate in activities that meet their interests and goals.

MOTOR-SKILL DEVELOPMENT THROUGH COMBINED-COMPONENT TRAINING

You can easily infuse various skill development activities as well as various games and recreational activities into many of these lessons. This approach allows you to extend the length of the activity, challenge all students, and provide variety. Many of the variations contain ideas for carrying out sport-specific variations so that students can connect fitness to other physical activities. See table 7.1 for a grid of activities in this chapter.

Table 7.1 Chapter 7 Activities Grid

Activity number	Activity title	Activity page	Concept	Middle school	High school	Reproducibles (on CD-ROM)
7.1	Health-Related Fitness Warm-Up	141	Health benefits	•		Team Health-Related Fitness Warm-Up Answer Sheet
						Health-Related Fitness Warm-Up Station Signs
7.2	Fitness Bingo	143	Defining health- and skill-related fitness	•		Fitness Bingo Task Cards
						Fitness Bingo Card
7.3	Component Countdown	145	Defining health- and skill-related fitness	•	•	Component Countdown Recording Sheet
						Component Countdown Fitness Tags
						Component Countdown Team Task Cards
						Component Countdown Teacher Key
7.4	Monopoly Fitness	148	Health-related fitness	•	•	Monopoly Fitness Station Signs
7.5	Health and Fitness Treasure Hunt	150	Health benefits	•		Health and Fitness Treasure Hunt Task Cards
7.6	Fortune Cookie Fitness	152	Exploring options and making choices	•		Fitness Fortunes
7.7	Circuit Training Choices	155	Exploring options and making choices		•	Circuit Training Choices Signs
7.8	Fitness Unscramble	157	Exploring options and making choices	•	•	Fitness Unscramble Task Signs
						Fitness Unscramble Worksheet
						Fitness Unscramble Worksheet Answer Key
7.9	Jump Band Fitness	160	Exploring options and making choices	•	•	None
7.10	Partner Racetrack Fitness	163	Exploring options and making choices	•	•	Racetrack Signs
7.11	12 Ways to Fitness	166	Exploring options and making choices	•		Add-On Cards
7.12	Sporting Fitness	169	Exploring options and making choices	•	•	Sporting Fitness Activity Cards
						Sporting Fitness Soccer Drills
7.13	Basketball Skills Fitness	171	Understanding health-related fitness	•	•	Circuit Station Cards
7.14	Mat Exercise Stations	174	Exploring options and making choices	•	•	None
7.15	Speed Circuit	177	Exploring options and making choices	•	•	None
7.16	Medicine Ball Circuit	179	Exploring options and making choices	•	•	Medicine Ball Circuit Station Signs

(continued)

Table 7.1 *(continued)*

Activity number	Activity title	Activity page	Concept	Middle school	High school	Reproducibles (on CD-ROM)
7.17	Fitness Adventure	182	Exploring options and making choices	•		Fitness Adventure Station Cards
						Fitness Adventure Worksheet
						Fitness Adventure Answer Key
7.18	Racetrack Fitness Using Stability Balls	185	Exploring options		•	Racetrack Fitness Station Signs
7.19	Know the Risks and Benefits	187	Healthy behaviors	•	•	Health Risk Station Signs
						Healthy Behavior Station Signs
						Health Risks and Benefits Worksheet
7.20	Body Image Museum Tour	189	Quackery and body image	•		Media Representation of Sport and Physical Activity

MIDDLE SCHOOL

Health benefits—Using a station format, students will enhance their knowledge through answering questions directly related to each component of health-related fitness while performing warm-up activities.

Purpose

Students will answer questions about aerobic fitness, muscular strength and endurance, flexibility, and body composition using small groups in a station format.

Relationship to National Standards

▶ Physical education standard 4: Achieves and maintains a health-enhancing level of physical fitness.

▶ Health education standard 1: Students will comprehend concepts related to health promotion and disease prevention.

Equipment

▶ Hula hoops, one for each station

▶ Cone markers, one for each station

▶ Jump ropes, two stations, enough for each student

▶ Resistance bands, one station, enough for each student

▶ Chairs or benches, one station, enough for each student

▶ Mats for floor work

▶ Music player with music

Procedure

1. Arrange stations around the perimeter of the gym, leaving space behind each area to allow the class to jog around the gym. At each station place one hula hoop, a station sign, and other specific equipment required for the activity.

2. Divide the class into groups of two or three students. Give each group a Team Health-Related Fitness Warm-Up Answer Sheet and pencil. Assign each group to a station; more than one group may be at each station.

3. On the start signal, students choose to perform one activity listed on the station sign for 45 seconds.

Reproducibles

Team Health-Related Fitness Warm-Up Answer Sheet, one per group.

Health-Related Fitness Warm-Up Station Signs (activities and questions).

4. At the conclusion of the activity time, the group writes down the answers to the questions on the answer sheet. After 60 seconds the signal to rotate is given.

5. When rotating, all groups jog one lap around the gym and stop at the next station to their right.

6. When all groups have arrived at their new station, start the 45-second activity.

Teaching Hint

Before beginning the activity review the FITT principle and components of health-related fitness. Ask students to give examples of activities that would fit into each component category and definitions of the FITT principle.

Sample Inclusion Tip

Pair able-bodied students with those with physical disabilities to work together at each station. In addition, modify equipment, tasks, and the environment at each station to allow all students to participate.

Variation

Exercises on the cards can change to be more sport or activity specific.

Home Extension

Students keep active while learning about the health benefits of various types of fitness activities.

Give each student a copy of the Team Health-Related Fitness Warm-Up Answer Sheet to take home. Give the assignment for students to ask family or friends what they think the answers are. Have students share the answers with the class and discuss the differences between the homework answers and those generated by teams during class.

Assessment

After completing the entire circuit and Team Health-Related Fitness Warm-Up Answer Sheet, have groups report their answers and discuss the concepts learned as they relate to the development and maintenance of lifelong health and fitness.

FITNESS BINGO

MIDDLE SCHOOL

Defining health- and skill-related fitness—Students enhance their knowledge of health-related fitness components through a series of challenging skill development activities.

Purpose

- ▶ Students will participate in a variety of physical activities to understand health-and skill-related fitness components.
- ▶ Students will be able to identify physical activities that involve health- and skill-related fitness components.

Relationship to National Standards

- ▶ Physical education standard 1: Demonstrates competency in motor skills and movement needed to perform a variety of physical activities.
- ▶ Physical education standard 4: Achieves and maintains a health-enhancing level of physical fitness.

Equipment

- ▶ Z ball (reaction time or random bounce ball)
- ▶ Jump ropes
- ▶ Basketballs
- ▶ Scarves
- ▶ Volleyballs
- ▶ Mats for floor work

Procedure

1. Students are given a Fitness Bingo Card with each component of health- or skill-related fitness written on it.

2. Students form a circle, leaving enough space between them to be active.

3. On the command to begin, students jog to the middle, pick up a Fitness Bingo Task Card, and bring it back to their place in the circle.

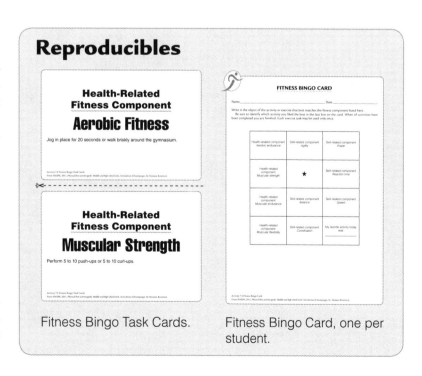

Fitness Bingo Task Cards.

Fitness Bingo Card, one per student.

4. The student performs the challenge task, determines where the task belongs on the Fitness Bingo Card, and writes down the name of the task or exercise.

5. After completion, the Fitness Bingo Task Card is brought back to the middle and the procedure is repeated.

6. The objective of the game is to fill the Fitness Bingo Card.

Teaching Hint

Before beginning the activity, review the components of health-related fitness and why each is important to the development of a healthy and active lifestyle.

Sample Inclusion Tips

▸ For students with physical disabilities, some physical activities may need to be adapted.

▸ For students with visual disabilities, a partner may be assigned.

▸ Use pictures to match written language on cards.

Variation

Reverse the procedure by having the student card reflect activities and the cards in the center reflect components of fitness.

Home Extension

Have students look in various magazines or newspapers and find pictures or articles related to the components of either health- or skill-related fitness. They can put the pictures or articles on a large sheet of paper with headings of health- or skill-related fitness. When they return the project to class, they can discuss each activity.

Students work on health- and skill-related fitness during Fitness Bingo.

Assessment

▸ Check the worksheet for accuracy of tasks and activities in the correct fitness component.

▸ Ask students to identify other activities or tasks for each fitness component.

COMPONENT COUNTDOWN

MIDDLE SCHOOL AND HIGH SCHOOL

Defining health- and skill-related fitness—This activity helps students review the health- and skill-related fitness components while they perform aerobic activities.

Purpose

▶ Students will learn how to apply these fitness components to various activities and games.

▶ Students will review health- and skill-related fitness components.

▶ Students will discuss the components and match them to indicate whether they are health related or skill related.

Reproducibles

COMPONENT COUNTDOWN RECORDING SHEET

Name _____ Date _____

Team Number _____

Team Members _____

Component related	Health or skill
1.	1.
2.	2.
3.	3.
4.	4.
5.	5.
6.	6.
7.	7.
8.	8.
9.	9.
10.	10.
11.	11.

Activity 7.3 Component Countdown Recording Sheet
From NASPE, 2011, *Physical Best activity guide: Middle and high school levels*, 3rd edition (Champaign, IL: Human Kinetics).

Component Countdown Recording Sheet, one per group.

COMPONENT COUNTDOWN TEACHER KEY

This key provides the poly spot numbers and health- or skill-related tags.

1. Body fatness—health
2. Coordination—skill
3. Flexibility—health
4. Strength—health
5. Balance—skill
6. Speed—skill
7. Muscular endurance—health
8. Agility—skill
9. Reaction time—skill
10. Power—skill
11. Aerobic fitness—health

Activity 7.3 Component Countdown Teacher Key
From NASPE, 2011, *Physical Best activity guide: Middle and high school levels*, 3rd edition (Champaign, IL: Human Kinetics).

Component Countdown Teacher Key.

Component Countdown Fitness Tag 1

Body Fatness (Composition)

The percentage of body weight that is made up of fat when compared with the other body tissues, such as bone and muscle.

Activity 7.3 Component Countdown Fitness Tags
From NASPE, 2011, *Physical Best activity guide: Middle and high school levels*, 3rd edition (Champaign, IL: Human Kinetics).

Component Countdown Fitness Tag 2

Coordination

The ability to use your senses together with your body parts or to use two or more body parts together.

Activity 7.3 Component Countdown Fitness Tags
From NASPE, 2011, *Physical Best activity guide: Middle and high school levels*, 3rd edition (Champaign, IL: Human Kinetics).

Component Countdown Fitness Tags; place one underneath each poly spot in random order; placing them numerically will eliminate all the fun.

Component Countdown Team Task Cards

Team 1

Search for Component Countdown Fitness Tags in the following order:
1 7 2 8 3 9 4 10 5 11 6

Activity 7.3 Component Countdown Team Task Cards
From NASPE, 2011, *Physical Best activity guide: Middle and high school levels*, 3rd edition (Champaign, IL: Human Kinetics).

Component Countdown Team Task Cards

Team 2

Search for Component Countdown Fitness Tags in the following order:
2 8 3 9 4 10 5 11 6 1 7

Activity 7.3 Component Countdown Team Task Cards
From NASPE, 2011, *Physical Best activity guide: Middle and high school levels*, 3rd edition (Champaign, IL: Human Kinetics).

Component Countdown Team Task Cards (six are provided; you can create more by mixing up the number order so that additional teams are not looking for the same numbers at the same time).

Relationship to National Standards

▶ Physical education standard 2: Demonstrates understanding of movement concepts, principles, strategies, and tactics as they apply to the learning and performance of physical activities.

▶ Physical education standard 5: Exhibits responsible personal and social behavior that respects self and others in physical activity settings.

Equipment

▶ Pedometers

▶ 11 poly spots

▶ Pencils

Procedure

1. Spread the poly spots out on the floor, with each one hiding a numbered Component Countdown Fitness Tag. Be sure to hide them in random order so that the order isn't obvious.

2. Divide students into six teams and provide each with a Component Countdown Team Task Card. This card gives each team their own order that they will need to find when they look through the poly spots. Each team is divided into three steppers and three seekers (you may have more if necessary, or you can create additional team cards). Make sure that students reset their pedometers before starting the activity. Each team should also receive a Component Countdown Recording Sheet.

3. When the teacher starts the music, the steppers start performing locomotor movements such as walking, jogging, skipping, hopping, and jumping, while one seeker runs in and turns over a poly spot. If the spot is not the correct number from their team card, the seeker returns to the team and tags the next seeker. The numbers must be found in the order given on the team card. The seekers continue to run to the poly spots until they find the spot with the correct number.

4. When a seeker finds the correct number, he or she takes the Component Countdown Fitness Tag and runs back to the group to write the word on the Component Countdown Recording Sheet. The team has to determine whether the word is health related or skill related and record the answer on the recording sheet before returning the Component Countdown Fitness Tag to the proper poly spot (an alternative would be to have many copies of each Component Countdown Fitness Tag at the poly spot locations so that the teams do not have to return the cards).

5. Now the steppers and seekers switch places, and the game continues until one group has found all the Component Countdown Fitness Tags and completed the Component Countdown Recording Sheet.

6. The first group to complete the task wins! Have the group stand up, recite the elements from the tags, and tell whether they are health related or skill related. If they get all the answers right have a reward for them! All other teams fill in their recording sheet as the winning group reads the answers.

Teaching Hint

Bring all the teams together and show a PowerPoint presentation that reviews the health- and skill-related fitness components.

Sample Inclusion Tip

Team a tutor with a student with disabilities. The tutor helps the student perform step patterns and participates with the student as a seeker.

Students team up to do aerobic activity while searching for health- and skill-related fitness components.

Variations

▶ You can incorporate any fitness activity into this game to make it fit your curriculum.

▶ Ask students to perform an activity that relates to each component as they work their way through the Component Countdown Fitness Tags.

Home Extension

Have students ask friends and family members what physical activities they participate in and how they relate to either health- or skill-related fitness. Students make a list and share it with the class.

Assessment

▶ Talk about what makes certain activities health related and others skill related.

▶ Have each team discuss various activities that they like to do and decide whether the activities are health related or skill related.

▶ Have each group share some of the activities that they listed.

▶ All teams turn in their Component Countdown Recording Sheets for participation points at the end of class.

Presented by Robyn Bretzing.

MONOPOLY FITNESS

MIDDLE SCHOOL AND HIGH SCHOOL

Health-related fitness—Using a fun game format, students become active while gaining knowledge in understanding the components of health-related fitness.

Purpose

▶ Students will be able to participate in a fitness routine that includes aerobic work, flexibility, strength development, and endurance using a variety of activities.

▶ Students will be able to determine which component of fitness is being worked at each station.

Relationship to National Standards

▶ Physical education standard 3: Participates regularly in physical activity.

▶ Physical education standard 4: Achieves and maintains a health-enhancing level of physical fitness.

Equipment

Possibilities include the following:

▶ Mats for floor work
▶ Stretch bands
▶ Pennies
▶ Rulers
▶ Table
▶ Basketballs
▶ Sticks
▶ Yardsticks
▶ Boards and round bases
▶ Jump ropes
▶ Jump bands
▶ Exercise tubes
▶ Body bars
▶ Aerobic steps
▶ Medicine balls
▶ Stability balls
▶ Cones (to hold the signs)
▶ Large set of foam dice

Procedure

1. Review the health-related fitness components (aerobic fitness, muscular fitness, flexibility, and body composition).

2. Students are arranged in groups of two or three at each station. A minimum of 10 stations are suggested.

Reproducible

Monopoly Fitness Station 1

• Jump into the air.
• While in the air, click your heels together twice before you hit the ground.
• Your feet must be at least 3 inches (8 cm) apart when you land.
• Take two tries.

Activity 7.4 Monopoly Fitness Stations Signs
From NASPE, 2011, Physical best activity guide: Middle and high school level, 3rd edition (Champaign, IL: Human Kinetics).

Monopoly Fitness Station Signs.

3. Students take turns rolling the dice. All students then add the numbers on the dice, jog clockwise the corresponding number of stations, and then perform the activities at that station. After performing the activity, students identify which component or components of fitness they worked on at that station.

Teaching Hints

▸ Music is always a motivational tool and can be used to time the workload at each station (45 seconds of music and 20-second intervals of no music). While music is playing, students exercise at the station. When the music stops, students move up to the next station in a clockwise direction.

▸ Some activities can be completed individually or with a partner.

▸ This fitness routine is an excellent way to incorporate a variety of pieces of equipment that have been taught throughout the school year.

▸ All students should do as many repetitions as possible within their ability level.

Monopoly Fitness helps students explore the areas of health-related fitness through activity stations set up throughout the gym.

▸ All students should be able to see progress no matter what the situation. Students have a choice at each station (weight of ball, weight of body bar, a variety of choices for abdominal and push-up exercises). For example, push-ups could include shoulder touch push-ups, over the line push-ups, or one-knee push-ups.

▸ Goals need to be SMART—specific, measurable, attainable, realistic, and timed.

Sample Inclusion Tips

▸ A partner can move with a physically challenged student to help count stations and help read aloud the directions for the exercise located on each instructional sign.

▸ A variety of different weighted balls and body bars could be included to help all students be successful.

▸ Use pictures to match written language on task cards and number your activity stations.

Variation

Vary locomotor activities from jogging to skipping, side stepping, hopping, jumping, or animal walks.

Home Extension

Have students work in small groups to develop their own stations and activities. During a future class, use the students' ideas for stations and activities.

Assessment

If you are using fitness journals, students can record how many repetitions they completed each day at each station. Encourage students to improve the number of repetitions each day as a part of the fitness component of the lesson. They should eventually try to increase the weight that they use in the activities.

From P. Darst & R. Pangrazi, 2009, *Dynamic physical education for secondary school students*, 6th ed. (San Francisco: Benjamin Cummings).

7.5 HEALTH AND FITNESS TREASURE HUNT

MIDDLE SCHOOL

Health benefits—This freestyle activity allows students to perform various exercises and activities as indicated by signs that describe either risky health behaviors or health-enhancing behaviors.

Purpose

To reinforce positive lifestyle choices and how they affect health and fitness.

Relationship to National Standards

▶ Physical education standard 4: Achieves and maintains a health-enhancing level of physical fitness.

▶ Physical education standard 6: Values physical activity for health, enjoyment, challenge, self-expression, and/or social interaction.

▶ Health education standard 1: Students will comprehend concepts related to health promotion and disease prevention.

Equipment

Task cards and equipment as determined by selected tasks. The sample task cards on the CD-ROM require these items:

▶ Several jump ropes

▶ Several tennis balls

▶ Mats for floor work

▶ Basketballs and hoop

Procedure

1. Develop a group of Health and Fitness Treasure Hunt Task Cards listing specific risky behaviors and health-enhancing behaviors along with fitness and motor skill activities that help students understand the relationship between physical activity and a healthy lifestyle. See the samples on the CD-ROM.

2. Have students form groups of two or three. Place the task cards face down in the center of the activity area.

3. On the start signal, all students begin to jog around the perimeter of the activity area. On a signal, one person from each group runs to the center and takes a card, returns to the group, and reads the card. The group members then perform the selected activity.

4. When they complete the activity, the group begins to jog. After they complete one lap, another member of each group returns the card to the center, places it facedown, and picks up another card.

Reproducible

Risky Behavior

The use of tobacco products has been shown to cause cancer, heart disease, and lung disease. Aerobic fitness also decreases when a person uses tobacco products.

Activity

Jump rope 100 turns: Jump rope 50 turns, walk a lap, and then jump 50 turns again. The second 50, when you are already tired, represent the effects of tobacco products.

Health and Fitness Treasure Hunt Task Cards.

5. Continue the activity for 5 to 10 minutes.

6. Use the first assessment as closure.

Teaching Hints

▶ Direct students not to read the card until they have returned to their group.

▶ If motor skills, such as the basketball spot shot, are used, designate a specific area for those activities.

▶ Keep tasks simple and modify them for varying ability and developmental levels.

▶ Use higher-level concepts with grades 9 through 12.

Sample Inclusion Tip

Pair students with lower reading or ability levels with peers capable of reading and explaining the information on the cards.

Variation

Rather than having students jog around the outside of the playing area, have them perform various locomotor movements either around the outside of the area or randomly.

Home Extension

Try combining this activity with Fitness Monopoly. Ask the students to develop this activity.

Students learn about risky and health-enhancing behaviors while performing exercises.

Assessment

▶ At the conclusion of the activity ask students to review what risky behaviors and health-enhancing behaviors they encountered. Ask for specific examples of both healthy and risky behaviors.

▶ Include some of the information learned in this activity on your next written assessment.

▶ If students use portfolios, have them list one or several health-enhancing or risky behaviors that were not used in the activity, and ask them to explain in their portfolios how exercise plays a role in each.

Adapted from J. Carpenter and D. Tunnell, 1994. *Elementary P.E. Teacher's Survival Guide* (West Nyack, NY: Parker Publishing). By permission of J. Carpenter.

FORTUNE COOKIE FITNESS

MIDDLE SCHOOL

Exploring options and making choices—Students enhance their knowledge of the components of health- and skill-related fitness through a fast-paced and challenging set of activities.

Purpose

▶ Students will explore and experience many types of exercise with various equipment while doing exciting and challenging physical fitness activities.

▶ Students will learn fitness activities that are personally appealing.

▶ Students will work cooperatively with partners.

Relationship to National Standards

▶ Physical education standard 4: Achieves and maintains a health-enhancing level of physical fitness.

▶ Physical education standard 5: Exhibits responsible personal and social behavior that respects self and others in physical activity settings.

▶ Physical education standard 6: Values physical activity for health, enjoyment, challenge, self-expression, and/or social interaction.

Equipment

▶ Music and player

▶ Equipment needed to complete the activities on the fortunes. If using fortunes provided on the CD-ROM, the following equipment is needed:

  • Resistance bands

  • Medicine balls

Procedure

1. Write various fitness activities on strips of paper (Fitness Fortunes) with the time period or number of repetitions on the other side (Lucky Number). You can also use the Fitness Fortunes provided on the CD-ROM, which were made to fold so that the Fitness Fortune will appear on one side and the lucky number on the other. Place them in a "cookie jar" (or shoebox) in the center of the activity area. The activities can cover health-related fitness components as well as manipulative and nonlocomotor skills.

2. Explain to students that they'll select a fortune and then do the activity listed on the fortune for the time period or number of repetitions specified on the Lucky Number side.

Reproducible

Fitness Fortunes.

Fortune Cookie Fitness adds a fun twist to station activities while helping students learn about health- and skill-related fitness.

3. Have students form groups of two.

4. If using music, start the music.

5. Partners take turns selecting Fitness Fortunes from the box. The partners return to their buddies, and the two students complete the activity that is listed on the fortune for the length of time or number of repetitions listed.

6. When both partners have completed the activity, the other partner comes to the box and exchanges the completed fortune for a new one.

Teaching Hint

If you do not include Lucky Numbers (the amount of time or number of repetitions) on your fortunes, you can instead use a recording that plays music for 30 seconds during which students exercise and then has 10 seconds of silence so that students can retrieve a new fortune.

Sample Inclusion Tip

For students with generally lower fitness levels, fortune cookies could contain two or more choices in the amount of activity (Lucky Numbers); this approach enhances the concept of allowing students to make choices.

Variations

▶ On a particular day all fortunes can emphasize one of the health-related fitness components (e.g., aerobic fitness).

▶ To incorporate progression and overload, encourage students to perform as many repetitions as possible while the music is playing and have them try to improve this number over time when revisiting the activity.

Home Extension

Have students research and discuss various activities and their relationship to the FITT principle.

Assessment

▶ Have students wear pedometers and record the number of steps that they take for the various fitness routines. Students can log their steps over a period of time and set some goals. They can graph the step counts and use them to compare activities and integrate math concepts with the routine.

▶ Read aloud a question related to the purposes and give partners a chance to discuss a correct response. Call on one pair to answer. Continue with several questions, soliciting answers from various pairs.

▶ Ask students to write about how much they did or did not enjoy each of the Fitness Fortunes and why. They could write about how the routines affect health-related fitness and the importance of personal choice and preference in achieving and maintaining health-related fitness.

HIGH SCHOOL

Exploring options and making choices—Students explore various fitness-related activities that enhance their knowledge and lead toward development of a personal health and fitness program.

Purpose

▶ Students will explore and experience many types of exercise with various equipment while doing exciting and challenging physical fitness activities.

▶ Students will learn fitness activities that are personally appealing.

▶ Students will work cooperatively with partners or in small groups.

Relationship to National Standards

▶ Physical education standard 3: Participates regularly in physical activity.

▶ Physical education standard 4: Achieves and maintains a health-enhancing level of physical fitness.

▶ Physical education standard 5: Exhibits responsible personal and social behavior that respects self and others in physical activity settings.

▶ Health education standard 3: Students will demonstrate the ability to practice health-enhancing behaviors and reduce health risks.

Equipment

▶ Music and player

▶ Equipment needed to complete the activities on the Circuit Training Choices Signs. If using stations provided on the CD-ROM, equipment needed includes the following:

• Jump ropes

• Step benches (or stairs)

• Resistance bands

• Mats for floor work

Procedure

1. Set up nine stations that each offers three choices. At each corner of the circuit is an aerobic fitness station (if using the Circuit Training Choices Signs on the CD-ROM, make two copies of each of the two aerobic choice stations). Another station is for abdominal strength. There are three flexibility stations—one for the legs, one for the torso area, and one for the upper body. An upper-body strength station completes the circuit.

2. Discuss with students the benefits of a circuit workout and of choice as it relates to fitness. (When you have a choice of exercises, you're more likely to find one that you like, and being able to do an activity that you like can help you be motivated to stay active.)

3. Have students get into equal-sized groups and have each group select a station at which to start.

Reproducible

Aerobic Choice

• Jog—around perimeter of area
• Jump rope—inside center of area
• Step-ups—use stairs, steps, or bleachers

Circuit Training Choices Signs.

155

4. Students complete one of the activities listed at each station and move to the next station in a predetermined rotation pattern, on a signal or when they have completed their activity of choice.

Teaching Hints

▶ Program a music recording with multiple series of 30 seconds of music (work phase) followed by 10-second pauses (when students move to the next station). You could also use a music player with a remote control for variable work and rest phases.

▶ Remind students about having choices and performing balanced workouts that include all the components of health-related fitness.

Sample Inclusion Tip

Circuit training stations allow students who are overweight or obese to adjust their personal intensity levels based on body type and current fitness level.

Variation

Focus on one component of health-related fitness by having all stations reflect that component.

Home Extension

Have students work in small groups to develop their own circuits and present them to the class during the next circuit activity session.

Assessment

Students get to practice making exercise choices during Circuit Training Choices.

▶ Have students respond to the following questions after completing the circuit:

• How is a circuit workout different from other workouts?

• What factors influenced you to make the choices that you did at each station?

• What other choices might you add?

• What are the benefits of working with others when you exercise?

▶ Have the students wear heart rate monitors, record their heart rates over the course of the circuit, and make observations regarding the various activities and stations.

▶ Ask students to write about how much they did or did not enjoy each of the circuit activities and why. Have them explain how circuit training affects health-related fitness. Also, students could write their answers to the assessment questions rather than responding to the questions aloud.

▶ If health-related fitness activities are done consistently throughout the year, students can measure their fitness levels using an appropriate fitness assessment (e.g., Fitnessgram). They can record their personal results in their journals and compare their results to previous assessments. Students can then set new fitness goals for future assessments.

FITNESS UNSCRAMBLE

MIDDLE SCHOOL AND HIGH SCHOOL

Exploring options and making choices—By experiencing a variety of fitness activities and then discussing them, students can gain an understanding of the importance of personal choices and preferences in maintaining lifetime physical activity.

Purpose

▶ Students will discriminate between health- and skill-related components of fitness.

▶ Students will participate in group fitness and cooperative activities.

Relationship to National Standards

▶ Physical education standard 1: Demonstrates competency in motor skills and movement patterns needed to perform a variety of physical activities.

▶ Physical education standard 5: Exhibits responsible personal and social behavior that respects self and others in physical activity settings.

▶ Health education standard 6: Students will demonstrate the ability to use goal-setting and decision-making skills to enhance health.

Equipment

▶ Foam ball

▶ 4-inch-by-8-inch (10 cm by 20 cm) mat

▶ Volleyball or beach ball

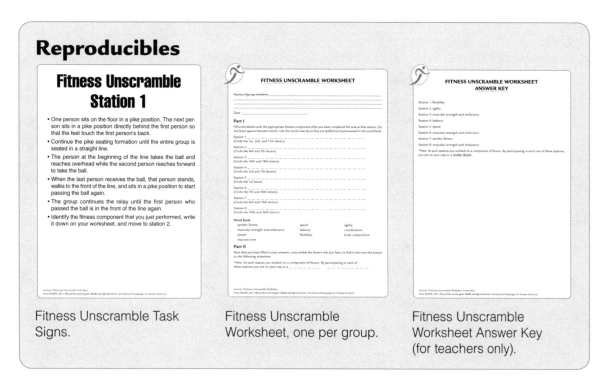

Reproducibles

Fitness Unscramble Task Signs.

Fitness Unscramble Worksheet, one per group.

Fitness Unscramble Worksheet Answer Key (for teachers only).

- ► Long jump rope
- ► Rope ladder laid flat on the ground for agility course (alternatively, can use hula hoops)
- ► Blocks, five or six (as many as the largest number of students in a group)
- ► Poly spots, five or six (as many as the largest number of students in a group)
- ► Weighted backpack
- ► Medicine ball or weighted objects for backpack
- ► Mats, enough for several students to use at once, connected together

Procedure

1. Review the health- and skill-related components of fitness as explained in activity 7.2. Explain that the object of the activity is for groups of students to travel from station to station performing group fitness activities. After completing the tasks, groups determine the health- or skill-related component used, and doing so gives them clues to complete the hint on the worksheet.

Group fitness activities are a fun way to introduce students to exercises they can explore and use throughout their lives.

2. Divide the class into small groups and send each group to a different station to begin.

3. Groups read the task card and perform the task given.

4. After completing the task, the group determines the health- or skill-related fitness component used. Using the worksheet, students fill in the component with the corresponding station.

5. On a signal, groups rotate to the next numerical station. After groups have rotated through every station, each group unscrambles the clues on the worksheet to solve the hint.

6. Reveal the answer to the hint. Assign each group a station and have them explain to the class why they chose the particular component that they chose for that station.

Teaching Hints

- ► Continually engage students by moving among the groups and asking questions as they generate their answers.
- ► As a class, students can create their own circuit by having each group design a station.

Sample Inclusion Tip

Allow a student using a wheelchair to choose the level and type of participation in the variety of station activities. A student using a wheelchair can develop upper-body strength by being the rope turner. At the agility station the student can self-propel and weave through cones. For the volleyball station, allow the student to catch the ball or let it bounce once before attempting to hit it back.

Variation

Have each member of the group write down their answers and present the rationale to the group before agreeing on a group answer.

Home Extension

As homework or a project, students can create an at-home fitness circuit that develops the health- or skill-related components of fitness. They can design the circuit around their favorite sport or lifestyle physical activity.

Assessment

▶ Have students discuss the differences between health- and skill-related fitness. Do some stations seem to include more than one component?

▶ Observe cooperation among students during the station activities and then ask the class what role group cooperation played in successful completion at stations.

JUMP BAND FITNESS

MIDDLE SCHOOL AND HIGH SCHOOL

Exploring options and making choices—Jump bands provide an excellent method of incorporating both aerobic fitness and rhythmic movement in a challenging activity for students.

Purpose

▶ Students will explore and experience many types of exercise with various equipment while participating in exciting and challenging physical fitness activities.

▶ Students will work cooperatively in small groups.

Relationship to National Standards

▶ Physical education standard 4: Achieves and maintains a health-enhancing level of physical fitness.

▶ Physical education standard 5: Exhibits responsible personal and social behavior that respects self and others in physical activity settings.

Equipment

▶ A set of jump bands (two) for every three students

▶ Music and player

Procedure

1. Divide the students into groups of three. Explain to students how to use the bands. Have two of the students in each group attach the jump bands around their upper ankles (they attach with Velcro). Have the third student step in and out of the bands as the students try to keep a 4/4 beat with the music. For the band holders, the movement is a constant repeated movement of out, out, in, in (see figure 7.1*a*).

2. Consider starting with music that has a clear beat, such as "We Will Rock You" or "Shrek #5." As the band holders begin jumping with their pattern, the middle jumper can begin with a simple in, in, out pattern with one foot. Then a two-foot pattern could be done the same way. Students switch from being a band holder to a middle jumper and back again as they get tired.

3. Although jump band activities will develop muscular strength and endurance in lower-body muscles, after several minutes of jumping, stop the entire class and have students perform a fun flexibility or upper-body muscular strength and endurance activity to switch the fitness focus. During each break, give students two or three of these exercises to choose from, such as modified push-ups, floor or bench dips, or a stretch. After the first break, put two groups together so that three students are holding the two sets of bands. One student has two sets of bands on his or her ankles. The remaining three students form a line and follow the leader through the two sets of bands (see figure 7.1*b*).

Reproducible

None.

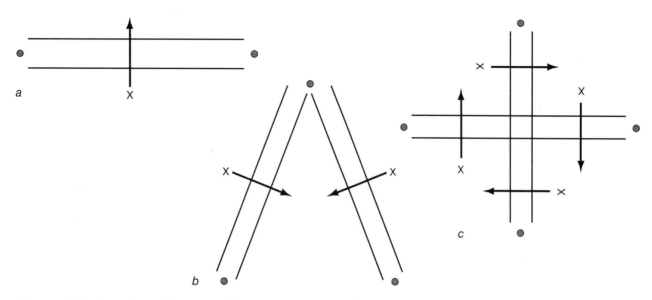

Figure 7.1 Jump band diagrams. The dots represent students holding the jump bands, and the X represents students jumping over the bands.

4. After a few minutes, take another break to do additional flexibility and upper-body muscular strength and endurance activities. Again, give students a variety of activities to choose from, such as calf stretches, hamstring stretches, push-ups, and curl-ups.

5. Finally, put the two groups together in a tic-tac-toe pattern and have the remaining two jumpers work their way around the pattern in front of the band holders. They could both go one direction and then change directions, or they could jump in opposite directions at the same time (see figure 7.1c).

Teaching Hints

▶ Program a music recording with multiple series of 30 seconds of music followed by 10-second pauses. Have students switch roles during the pause and then start jumping when the music starts.

▶ Tell students that jumping is primarily an aerobic fitness activity. The activities that they did during the breaks incorporated other components of health-related fitness.

Sample Inclusion Tip

Because this activity includes a lot of jumping, for students with disabilities needing assistance with jumping and balance, consider using minitrampolines with braces or handles or provide a peer to extend a hand of support so that the student can simulate the jumping technique.

Variations

▶ Use long jump ropes as your equipment.

▶ Place students in groups of three with a long jump rope for each group. The turners start turning the rope, and the jumpers come in and out of the rope with a front-and-back-door entrance. After each student has a chance to try each position, have the jumper enter the rope, make three jumps, exit, go around one of the turners, and then come back in to the rope for three more jumps. Soon the jumping student will be making a figure eight around the turners, taking three jumps in the middle, and continuing out to make the continuing figure eight. Students should do this for 30 seconds, change positions, and begin again. Jumping in this fashion is a demanding aerobic activity. Students get a rest while they are the turners of the rope.

Home Extension

Have students create their own jump band routines.

Assessment

▶ Have the students wear pedometers and record the number of steps that they take during this activity. Ask students how many steps they took and whether they are surprised by the number (which will likely be high). They can graph the step counts and use them to compare activities and integrate math concepts.

▶ Have students describe how they could tell that this was an aerobic fitness activity and explain how aerobic fitness affects health-related fitness. Ask students to comment on which of the break, or choice, activities aligns with each fitness component, separating those that are skill-related from those that are health-related.

▶ Lead a discussion related to the cooperation and team building necessary to experience success in this activity. What happened when they didn't listen to each other? How can cooperation and support be helpful in sticking with a physical activity plan?

MIDDLE SCHOOL AND HIGH SCHOOL

Exploring options and making choices—Partner Racetrack Fitness provides a fast-paced and challenging set of activities for both middle and high school students. This activity focuses on aerobic and muscular strength components of health-related fitness.

Purpose

▶ Students will explore and experience many types of exercise with various equipment while doing exciting and challenging physical fitness routines.

▶ Students will learn fitness activities that are personally appealing.

▶ Students will work cooperatively with partners.

Relationship to National Standards

▶ Physical education standard 4: Achieves and maintains a health-enhancing level of physical fitness.

▶ Physical education standard 5: Exhibits responsible personal and social behavior that respects self and others in physical activity settings.

▶ Physical education standard 6: Values physical activity for health, enjoyment, challenge, self-expression, and/or social interaction.

Equipment

▶ Music and player

▶ If using the signs provided on the CD-ROM, equipment needed includes the following:

  • Resistance bands

  • Free choice equipment such as step benches and dumbbells

  • Mats for floor work

Procedure

1. Arrange six stations in a circle or rectangle. At each station post a Racetrack Sign with several exercises or stretches to perform. Use those provided on the CD-ROM or design your own. If designing your own, include two aerobic, two muscular strength and endurance, and two flexibility stations.

2. Have students form groups of two and select a station at which to begin. More than one pair might be at a station at one time.

3. On the start signal, one partner begins the first exercise or stretch at the sign while the other partner jogs around the perimeter of the stations.

Reproducible

Aerobic Fitness

⚑ High knees
⚑ Side shuffles
⚑ Jumping jack variations
⚑ Free choice—aerobic

Racetrack Signs.

Students work in pairs, one jogging around the gym while the other performs tasks at a station, to get around the racetrack.

4. After the jogging partner returns, the partners switch roles and pick a new exercise to perform. They repeat for each exercise.

5. After completing all the activities at one station, students run one lap and move to the next station.

Teaching Hint

This activity works well outdoors. Signs can be attached to slotted cones.

Sample Inclusion Tip

Students using a wheelchair can self-propel around the racetrack while a partner is exercising, recording time, or recording distance traveled.

Variations

▶ To add variety, change the locomotor skill for the students moving around the racetrack (e.g., jumping rope, sliding, carioca, or race walking).

▶ Let students design their own racetrack signs by creating a variety of manipulative activities (such as juggling, ball skills, or beanbag activities).

Home Extension

Have students develop their own Partner Racetrack activities and use them in class.

Assessment

▶ Students can use a scale of 1 to 10 to determine their level of intensity during this activity. They could record their performance on their activity logs.

▶ If fitness activities are performed consistently throughout the year, students can measure their fitness levels using an appropriate fitness assessment (e.g., Fitnessgram). They can record their personal results in their journals and compare the results to previous assessments. Students can then set new fitness goals to reach for future assessment situations.

▶ After students have completed all activities, lead a discussion to encourage them to talk about what positive interactions emerged during the lesson. Did students get positive or negative feedback from their classmates, and how did this affect their motivation to continue participating?

▶ Have students record which activities they liked the least, which they liked the most, and how they could incorporate the activities that they enjoyed into their physical activity plan.

MIDDLE SCHOOL

Exploring options and making choices—Using a variety of physical challenges, students enhance their knowledge of various activities designed to improve fitness and activity patterns while having fun.

Purpose

▶ Students will explore and experience a variety of physical activities.

▶ Students will demonstrate and lead the class in activities.

Relationship to National Standards

▶ Physical education standard 4: Achieves and maintains a health-enhancing level of physical fitness.

▶ Physical education standard 5: Exhibits responsible personal and social behavior that respects self and others in physical activity settings.

▶ Health education standard 3: Students will demonstrate the ability to practice health-enhancing behaviors and reduce health risks.

Equipment

▶ Mats for floor work

▶ Music and player

Procedure

1. This is an add-on fitness game that uses 12 student leaders. Select the leaders and give each an Add-On Card.

2. The leaders present the activity on their cards one at a time, and the class and leader perform repetitions of the exercise to match the leader number. For example, if leader #3 is presenting an exercise, that leader and the entire class perform that exercise three times. Each new exercise is added to the ones before it, and each exercise retains its number of repetitions. The sidebar on page 167 shows an example.

Teaching Hint

Before introducing the activity, review the various locomotor movements listed. Have fun with the animal walks and movements by allowing students to make the sound of the animal.

Sample Inclusion Tip

For students with cognitive or learning disabilities, use pictures or a mnemonic memory device (abbreviation or acronym) to help students remember what activity or skill is coming next.

Add-On Cards.

SAMPLE PROGRESSION FOR ADD-ON CARDS

Leader #1: Push-Up
The leader and the class do 1 push-up.

Leader #2: Curl-ups
The leader and the class do 2 curl-ups and 1 push-up.

Leader #3: Coffee Grinders
The leader and the class do 3 coffee grinders, 2 curl-ups, and 1 push-up. In a coffee grinder, students are in a side-leaning position, with one hand and the same-side leg on the floor, and they pivot around the supporting hand.

Leader #4: Crab Kicks
The leader and the class do 4 crab kicks, 3 coffee grinders, 2 curl-ups, and 1 push-up. In a crab kick, students in a crab-walk position lift one leg, hold, and switch legs.

Leader #5: Golden Rests
The leader and the class do 5 counts of golden rest, 4 crab kicks, 3 coffee grinders, 2 curl-ups, and 1 push-up. In a golden rest, students simply rest for the number of counts desired.

Leader #6: Leaping Leaps
The leader and the class do 6 leaping leaps, 5 golden rests, 4 crab kicks, 3 coffee grinders, 2 curl-ups, and 1 push-up. In a leaping leap, students alternate the leading foot from right and left, leaping to the side.

Leader #7: Jumping Jacks
The leader and the class do 7 jumping jacks, 6 leaping leaps, 5 golden rests, 4 crab kicks, 3 coffee grinders, 2 curl-ups, and 1 push-up.

Leader #8: Forward Lunges
The leader and the class do 8 forward lunges, 7 jumping jacks, 6 leaping leaps, 5 golden rests, 4 crab kicks, 3 coffee grinders, 2 curl-ups, and 1 push-up.

Leader #9: Carioca Steps
The leader and the class do 9 carioca steps, 8 forward lunges, 7 jumping jacks, 6 leaping leaps, 5 golden rests, 4 crab kicks, 3 coffee grinders, 2 curl-ups, and 1 push-up.

Leader #10: Skipping Skips
The leader and the class do 10 skipping skips, 9 carioca steps, 8 forward lunges, 7 jumping jacks, 6 leaping leaps, 5 golden rests, 4 crab kicks, 3 coffee grinders, 2 curl-ups, and 1 push-up.

Leader #11: Rooster Hops
The leader and the class do 11 rooster hops, 10 skipping skips, 9 carioca steps, 8 forward lunges, 7 jumping jacks, 6 leaping leaps, 5 golden rests, 4 crab kicks, 3 coffee grinders, 2 curl-ups, and 1 push-up. In a rooster hop, students hop on one foot.

Leader #12: Running Steps
The leader and the class do 12 running steps, 11 rooster hops, 10 skipping skips, 9 carioca steps, 8 forward lunges, 7 jumping jacks, 6 leaping leaps, 5 golden rests, 4 crab kicks, 3 coffee grinders, 2 curl-ups, and 1 push-up. In running steps, students jog in place.

Variations

▶ Have student leaders select movements of their choice. You might have them select a movement from a sport or activity that they enjoy.

▶ Select a dance that can be broken up into 12 parts (steps) and use as each add-on piece.

▶ Use manipulative activities for each new add-on movement, such as juggling, ball skills, and beanbag activities.

An add-on game allows students to get firsthand experience with a variety of health-related fitness activities.

Home Extension

Have students discuss the components of health-related fitness with their families and friends. Through these conversations, they could develop a list of additional activities to be presented to the class.

Assessment

▶ Ask students to write about how much they did or did not enjoy the add-on activity. How does each of the activities performed today contribute to health-related fitness? Which activities did they enjoy the most? How might they incorporate those activities into their physical fitness plans?

▶ Ask the class these questions: Which of the add-on activities did you enjoy the most? What other activities would you like to include the next time the class does this activity? How could you use the add-on concept in the fitness activities that you do outside of class?

▶ Observe and record physical and affective information. Which of the add-on activities do students need to improve in? Which students need direction in developing leadership skills?

MIDDLE SCHOOL AND HIGH SCHOOL

Exploring options and making choices—Sport and fitness are not separate. To play a sport, a person must learn the skills and achieve a certain level of fitness. In this activity, students enhance their knowledge of health-related fitness while enhancing their skills in various sports.

Purpose

Students will develop health-related fitness components as they practice sport skills. (This activity is written for soccer, but the same concept could be used in a variety of sports.)

Relationship to National Standards

▶ Physical education standard 1: Demonstrates competency in motor skills and movement patterns needed to perform a variety of physical activities.

▶ Physical education standard 4: Achieves and maintains a health-enhancing level of physical fitness.

Equipment

Equipment will vary based on the sport skills being taught. For the soccer activities presented in this activity, the following equipment is needed:

▶ Agility ladder

▶ Mats for floor work

▶ Aerobic steps or benches

▶ Soccer balls

▶ Cones (or lines)

Procedure

1. Place the cards around the playing field, starting with a drill station and alternating with health-related fitness component stations. You will have 10 stations.

2. Make sure that students know what to do at each of the stations. Demonstrate how to do the sport-specific drills, and explain that students have a choice of exercises at the fitness component stations.

3. Divide students into 10 groups and place each group at one of the stations.

Sporting Fitness Activity Cards.

Sporting Fitness Soccer Drills.

4. On your cue, have the students begin the activity labeled at their station.

5. After one to two minutes, cue the groups to switch stations in a clockwise fashion.

6. After students have completed all stations, conduct a heart rate check. As time permits, have students continue through each station again. After the second round, conduct another heart rate check.

Teaching Hint

Increase the length of time at each station or the number of stations over time, when revising the activity.

Sample Inclusion Tips

▶ For students with low fitness levels, vary the activities on the station cards to build in success and serve as motivation to continue to the next station. For example, use wall push-ups as a muscular strength and endurance activity option.

▶ For students with high fitness levels, offer variations with greater challenge. For example, students could do push-ups with the feet slightly elevated or with one ankle crossed over the other.

Students learn about health-related fitness components while participating in sports like soccer.

▶ Using modified equipment (e.g., lighter weights, brightly colored balls, or a buddy system) will help students with special needs participate fully.

Variations

▶ Make your own skill-drill station cards for other sports and use this activity as a warm-up or conditioning activity for a variety of sports throughout the year.

▶ Combine skills from various sports in the setup.

Home Extension

Have students research two sports, one an individual sport and one a team sport, and determine what components of health-related fitness are required to participate.

Assessment

▶ Discuss with the students, or ask them for a written assessment as a homework assignment or in their journals, how health- and skill-related fitness components affect soccer performance.

▶ Discuss how students felt in the second round of stations compared with the first round. Did their aerobic and muscular endurance start to fade in the second round? What was their heart rate in the second round compared with the first? Did they feel more warmed up and flexible in the second round?

▶ Ask students which activities they enjoyed the most and how they could incorporate those activities into their daily physical activity plans.

BASKETBALL SKILLS FITNESS

MIDDLE SCHOOL AND HIGH SCHOOL

Understanding health-related fitness—This general fitness and skill development activity is designed to enhance knowledge of health-related fitness and basketball skills.

Purpose

Students will develop health-related fitness (i.e., aerobic, muscular strength and endurance, flexibility) while practicing basketball skills.

Relationship to National Standards

- ▶ Physical education standard 1: Demonstrates competency in motor skills and movement patterns needed to perform a variety of physical activities.
- ▶ Physical education standard 4: Achieves and maintains a health-enhancing level of physical fitness.

Equipment

- ▶ Basketball hoops
- ▶ Basketballs (one for each student)
- ▶ Mats for floor work
- ▶ Timed music (45 seconds of music and 10 seconds of silence) and a music player
- ▶ Cones (to hold signs)

Procedure

1. Ask students to pair up. Each student should have a basketball and go to a basket (you need to have an even number of partnerships at each basket and no more than four partnerships at each).

2. When the music starts, one partnership works on the basketball skill (listed on the basketball figure: shooting, layups, two-ball passing, key dribbling, one-on-one, and your choice) while the other partnership works on the basketball fitness activity. Students perform basketball skills at each basketball hoop and do fitness activities in the middle of the basketball court (see Basketball Skills Fitness, figure 7.2 on page 172, and the sidebar "Basketball Skills Fitness Activities" on page 172 for details).

3. When the music stops, partnerships change places.

4. Partnerships rotate through stations until they complete each basketball skill and fitness activity.

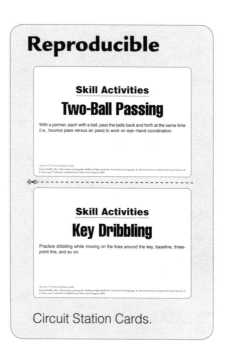

Reproducible

Skill Activities
Two-Ball Passing

With a partner, each with a ball, pass the balls back and forth at the same time (i.e., bounce pass versus air pass) to work on eye–hand coordination.

Activity 7.13 Circuit Stations Cards.
From NASPE, 2011, *Physical Best activity guide: Middle and high school level, 3rd edition* (Champaign, IL: Human Kinetics). Reprinted, by permission of P. Davis and T. Johnson, modified from Davis and Tangen 2009.

Skill Activities
Key Dribbling

Practice dribbling while moving on the lines around the key, baseline, three-point line, and so on.

Activity 7.13 Circuit Stations Cards.
From NASPE, 2011, *Physical Best activity guide: Middle and high school level, 3rd edition* (Champaign, IL: Human Kinetics). Reprinted, by permission of P. Davis and T. Johnson, modified from Davis and Tangen 2009.

Circuit Station Cards.

BASKETBALL SKILLS FITNESS ACTIVITIES

Skill Activities

- Two-ball passing—Two students, each with a ball, pass the balls back and forth at the same time (i.e., bounce pass versus air pass) to work on eye–hand coordination.
- Key dribbling—Students practice dribbling while moving on the lines around the key, baseline, three-point line, and so on.
- Shooting—Students work on shooting skills from various distances.
- One-on-one—Two students play a short game of one-on-one.
- Your choice—Students can practice whatever skills they want here.
- Layups—Students work on various layups such as right- versus left-handed, baseline, reverse, underhand, and so on.

Fitness Activities

- Push-ups—With hands on a basketball, perform push-ups on the toes or knees.
- Basketball squats—Hold a basketball in front and perform squats. Go down until the legs are parallel to the floor.
- Plank—In prone position, elevate the body with only the forearms and toes touching the floor. Hold this position. Keep the body parallel to the floor.
- Overhead jumps—Hold a basketball overhead and jump as high as possible.
- Push-up coffee grinders—With hands on a ball in push-up position, travel with the feet in a circle around the ball using an even pace.

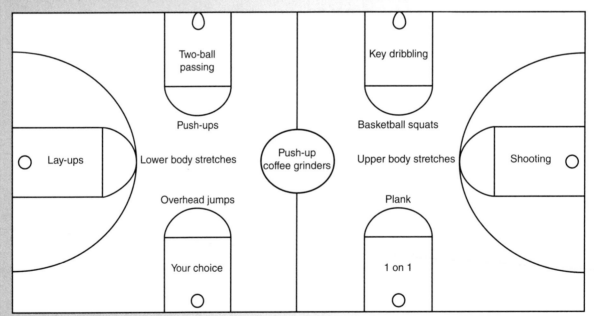

Figure 7.2   Floor diagram for Basketball Skills Fitness.

Reprinted, by permission of P. Darst and T. Johnson; modified from Darst and Pangrazi 2009.

Teaching Hints

▶ Use timed music to make transitions easier.

▶ Use your time to teach and coach students who need the most assistance.

Sample Inclusion Tips

▶ Adjust skill and fitness activities to meet the developmental needs of students.

▶ Supplying different sizes of basketballs can help meet the developmental needs of all students. For example, use a bigger ball, a softer ball, or a lower basket so that students can be successful at each station.

▶ Students can work with an aide or with another student to work at their own level at each station.

Variation

Because basketball, soccer, and floor hockey are similar activities, try alternating stations among the three activities.

Home Extension

Have students keep journals of skill development activities and related fitness enhancement activities done at home. In their journals they should state why and how the fitness activities will enhance their ability to participate in the skill-related activity.

Assessment

At the conclusion of the activity, ask the class the following questions.

▶ Which fitness activities focused on muscular strength? Which focused on aerobic fitness?

▶ Which component of health-related fitness could be enhanced by playing basketball? Why?

Discuss each of the answers and the rationale used to determine the answers.

Reprinted, by permission of P. Darst and T. Johnson; modified from Darst and Pangrazi 2009.

MAT EXERCISE STATIONS

MIDDLE SCHOOL AND HIGH SCHOOL

Exploring options and making choices—This general fitness activity for students is designed to target two components of health-related fitness—aerobic capacity and muscular strength and endurance.

Purpose

Students will focus on aerobic fitness and muscular strength and endurance to determine how exercise could affect fitness through challenging and targeted activities.

Relationship to National Standards

▶ Physical education standard 1: Demonstrates competency in motor skills and movement patterns needed to perform a variety of physical activities.

▶ Physical education standard 3: Participates regularly in physical activity.

▶ Physical education standard 5: Exhibits responsible personal and social behaviors that respect self and others in physical activity settings.

Equipment

▶ 5-foot-by-10-foot (1.5 by 3 m) folding mats, one for every six students, or two aerobic steps with two or three risers and one flat mat or individual mat for curl-ups

▶ Two jump ropes per mat

Procedure

1. Place folded mats in various locations throughout the gym. Place one jump rope about 4 feet (120 cm) back from each end. Divide students into groups of six and have each group go to a mat. Each mat has six stations—one on each end, one on each side, and the two jump rope areas.

   • End 1—Students place their hands on the mat or step and perform push-ups.

   • Side 1—Students lie down with their knees bent and heels off the ground and perform curl-ups.

   • End 2—Students stand on the floor and do step-ups on the end of the mat.

   • Side 2—Students sit down with their feet facing away from the mat, place their hands on the mat behind them, and do dips.

2. Before students begin, ask them to think about the FITT principle at each station—which exercise is most intense, what specific muscle group and area of fitness are the focus of the stations, and how time affects the intensity. Before starting the activity have all students take their 30-second resting heart rates.

3. On the go signal, students at the mat stations and jump rope stations begin their assigned activities. After 60 seconds the students rotate one station to the right; those at the side stations rotate to the jump rope sta-

Reproducible

None.

Students combine aerobic activity with muscular fitness activity to determine the effect on their heart rates.

tions, those at the ends rotate to the sides, and those at the jump rope stations rotate to the ends.

4. After the first complete rotation, have the students take their 30-second heart rates and compare them with the rates taken before they started the circuit.

5. The rotation continues until all students have completed two full rotations.

6. At the conclusion of the rotations, have the students take their 30-second heart rates again, jog one slow lap, and return to their mats to take their heart rates one more time.

Teaching Hint

When arranging stations at each mat or step, make sure that the push-up and curl-up stations are located at the ends of the mat, which helps keep the mat from sliding.

Inclusion Tips

▶ Students work at their level of ability, allowing them to participate at their intensity level.

▶ Provide jump ropes that have been cut or folded in half for students with ambulatory limitations.

Variation

After they complete each station have students jog one lap of the gym before rotating to the next station at their mat or step.

Home Extension

Have students write how the FITT principle was used, or not used, in this activity; which activities were the most intense; and how each activity focused on one fitness component—frequency, intensity, type, or time.

Assessment

After they take their heart rates have the students sit around their mats and participate in a class discussion. Use the following topical areas to begin the discussion:

▸ Did your heart rate go up after the first rotation? How much?

▸ How about after the second rotation? Was it higher than it was after the first?

▸ Did your heart rate go down after jogging the slow lap? If so, why do you think that took place?

▸ What station was the most intense? Why? What was the least intense? Why?

▸ Discuss how time affected the intensity by asking how a duration of 30 seconds or 2 minutes would affect intensity.

Adapted, by permission, from J. Carpenter, 2000, *PE teacher's complete fitness and skills development activity program* (Parker Publishing). By permission of J. Carpenter.

SPEED CIRCUIT

MIDDLE SCHOOL AND HIGH SCHOOL

Exploring options and making choices—Students perform a fast-paced aerobic activity for a specified period and then do a muscular strength and endurance activity before returning to an aerobic activity.

Purpose

This activity will focus on enhancing student knowledge of the FITT principle through active participation in a fast-paced circuit consisting of alternating aerobic fitness and muscular strength and endurance activities.

Relationship to National Standards

▶ Physical education standard 2: Demonstrates understanding of movement concepts, principles, strategies, and tactics as they apply to the learning and performance of physical activities.

▶ Physical education standard 3: Participates regularly in physical activity.

Equipment

▶ One jump rope for each student

▶ One aerobic step or folded mat for every two students

Procedure

1. Arrange aerobic steps around the sides of the gym. Place two jump ropes at the end of each bench. Have two students stand at each step.

2. Table 7.2 shows a sample routine that you can use for this activity. On the start signal, students begin the first aerobic set by jumping rope. At the end of the period, the students put down the jump rope and immediately move into the alternating activity. The rotation between aerobic activity and muscular endurance activity continues until the routine is completed. Have students monitor their pulse rates after completing three rotations; they should note whether their heart rates stay in the target zone throughout the routine. Ask them to remember which activities caused the greatest increase.

Teaching Hints

▶ Have students walk for 2 minutes after the complete rotation and repeat the activity using 60 seconds for the aerobic activity.

▶ Discuss the FITT principle in relation to intensity and time.

Table 7.2 Sample Routine

Movement	Time
Rope jumping	90 seconds
Push-ups	30 seconds
Bench step-ups*	90 seconds
Curl-ups	30 seconds
Rope jumping	90 seconds
Rowing**	30 seconds
Bench step-ups	90 seconds
Triceps push-ups	30 seconds
Rope jumping	90 seconds
Curl-ups	30 seconds
Bench step-ups	90 seconds
Plank	30 seconds
Jog	90 seconds
Walk	60 seconds

*Bench step-ups are done with both partners performing at the same time on opposite sides of a bench.

**Rowing is done from a seated position on the floor. Students should be balanced with both legs off the ground. Begin a rowing motion by extending the legs while pulling the arms back to the side. Alternate legs back, arms extended.

Reproducible

None.

Sample Inclusion Tips

▶ Decrease time on task.

▶ Cut or fold jump ropes in half for students not able to jump independently.

Variation

Rather than including muscular strength and endurance activities, add skill development activities such as throwing and catching, dribbling a basketball, or passing a basketball.

Home Extension

Have students do this activity sequence over the weekend with a family member or friend. Students should explain the FITT principle to the family member or friend, ask the person which activities were the most intense, and compare that answer to their own.

Assessment

At the conclusion of the activity, have the class discuss how their heart rates varied between activities. Relate this to the FITT Principle components of intensity, time, and type. The following could be used to begin the discussion.

▶ Did your heart rate increase or decrease as the rotation continued?

▶ Which of the activities seemed to be more intense?

▶ How did time affect the intensity? Aerobic activities were performed for 90 seconds, and muscular strength activities were performed for 30 seconds.

▶ Did your heart rate change between the aerobic and muscular strength activities? Why?

Students use the FITT principle to explore the effect of several fast-paced exercises on their target heart rate zones.

Adapted from J. Carpenter and D. Tunnell, 1994, *Elementary PE teacher's survival guide* (Parker Publishing). By permission of J. Carpenter.

MEDICINE BALL CIRCUIT

MIDDLE SCHOOL AND HIGH SCHOOL

Exploring options and making choices—Students enhance muscular strength and endurance, aerobic fitness, and flexibility while using a combination of medicine balls and traditional exercises in a challenging circuit designed to allow for individual differences and goal setting.

Purpose

Student will be able to develop aerobic fitness, flexibility, and muscular strength and endurance by participating in a wide variety of exercises using medicine balls (or substituted balls).

Relationship to National Standards

► Physical education standard 3: Participates regularly in physical activity.

► Physical education standard 4: Achieves and maintains a health-enhancing level of physical fitness.

Equipment

► One medicine ball, or alternative equipment (see "Teaching Hints") for every two students

► Jump ropes for station 3

► Mats for floor work

► Cone markers for each station

► Upbeat music and player (optional)

Procedure

1. Set up a five-station circuit around the teaching area.

2. Use cones to designate each station. Place students in small groups and assign each to a station.

3. Students do aerobic fitness activities both at the station and in the perimeter of the area.

4. Lead a class warm-up before having students begin to rotate through the stations. Have all students spread out randomly around the gym. On the "go" signal, have everyone begin to jog slowly, without bumping into anyone else. After 20 seconds of jogging tell them that they have 5 seconds to find one other person and stand toe to toe with her or him. Repeat and have them stand shoulder to shoulder with a different partner. Repeat the jogging and have them stand back to back with a partner; this person will be their partner for the day.

5. Have all students standing together. Give the direction that when you say the number 5, one partner should sit. Have the standing partner run and get a medicine ball while the other goes to the group's first station.

Reproducible

Station 1

Around the World

Partners stand back to back, and one holds a medicine ball. Holding the ball at waist height, they pass the ball while their feet remain stationary. The partners continue to pass the ball from one to the other. They go first to the right five times and then to the left five times.

Good Mornings

Partners face each other, and one partner has a medicine ball. The partner with the ball holds it above his or her head while the other partner places a hand above his or her head. Both partners bend forward at the waist, moving their hands down toward the floor. When they reach a full stretch position, they hold for the count of 10 and stand back up. They repeat six times, switching partners with the ball each time.

Wood Choppers

The student holds the ball between the legs, brings it up above the head, and returns it down between the legs (simulating a wood-chopping motion). The knees should be kept slightly flexed to protect the lower back.

Activity 7.16 Medicine Ball Circuit Station Signs
From NASPE, 2011, *Physical best activity guide: Middle and high school level, 3rd edition* (Champaign, IL: Human Kinetics). Reprinted, by permission of P. Harris and T. Johnson, *models.k.from Tuscr and Penguins 2008.*

Medicine Ball Circuit Station Signs.

Introduce the use of various types of equipment, such as medicine balls, to help students discover new ways to address aerobic, muscular strength and endurance, and flexibility fitness.

6. Students do each of the activities at the station. If they complete all activities before the signal to rotate is given, they begin doing the first activity again.

7. Groups have three minutes at each station. Then all students run one lap of the gym before stopping at the station to the right of their previous one.

8. Lead a class cool-down after all groups have completed the five stations. Have partners sit facing each other on the floor with their feet spread in a straddle position. The partner with the medicine ball extends the ball with the fingers toward the partner, stretching the hamstrings and lower back. At the peak of the stretch, he or she slowly rolls the ball to the partner, who receives the ball and repeats the stretch. The partners stretch and roll the ball five times each.

Teaching Hints

▶ Some activities can be done individually or with a partner.

▶ If only a few medicine balls are available, design your circuit to include a variety of stations that do not need the medicine balls and a few that use them. If no medicine balls are available, try substituting playground balls, basketballs, or volleyballs for some of the activities (such as push-up partner roll). Substituting unweighted balls will change the intensity and specificity of the activity, but students will find success, learn correct form, and may eventually be able to use a weighted medicine ball. Discuss with the class the components of the FITT principle and ways in which intensity may be changed by using different equipment even when time and type of activity remain the same.

▶ Playing continuous music helps maintain the enthusiasm and effort of your students.

▶ Provide a variety of different weighted balls at each station to challenge all levels of students.

▶ Students should start with a partner of about the same height or strength. Most girls should start with a 2-kilogram (4.4 lb) ball, and most boys should start with a 3-kilogram (6.6 lb) ball.

Sample Inclusion Tip

Students with disabilities will find success by using a larger or softer ball and being paired with an aide.

Variations

Music is always a motivational tool and can be used to time the workload at each station (45 seconds of music followed by 45 seconds of no music). In this variation, students should disregard the number of repetitions recommended in the instructions and instead perform as many repetitions as they safely can during the 45 seconds of music.

▶ While music is playing, students move around the circuit in a teacher-designated movement that works the aerobic endurance component of fitness (jog, slide, carioca, power skips, and so on).

▶ When the music is paused, students perform the exercise with the medicine balls.

Home Extension

Ask students to try one activity from each station at home, with or without equipment. Have them write down what activity they did and with what equipment and share their experience with the class.

Assessment

Each station lists the number of repetitions that should be done, but students should be encouraged to go beyond that goal. Have students record in their fitness journals how many repetitions they completed each day at each station and whether they exceeded or were under the goal set for the class. If they were above or below the goal, they should set new personal goals for the next time the activity is presented. Encourage students to increase the number of repetitions that they perform each time as a part of the fitness component of the lesson.

Students could also be evaluated by a peer at teacher-designated stations. A rubric could be developed about what to look for relative to the particular skill.

FITNESS ADVENTURE

MIDDLE SCHOOL

Exploring options and making choices—Middle level students will work together to complete various fitness challenge tasks as well as to assess knowledge and understanding of nutrition and health-related fitness components.

Purpose

▶ Students will be able to work collaboratively to complete fitness activity challenges.

▶ Students will have an opportunity to participate in a variety of physical activities for the purpose of increased enjoyment and social interaction.

▶ Students will have the opportunity to demonstrate knowledge of health-related fitness concepts and health-enhancing behaviors.

Relationship to National Standards

▶ Physical education standard 3: Participates regularly in physical activity.

▶ Physical education standard 5: Exhibits responsible personal and social behavior that respects self and others in physical activity settings.

Equipment

▶ Six to eight cones or line markers

▶ Four jump ropes

▶ Poly spots, enough to create an area for teams to cross

▶ Blocks or beanbags, as many as possible, for one end of shuttle runs

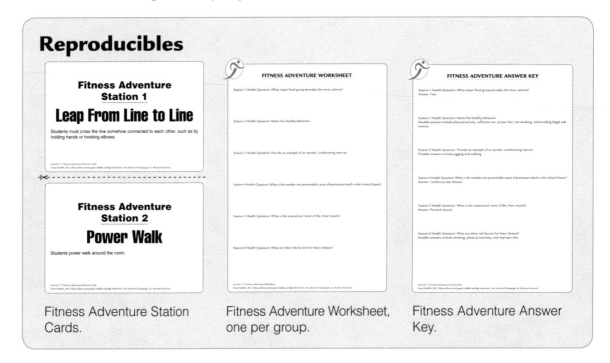

Fitness Adventure Station Cards.

Fitness Adventure Worksheet, one per group.

Fitness Adventure Answer Key.

- 1-inch-by-2-inch (2.5 by 5 cm) wooden blocks, board erasers, or juggling cubes, as many as possible, for one end of shuttle runs
- One scooter or carpet square
- Pencil, one per team

Procedure

1. Set up stations around the room.
   - Station 1—Set up six to eight line markers approximately 5 to 6 feet (1.5 to 1.8 m) apart.
   - Station 2—No setup required.
   - Station 3—Provide jump ropes, enough so that each member of a team has one.
   - Station 4—Evenly space poly spots approximately 3 to 4 feet (1 to 1.2 m) apart or more, if desired. Students will be instructed to cross the poly spots, maintaining their balance.
   - Station 5—Set up several shuttle run piles 10 to 15 feet (3 to 4.5 m) apart. Place piles of beanbags on one end and piles of blocks on the other.
   - Station 6—Place a carpet square or scooter in an empty area.

2. For a warm-up, students should form teams of three or four and play tag. After being tagged, the tagged student spins around twice and then reenters the game. Have students play for about two minutes before coming together to discuss the health topic "Describe how exercise helps maintain a healthy heart."

3. After the warm-up, assign teams to different stations around the room that describe an activity and ask a health question. When a team is done with a station, they come back to the teacher to answer the question given at the station. A correct answer earns a health point toward immunity or disease prevention. An incorrect answer gets an unhealthy point deduction from the team's score.

4. Students move on to the next station.

Fitness Adventure guides students through various types of activities while they collect, or lose, fitness points from challenges.

Teaching Hints

▶ Allow a certain amount of time for each team to complete the task.

▶ Keep a chart of fitness points and immunity points for each team.

▶ To avoid excessive competition, modify scoring so that all teams that complete the tasks in a prescribed amount of time earn a point.

Sample Inclusion Tips

▶ Students with limited mobility may require the assistance of an aide.

▶ Students work to their level of ability, allowing them to participate at their intensity level.

Variation

Redirect the health questions to be related to the FITT principle (e.g., how does frequency of physical activity help you become more fit?).

Home Extension

Have students research three different health questions, write down the answers, and present them in class.

Assessment

▶ Discuss the answers and relevant information concerning the health and fitness concepts.

▶ Ask students to write a reflective journal about their experience of working collaboratively.

RACETRACK FITNESS USING STABILITY BALLS

HIGH SCHOOL

Exploring options—Students practice aerobic fitness, muscular strength and endurance, and flexibility using stability balls on an exercise circuit.

Purpose

Students will participate in a fitness activity using stability balls. The activity will affect aerobic endurance, muscular strength and endurance, and flexibility. Stability balls are a fun and motivating change of pace activity for developing core strength through maintaining balance in a variety of dynamic movements. Flexibility is also enhanced through maintaining balance in a wide variety of movements.

Relationship to National Standards

- ▶ Physical education standard 3: Participates regularly in physical activity.
- ▶ Physical education standard 4: Achieves and maintains a health-enhancing level of physical fitness.

Equipment

- ▶ Nine cones, one for each station
- ▶ Six mats for stations with floor exercises
- ▶ Stability balls for half of your largest class
- ▶ Upbeat music and player (optional)

Procedure

1. Set up a circuit around the area with a variety of stations that require aerobic and muscular fitness as well as flexibility. Remember to use mats for all exercises in which students are on the floor.

2. One partner performs the aerobic activity designated by the station signs around the outside of the cones while partner 2 works on the stability balls at one station.

3. When partner 1 arrives back at the starting point, she or he high-fives partner 2, who then does the aerobic activity around the area while partner 1 does the designated stability activity.

4. After partner 2 comes back and high-fives partner 1, they move up one station and continue alternating the aerobic and stability ball activities.

Teaching Hints

- ▶ Playing continuous music helps maintain the enthusiasm and effort of your students. Select a variety of stability ball activities that your students have been taught.

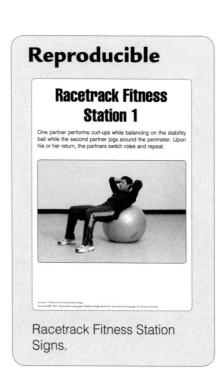

Reproducible

Racetrack Fitness Station 1

One partner performs curl-ups while balancing on the stability ball while the second partner jogs around the perimeter. Upon his or her return, the partners switch roles and repeat.

Activity 7.18 Racetrack Fitness Station Signs
From WAHPE, 2011, *Physical Best activity guide: Middle and high school levels,* 3rd edition (Champaign, IL: Human Kinetics)

Racetrack Fitness Station Signs.

Students get practice using all three fitness components in Racetrack Fitness Using Stability Balls.

▶ This approach allows you to get by with fewer stability balls and still provides a fun, positive fitness experience with a variety of aerobic, strength, and flexibility activities using novel equipment.

▶ Remind students to be aware of their position on the ball. They should ask their partners or you to correct their position if necessary.

Sample Inclusion Tip

Students with physical disabilities can be paired with a helper who will aid them in moving around the outside of the racetrack and help them position themselves on the ball so that they can achieve correct form.

Variation

These suggestions are just a few of the possible stability ball exercises. As students improve, continue to challenge them with new and different exercises. A helpful resource is John Byl's *Having a Ball: Stability Ball Games* published by Human Kinetics.

Home Extensions

▶ Have student find places in the community where they could buy or use a stability ball. This may even include looking online, such as on craigslist, for inexpensive stability balls that people might sell or donate.

▶ If students have a stability ball, it could be used to sit on instead of a desk chair when they are doing homework. Students can also keep a stability ball in the TV room so they can do exercises while they watch TV or during commercials.

Assessment

All students should be working at their own individual level. Students can keep track of how many repetitions they completed at each station.

Adapted from P. Darst and R. Pangrazi, 2009, *Dynamic physical education for secondary school students,* 6th ed. (San Francisco: Benjamin Cummings). By permission of P. Darst.

KNOW THE RISKS AND BENEFITS

MIDDLE SCHOOL AND HIGH SCHOOL

Healthy behaviors—Making healthy lifestyle choices is an important part of minimizing cardiovascular disease risks.

Purpose

▶ Students will gain an understanding of the risk factors for cardiovascular disease.

▶ Students will be able to identify healthy behaviors that may minimize risks for cardiovascular disease.

Relationship to National Standards

▶ Physical education standard 4: Achieves and maintains a health-enhancing level of physical fitness.

▶ Physical education standard 6: Values physical activity for health, enjoyment, challenge, self-expression, and/or social interaction.

Equipment

Equipment for each station should be sufficient so that all students in a small group can participate at the same time.

▶ Bench steps, 12 to 16 inches (30 to 45 cm) high

▶ Small exercise mats

▶ Elastic bands or weights

▶ Various balls: sponge ball, soccer ball, volleyball, basketball

Reproducibles

Health Risk Factor
Smoking
Health Risk
Increases risk of lung cancer and decreases the ability to breathe.
Activity
Jog in place for one minute while breathing through a straw.

Health Risk Station Signs.

Healthy Behaviors
Exercise
Health Benefit
Increases aerobic fitness and strengthens the heart and lungs.
Activity
Jump rope or skip in place for one minute.

Healthy Behavior Station Signs.

HEALTH RISK AND BENEFITS WORKSHEET

Name _____ Date _____

Directions: Briefly state the health risk or benefit associated with the behavior.

Smoking
Health risk _____

Excessive body fat
Health risk _____

Substance abuse
Health risk _____

Physical inactivity
Health risk _____

Health Risks and Benefits Worksheet, one per group.

▶ Jump ropes

▶ Straws, one per student in class

▶ Pencil, one per group

▶ Hula hoop taped to the wall

Procedure

1. Set up a circuit around the perimeter of the gymnasium, alternating Health Risk Station Cards and Healthy Behaviors Station Cards.

2. Organize students into groups of two or four at each station.

3. Give each group a worksheet and a pencil or marker

4. Each group reads the risk factor or healthy behavior located at their station and at the "go" signal or start of music performs the task for 60 seconds. When time is called, students mark on their worksheet the health risk factor that is associated with unhealthy behavior or the health benefit associated with the healthy behavior.

Teaching Hints

▶ Demonstrate unfamiliar tasks.

▶ Be sure to instruct groups to rotate in the same direction to avoid collisions.

Sample Inclusion Tip

Have a partner assist students with visual difficulty or include both written and pictorial cues to completion.

Variation

Allow student choice by listing and providing equipment for two or three activity options on each Healthy Behavior Station Card.

Home Extension

Have students identify an activity that they could do at home for each health-related fitness component.

Assessment

▶ Check worksheets for accuracy and correct answers.

▶ Ask students to review other types of behaviors that may minimize the risks of cardiovascular disease.

Students learn about the health risks associated with unhealthy behavior and the health benefits associated with healthy behavior while performing aerobic, muscular fitness, and flexibility activities.

BODY IMAGE MUSEUM TOUR

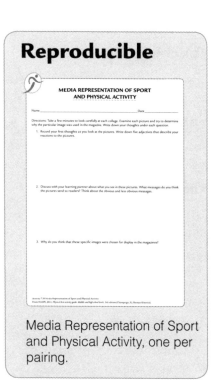

7.20

MIDDLE SCHOOL

Quackery—A method of advertising or selling that uses false claims to lure people into buying products that are worthless or even harmful.

Body image—Media images of beauty can be unrealistic and unattainable for all but a small number of people.

Purpose

▶ Students will understand the importance of staying active on most days of the week.

▶ Students will analyze the messages that the media place on body image.

▶ Students will examine strategies that promote an active lifestyle.

Relationship to National Standards

Physical education standard 3: Participates regularly in physical activity.

Equipment

▶ Two magazines per group (magazines that include images of men and women being active)

▶ One large sheet of paper per group

▶ Glue sticks

Procedures

1. Facilitate a class discussion on the messages being portrayed by the media in relation to body image. Specifically, focus the discussion on how the health-related fitness components are represented by various media sources.

2. Arrange the class into groups of four and explain to the class that they will be going on a body image museum tour.

3. Provide each group of four with two magazines of men and women being physically active. Explain to the groups that each will be making a collage representing images of people in various activity situations. Emphasize that the collages must include both genders.

4. After the collages are completed, have the groups place their collages in various parts of the room. Have each student pair up with a partner from the same group. Each pair will have a Media Representation of Sport and Physical Activity handout.

5. Explain to the class that each pair will be touring the museum collages. Each pair should visit all the collages to assist them in completing the handout.

Reproducible

MEDIA REPRESENTATION OF SPORT AND PHYSICAL ACTIVITY

Name_____ Date_____

Directions: Take a few minutes to look carefully at each collage. Examine each picture and try to determine why the particular image was used in the magazine. Write down your thoughts under each question.

1. Record your first thoughts as you look at the pictures. Write down five adjectives that describe your reactions to the pictures.

2. Discuss with your learning partner about what you see in these pictures. What messages do you think the pictures send to readers? Think about the obvious and less obvious messages.

3. Why do you think that these specific images were chosen for display in the magazines?

Media Representation of Sport and Physical Activity, one per pairing.

Distinguishing between the idealized body images portrayed in the media and what represents an actual healthy body is an important life skill for any student. Body Image Museum Tour gives you the chance to help students explore media images and the impact of those images on their own beliefs about body image.

6. When pairs have visited all the collages, facilitate a class discussion based on the responses from the handout. Throughout the discussion, emphasize that people come in different shapes and sizes. The important message is that everyone may benefit from regular bouts of physical activity to maintain or improve components of health-related fitness.

7. Have the pairs examine strategies that promote an active lifestyle both in and out of school.

Teaching Tip

In selecting the magazine ad in the initial class discussion, include photos and information on people with different disabilities.

Sample Inclusion Tip

Students of all abilities can be actively involved in this activity. Consult with the special education teacher for techniques that promote a positive, safe learning environment.

Variation

Select a fitness-related magazine and a news-related magazine for each group. Ask students to compare images in both.

Home Extension

Ask students to discuss what they have learned with family and friends. During the next class, discuss the various ideas presented at home.

Assessment

Explain to the class that there is no ideal body type and that everyone may benefit from regular physical activity.

PART III

Personal Fitness Connections

Andres Rodriguez

Self-Management and Goal Setting

Bananastock

A fter your students learn about the benefits of physical activity and how much physical activity they need to get those benefits (see *Physical Education for Lifelong Fitness: The Physical Best Teacher's Guide, Third Edition*), the next concepts to teach are how students can learn to become active if they are not already active and how they can stay active if they are currently active on a regular basis. To help you do this, we have provided sample lesson plans,

with support materials and suggested activities, for teaching self-management and goal setting.

This chapter includes lessons that are structured as a combination of class presentations, discussion, and activity. Getting across key concepts of self-management and goal setting is important, but we also want to provide an opportunity for students to be physically active. See table 8.1 for a grid of activities in this chapter.

Table 8.1   Chapter 8 Activities Grid

Activity number	Activity title	Activity page	Concept	Middle school	High school	Reproducibles (on CD-ROM)
8.1	Learning Self-Management Skills	195	Self-management skills	•	•	What Stage Am I?
						Physical Activity Pyramid for Teens
	Enrichment Activity: Fitness Trail	198	Exercise	•	•	Fitness Trail Station Signs
8.2	Goal Setting	200	Goal setting	•	•	Setting Goals
						Short-Term Versus Long-Term Goals
8.3	Using Pedometers to Set Goals and Assess Physical Activity	202	Pedometer use and goal setting		•	Assessment record sheet
8.4	Using Heart Rate Monitors	204	Heart rate monitor use and goal setting	•	•	Activity Template and Record Sheet
8.5	Fitness Olympics	206	Goal setting	•		Fitness Olympics Scorecard
						Basketball Station Cards
8.6	Power Team Training	208	Goal setting		•	Power Team Challenge Score Card
						Power Team Challenge Station Task Cards

LEARNING SELF-MANAGEMENT SKILLS 8.1

MIDDLE SCHOOL AND HIGH SCHOOL

Self-management skills—These skills are used by a person to take control of his or her lifestyle or behavior to stay physically active.

Objectives

▶ Describe the stages of physical activity change.

▶ Describe several self-management skills.

▶ Explain how to use self-management skills for living a healthy life.

Relationship to National Standards

▶ Physical education standard 3: Participates regularly in physical activity.

▶ Physical education standard 4: Achieves and maintains a health-enhancing level of physical fitness.

▶ Physical education standard 5: Exhibits responsible personal and social behavior that respects self and others in physical activity settings.

Opener

Introduce the lesson by using one of the following ideas:

▶ Show the class two contrasting photos—one of a person watching television, the other of a person being physically active in a small-group exercise. Have students provide ideas about why they are behaving the way they are.

▶ Divide students into small groups and have them place famous people they know onto a physical activity spectrum (high amount of physical activity to low amount of physical activity).

▶ Place students in pairs and have them compare how each of them manages and organizes the sports or physical activities that they do. For example, do some students use a calendar to schedule their activity times? Do some students plan recreational activities for the days on which they don't have a sport practice session? (See table 8.2 on page 196 for other self-management skills.)

▶ Use the following worksheet as homework or have students do it in class so that you can help them with questions.

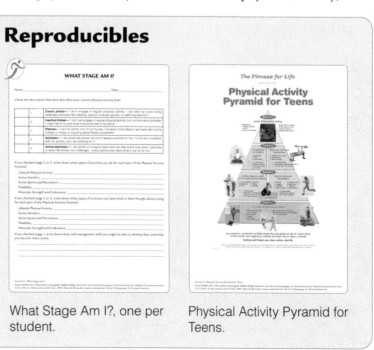

What Stage Am I?, one per student.

Physical Activity Pyramid for Teens.

195

Table 8.2 Self-Management Skills for Active Living, Health, and Wellness

Skill	Definition
Self-assessment	This skill allows you to test your own fitness to help you see where you are and to help you get to where you want to be.
Building self-confidence	This skill helps you build the feeling that you are capable of being active for life.
Identifying risk factors	This skill helps you identify, assess, and reduce health risks.
Choosing good activities	This skill helps you select activities that are best for you personally.
Goal setting	This skill helps you set realistic and practical goals for being active and achieving physical fitness.
Building positive attitudes	This skill allows you to identify and build attitudes that will help you to be active throughout life.
Self-monitoring	This skill helps you learn to keep records (or logs) to see whether you are in fact doing what you think you are doing.
Finding social support	This skill helps you find ways to get the help and support of others (your friends and family) to adopt healthy behaviors and to stick with them.
Building performance skills	These skills help you to be good at and enjoy sports and other physical activities.
Building intrinsic motivation	This skill helps you learn to enjoy physical activity for your own personal reasons rather than because others think it is good for you.
Preventing relapse	This skill helps you stick with healthy behaviors even when you have problems getting motivated.
Managing time effectively	This skill helps you learn to schedule time efficiently so that you will have more time for important things in your life.
Building positive self-perceptions	This skill helps you think positively about yourself so you can stay active for a lifetime.
Learning to say no	This skill helps keep you from doing things you don't want to do, especially when you are under pressure from friends or other people.
Thinking critically	This skill helps you find and interpret information that will be useful in making decisions and solving problems.
Overcoming barriers	This skill helps you find ways to stay active despite barriers such as lack of time, unsafe places to be active, and weather.
Finding success	This skill helps you find success in physical activity.
Overcoming competitive stress	This skill helps you prevent or cope with the stresses of competition or the tension you feel when performing some types of activity.

Adapted, by permission, from C. Corbin and R. Lindsey, 2004, *Fitness for life,* 5th ed. (Champaign, IL: Human Kinetics), 79.

Target Questions

1. What is the difference between a dream and a goal?
2. How do you feel when you achieve a goal that you have set for yourself?
3. How do you feel when you don't achieve a goal that you've set for yourself? What can such an experience teach you?

Question Outline to Guide the Lesson

1. Why do you think that some people are more active than others?
2. Do you think that people are more active while they are teenagers or after they leave school and begin working? Take a guess at the following: (*a*) _____ out of every 100 teens do no physical activity (answer: 14); (*b*) _____ out of every 100 adults do no physical activity (answer: 40).

Figure 8.1   Five stages of physical activity behavior.

Adapted, by permission, from C. Corbin and R. Lindsey, 2004, *Fitness for life,* 5th ed. (Champaign, IL: Human Kinetics), 78.

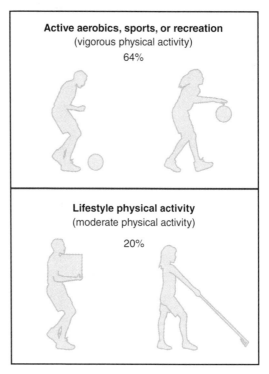

Figure 8.2   Percentage of teens classified as active exercisers for each of the different types of physical activity.

Adapted, by permission, from C. Corbin and R. Lindsey, 2004, *Fitness for life,* 5th ed. (Champaign, IL: Human Kinetics), 77.

3. People can be placed into one of five stages in terms of their physical activity behaviors: *couch potato* describes people in the first stage; *active exerciser* describes people in the fifth stage. Can you speculate on what might characterize the other three stages? (See figure 8.1.)

4. The Physical Activity Pyramid shows different kinds of activity. The stage of behavior that you are in depends on the kind of activity that you are talking about. Look at the Active Sports and Recreation level of the Physical Activity Pyramid. What stage do you think many teenagers are in if you evaluate them within the Active Sports and Recreation level? (See figure 8.2.)

5. What do you think is meant by the term *self-management*?

6. How do self-management skills relate to physical activity behaviors?

7. What are some essential things that people with good self-management skills do?

8. As you know, when learning sport skills, practice makes perfect. If you practice the right skills correctly, you'll get better at playing the sport. Is the same true for self-management skills? What might you need to practice to get better at self-management?

9. How can good self-management skills enable you to move to a more active stage of physical activity behavior?

Closing Discussion

Review with the class key facts about what happens to physical activity participation as people get older. Reinforce students' understanding of the five stages of physical activity behavior and the way that each stage differs depending on the kind of activity referred to. Finish by highlighting the new concept, self-management skills. Emphasize the relationship between good self-management skills and lifetime physical activity behaviors.

Enrichment Activity: Fitness Trail

When they reach adulthood, your students will face many obstacles in their ability to self-manage their physical activity. Certainly one such barrier will be gaining access to exercise venues when traveling, either for work or for vacation. More and more hotels are offering fitness trails for guests. These trails provide a good way for people to stay active while on the road. In this activity students learn how to take advantage of fitness trails.

Objective

For students to perform a complete workout on a fitness trail.

Equipment

The following equipment is needed for the stations described on the Fitness Trail Station Signs. You can modify the stations and worksheet as needed to fit your situation.

▶ One yardstick (or meter stick), for the back-saver sit-and-reach

▶ One 12-inch-high (30 cm high) box, for the back-saver sit-and-reach

▶ Two posts, driven into the ground

▶ Hula hoops, enough to make a hopscotch course (could instead draw the course on the ground)

▶ One chin-up bar

▶ One sloping bar

▶ One log or bar, for curl-ups

▶ Three bars of three different heights, for push-ups

▶ Mats for floor work

▶ One slant board

▶ One tree or post, to lean against for calf stretcher

Procedure

1. Before class, place an identifying sign (a Fitness Trail Station Sign) and necessary equipment at each station.

2. Divide the class into 14 groups, or the number of stations that you have. Assign each group a starting station.

Fitness Trail Station Signs.

3. Have groups follow the instructions on their sheets to complete the fitness trail, rotating through all the stations.

4. Have students cool down after completing the fitness trail.

Sample Inclusion Tips

▶ Use a peer or teaching assistant to help complete the worksheets.

▶ Use verbal prompting to repeat directions and questions and to check for understanding.

Assessment

Students will complete the reproducible worksheets for teacher feedback.

Adapted, by permission, from C. Corbin and R. Lindsey, 2004, *Fitness for life,* 5th ed. (Champaign, IL: Human Kinetics), 77.

GOAL SETTING

MIDDLE SCHOOL AND HIGH SCHOOL

Goal setting—Planning to determine ahead of time what you expect to accomplish and how you can accomplish it.

Objectives

▶ Students will explain how goal setting can help you plan your fitness program.

▶ Students will identify some guidelines that you should follow when setting goals.

Relationship to National Standards

▶ Physical education standard 3: Participates regularly in physical activity

▶ Physical education standard 4: Achieves and maintains a health-enhancing level of physical fitness.

▶ Physical education standard 5: Exhibits responsible personal and social behavior that respects self and others in physical activity settings.

Opener

Introduce the lesson by using one of the following ideas:

▶ Have students work individually to write out the goals that they have for physical activity, a sport, or other interest area, for six months, one year, and five years beyond this point in time. Ask each student to list three tasks required to achieve these goals.

▶ In small groups, students list features of a good goal (measurable, worthy, achievable, has a time line).

▶ In small groups, students think of a sports player or media personality and then create a list of the goals that this person may have written down five years ago.

▶ For the entire class, create a nonsensical set of goals on the board and have students critique and refine these goals to make them more realistic, with a better time frame, a measurable objective, and so forth.

▶ Both reproducibles should be handed out to students to use as a reference as they are writing their own goals.

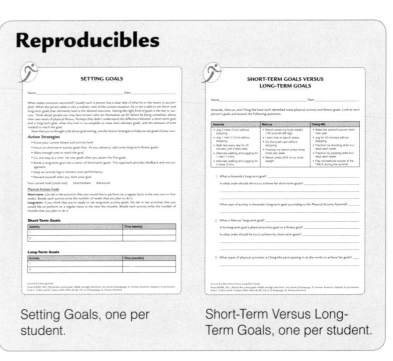

Setting Goals, one per student.

Short-Term Versus Long-Term Goals, one per student.

Question Outline to Guide the Discussion

(Teachers: For more information on this topic, see pages 84–85 of the *Fitness for Life* student textbook.)

1. Explain how successful people use goal setting to achieve something that they deem important.

2. What are the differences between short-term goals and long-term goals?

3. What are the important things to remember about setting a long-term physical activity goal?

4. Explain whether it is necessary to set long-term goals to improve your fitness, and why.

5. Why do experts recommend writing down your long-term fitness goals?

6. Often, a pad and paper is all that some people need to list their long-term goals. What electronic devices are also available to help you with goal setting? What is an advantage of these electronic devices? What is a disadvantage?

7. What are the characteristics of short-term goals?

8. What is an example of a short-term physical activity goal?

9. What might be a problem with listing "improving my fitness" as a short-term goal?

10. What is the best way of using short-term goals to improve your fitness?

11. What are some general guidelines for setting physical activity goals?

12. List some additional guidelines for people with different levels of physical activity goal-setting experience: beginners, intermediate, and advanced.

Closing Discussion

Emphasize the importance of goal setting as a self-management skill critical to lifetime physical activity behaviors. Review the difference between short-term goals and long-term goals. Finish by explaining that becoming proficient at goal setting increases the chances of becoming successful in physical activity and other areas of life.

Teaching Hint

Teachers are encouraged to complete Fitnessgram testing before completing this exercise so that students can use their Fitnessgram scores to set goals for improvement.

Sample Inclusion Tips

▶ Use a peer or teaching assistant to help complete worksheets.

▶ Use verbal prompting to repeat directions and questions and to check for understanding.

Assessment

Students will complete the reproducible worksheets for teacher feedback.

Adapted, by permission, from C. Corbin and R. Lindsey, 2004, *Fitness for life,* 5th ed. (Champaign, IL: Human Kinetics), 83.

Students must learn how to set and work toward long-term goals.

HIGH SCHOOL

Pedometer use and goal setting—Using the goal setting process, students will use pedometers to measure progress towards achieving a goal of increased physical activity.

Purpose

Students will learn to describe ways in which goal setting enhances motivation for physical activity, to value the use of pedometers as an assessment and teaching tool for physical education, and to quantify moderate to vigorous physical activity (MVPA) using steps and activity time.

Relationship to National Standards

▸ Physical education standard 3: Participates regularly in physical activity.

▸ Physical education standard 4: Achieves and maintains a health-enhancing level of physical fitness.

▸ Physical education standard 5: Exhibits responsible personal and social behavior that respects self and others in physical activity settings.

Equipment

▸ Pedometer for each person

▸ Pencil, one per person

Procedure

Explain to students how pedometers are used and what purpose they serve in helping them set personal goals and implement the components of the FITT principle into various activities.

After all students have been given a pedometer, explain how to set, read, and record the number of steps taken in the specified period.

Activity 1

1. Students put on pedometers (if this is a new task, you must first teach them how the pedometers work).

2. Put on fun music and ask students to walk around the gym or area until the music stops (two minutes). They record the number of steps on their sheets.

3. Then, again with music, ask students to run until the music stops (two minutes). They record the number of steps on their sheets.

Discuss and ask which activity was more vigorous:

▸ Explain that the national physical activity goal is to perform more than 60 minutes of physical activity daily.

▸ Ask them to think about how pedometers can help them achieve that goal.

▸ If they were active for a total of 2 minutes to take the number of steps shown on their pedometers, how many steps do they need to achieve the national goal (multiply by 30). Have them write this down as a daily step goal.

Assessment Record Sheet, one per student.

Activity 2

1. Ask them to write down on their paper how many steps they think they can take in the next two minutes. Explain that this is their new goal.

2. Put music on and challenge students to meet or exceed their goal.

Discuss:

▶ Explain that having a goal in any activity helps us to direct our learning and stay on task.

▶ Goals need to be increasingly more difficult to help us perform better and learn more.

▶ Assessing and thinking about our goals helps us to come up with new strategies to accomplish important tasks and goals.

Teaching Hint

Ask students to be prepared to set goals in their next physical education class.

Sample Inclusion Tips

▶ A teacher may assist with putting on heart rate monitors.

▶ Use a peer or teaching assistant to help complete worksheets.

▶ Use verbal prompting to repeat directions and questions and to check for understanding.

Students use pedometers to learn how to set, measure, and record their progress on goals.

Variation

Have students form groups of three or four and repeat the walking and running activities. Before beginning, have each group write down their prediction of how many total steps the group will do in the specified time. After each session have them add the total number of steps made by their group and compare the total with their prediction.

Home Extension

Ask students to think about and share ways in which they can use goal setting at home or in school.

Assessment

▶ Ask students how many met or exceeded their goals (show of hands).

▶ Ask them to suggest ways to increase the level (moderate or vigorous) of activity in the next two minutes.

　• For those who met or exceeded their goals, ask what they did differently and have them share with the class.

　• For those who did not meet or exceed their goals, ask what they might do differently to accomplish their goals.

▶ Explain that this is the concept of progression and involves the process of setting goals.

USING HEART RATE MONITORS

MIDDLE SCHOOL AND HIGH SCHOOL

Heart rate monitor use and goal setting—Heart rate monitors provide an excellent and simple means of allowing students to self-assess and set personal goals.

Purpose

Students will learn to identify benefits of goal setting for achieving MVPA, to describe ways in which goal setting increases the chances for achieving fitness goals, to value the use of heart rate monitors as an assessment and teaching tool for PE, and to quantify MVPA using time in the zone.

Relationship to National Standards

- ▶ Physical education standard 3: Participates regularly in physical activity.
- ▶ Physical education standard 4: Achieves and maintains a health-enhancing level of physical fitness.
- ▶ Physical education standard 5: Exhibits responsible personal and social behavior that respects self and others in physical activity settings.

Equipment

- ▶ One heart rate monitor for every two students
- ▶ Pencils, one per student

Procedure

Before handing out the heart rate monitors, review the FITT principle and the purpose of monitoring heart rate during exercise—to examine the effects of intensity and time. Explain how the heart rate monitor works and how the students will record their heart rates.

Activity 1

1. One student puts on the heart rate monitor strap. A partner wears the monitor.

2. Put on fun music and ask students to walk around the gym or area until the music stops (two minutes). The partners record the average HR on the record sheet for walking.

3. Then, again with music, ask students to run until the music stops (two minutes). The partners record on the record sheet the average heart rate while running.

4. Partners exchange roles.

Discuss and ask which activity was more vigorous:

- ▶ Explain that the national physical activity goal is to perform more than 60 minutes of moderate to vigorous physical activity daily.
- ▶ Walking is considered moderate activity; running is considered vigorous activity.

Reproducible

ACTIVITY TEMPLATE AND RECORD SHEET

Activity Template and Record Sheet, one per pair.

▶ Ask students to think about how heart rate monitors can help them achieve that goal.

Activity 2

1. Have students estimate their target HR zone (see formula on the template).

2. Ask them to write down on their papers how long they think they can stay in their healthy heart rate zone in the next 10 minutes by walking or running. Explain that this is their new goal for intensity.

3. Put music on and challenge students to meet or exceed their goal.

4. Partners need to give regular feedback when students are in their target zone.

5. Partners change roles and repeat.

Teaching Hints

▶ Explain that having a goal in any activity helps us direct our learning and stay on task.

▶ Goals need to be increasingly more difficult to help us perform better and learn more.

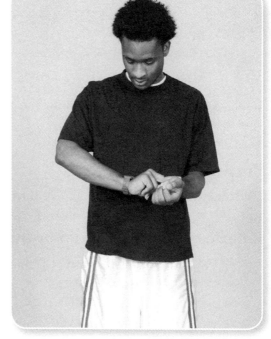

Students use their heart rates to set and monitor their goals.

▶ Assessing and thinking about our goals can help us come up with new strategies to accomplish important tasks or goals.

Sample Inclusion Tips

▶ A teacher may assist with putting on heart rate monitors.

▶ Use a peer or teaching assistant to help complete worksheets.

▶ Use verbal prompting to repeat directions and questions and to check for understanding.

Variation

Have one student wear both the chest band and the monitor for an entire period and record the activity done and her or his heart rate during that time.

Home Extension

Check out monitors to students and ask that they wear them until they go to bed. They should maintain journals and record their various activities and heart rates during both physical activity and rest.

Assessment

▶ Ask students how many met their goal (show of hands).

▶ Ask them to suggest ways to increase the level (moderate or vigorous) of activity in PE.

- For those who met or exceeded their goals, ask what activities they did and have them share with the class.

- For those who did not meet their goals, ask what they might do differently to accomplish their goals.

- Explain that this is the concept of setting and monitoring goals. We must set goals and measure them, and then modify or change our behaviors to make progress toward health and lifelong physical activity goals.

FITNESS OLYMPICS

MIDDLE SCHOOL

Goal setting—Students will focus on the enhancement of general fitness levels while doing skill development activities.

Purpose

Students will work on health- and skill-related activities to determine how they could use these activities in setting goals for health- or skill-related fitness.

Relationship to National Standards

► Physical education standard 1: Demonstrates competency in motor skills and movement patterns needed to perform a variety of physical activities.

► Physical education standard 3: Participates regularly in physical activity.

► Physical education standard 6: Values physical activity for heath, enjoyment, challenge, self-expression, and/or social interaction.

► Health standard 7: Students will demonstrate the ability to practice health-enhancing behaviors and avoid or reduce health risk.

Equipment

The equipment used may vary depending on the skill development focus; for example, a basketball unit would require basketballs, hoops, cones, and mats.

► Three Nerf soccer or playground balls

► Six jump ropes

► A pencil for each group

Procedure

1. Set up a 10-station circuit to include skill-based activities and fitness enhancement activities (see sample reproducibles of station cards on the CD-ROM). Each station should have enough equipment for three students or for an equal division of students in the class.

2. Place students in groups of three and give each a Fitness Olympics Scorecard and pencil. Have each group go to a station.

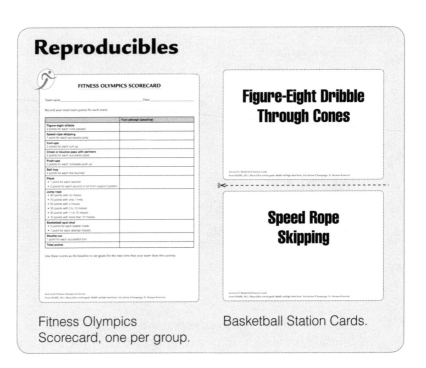

Reproducibles

Fitness Olympics Scorecard, one per group.

Figure-Eight Dribble Through Cones

Speed Rope Skipping

Basketball Station Cards.

Sports such as basketball provide a format through which students can set and work on goals.

3. At the start signal, students begin performing the activity at their stations, keeping track of their total repetitions. After 90 seconds the students stop the activity and record their total team points or number of repetitions on their scorecards. After recording their scores, students rotate and begin the next activity.

4. After completing the entire rotation, students add their total points and make comments related to which areas of health-related fitness were emphasized at each fitness station and whether the skill activity had any effect on fitness.

Teaching Hint

Rather than using a team approach, have individuals keep their own scores. Using the individual scores as a goal-setting baseline, have students set personal goals for the next time the activity is done.

Variation

Change the station format to reflect either summer or Olympic events, such as track and field events, floor hockey, agility runs (for skiing), and swimming movements on scooters.

Home Extension

Have students research Olympic events and develop an outline of potential training activities that the athletes would use to prepare.

Inclusion Tip

To include students with disabilities, use the buddy system by having them partner with another student (or two, depending on their abilities), who will assist them in modifications of each station.

Assessment

When using the activity for goal setting, determine whether goals are realistic and what activities each student would do to achieve her or his goal. See *Physical Best Teacher's Guide*, pages 27-32, for goal-setting ideas.

POWER TEAM TRAINING

HIGH SCHOOL

Goal setting—This cooperative activity provides students with an activity designed to begin setting personal goals while setting the stage for the development of a personal health and fitness plan.

Purpose

▶ Students will practice the goal-setting process and enhance knowledge of the FITT principle through an intense set of aerobic fitness and muscular strength and endurance activities conducted in a team format.

▶ Students will be able to begin setting realistic goals for the development of a personal health and fitness plan through the recording of scores during their initial participation in the activity and subsequent participation.

Relationship to National Standards

▶ Physical education standard 2: Participates regularly in physical activity.

▶ Physical education standard 4: Achieves and maintains a health-enhancing level of physical fitness.

▶ Physical education standard 5: Exhibits responsible personal and social behavior that respects self and others in physical activity settings.

▶ Health education standard 7: Students will demonstrate the ability to practice health-enhancing behaviors and avoid or reduce health risk.

Equipment

Equipment used varies based on school inventory; use what is available. For example, for a class of 30 students, you might use the following:

▶ Two heavy medicine balls

▶ Eight step benches with three risers on each end

▶ Six jump ropes

▶ Six weighted jump ropes (a heavy rope, usually a rubber tube filled with sand)

▶ Eight 6- to 8-pound (2.5 to 3.5 kg) dumbbells

▶ Mats for floor work

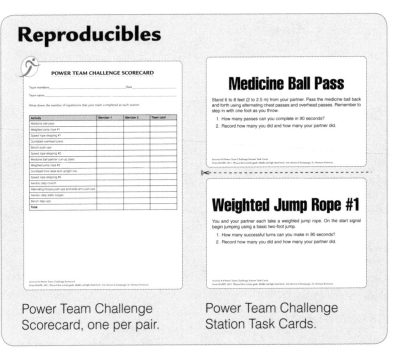

Power Team Challenge Scorecard, one per pair.

Power Team Challenge Station Task Cards.

Procedure

1. Set up stations around the gym, each with a specific task card.
2. Have students each find a partner and a scorecard before going to their beginning stations.
3. On the go signal, students begin working continuously at the stations for 90 seconds. After time is called, they write their scores on the Power Team Challenge Scorecard and immediately move to the next station on their right; allow no more than 30 seconds. After the rotation give the signal to begin.
4. The rotation continues until students have completed all stations and recorded their scores.

Teaching Hints

▶ Have students think about the FITT principle at each station and remember the intensity of each as well as the cumulative effect of the total circuit on the intensity. They should consider how that fits into the time principle.

▶ Ask students to review their team scores and think about what they might be able to accomplish at each station if they performed the activity in the same format the following week. The first scores would be a baseline on which to set goals for the next circuit.

Sample Inclusion Tip

For classes that have students with a cognitive or learning disability, assign a peer leader to read aloud, interpret the activities, and guide the team in performing the activities.

Assessment

At the conclusion of the activity, partners should total their individual scores and answer the questions related to the FITT principle and goal setting at the bottom of their Power Team Challenge Scorecard. The teacher should collect the Power Team Challenge Scorecards and review the scores and comments. On the following day, conduct a class discussion related to the FITT principle using the comments made on the scorecards as a focus.

The basis of the discussion should be a review of the goal-setting process—establishing short-term and long-term goals that are realistic and measurable. A review

Students apply the FITT principle to the creation of their own health and fitness goals.

of scorecards should include teacher comments and student feedback related to the goals being realistic for individual students or the team.

Being a Good Health and Physical Activity Consumer

Acomprehensive health-related fitness program must not only teach basic training
principles of health-related fitness, fitness safety,
nutrition, and benefits of physical activity but
also include fitness consumer awareness education. Students need to know the truth about fitness, weight control, and nutritional supplements
and other products as well as how to discern fact
from fiction in advertising. Students have seen
and heard newspaper, magazine, radio, and television advertisements for health and fitness products and services. But do they have the knowledge
to tell whether a product or service is really safe
and effective? In this chapter we provide lessons,
resource materials, and activities that will help
your students learn how to become wise purchas-
ers and consumers of health and fitness products.
See table 9.1 for a grid of activities in this chapter.

The following consumer education resources
may also be helpful:

▶ *Fitness for Life*—This widely used lifetime
personal fitness program is designed as a
foundational course in middle school and
high school physical education that includes

consumer education. The emphasis of the
course is helping students become responsible for their own activity, planning, fitness,
and health. For more information visit www.
fitnessforlife.org or www.HumanKinetics.
com.

▶ Centers for Disease Control—www.cdc.gov/
HealthyLiving. This Centers for Disease
Control Web site is designed to provide up-
to-date credible health information across a
wide variety of relevant topics.

▶ Teen Consumer Scrapbook—www.atg.wa.gov/
teenconsumer. Teen Consumer Scrapbook is
designed by a group of high school students
who want to share consumer knowledge. All
the articles found on this site are written
about topics that teenagers are interested in.
Information in several consumer areas can be
found: buying goods and services, finances,
health and safety, transportation, and recreation. The site, developed for the Washington
State Attorney General's Office through a
special project by Mt. Rainier High School
students, covers issues that are useful to all.

Table 9.1 Chapter 9 Activities Grid

Activity number	Activity title	Activity page	Concept	Middle school	High school	Reproducibles (on CD-ROM)
9.1	Health and Fitness Quackery	213	Quackery and passive exercise	•	•	Evaluating Exercise Devices
						Fitness-Related Experts
9.2	Evaluating Health Products	215	Quackery and self-motivated exercise	•	•	Sense and Nonsense
						Evaluating Health and Fitness Information and Services
	Enrichment Activity: Exercise at Home	216	Exercise	•	•	Exercising at Home Worksheet

MIDDLE SCHOOL AND HIGH SCHOOL

Quackery—A method of advertising or selling that uses false claims to lure people into buying products that are worthless or even harmful.

Passive exercise—Being moved by a machine rather than using your own muscles to produce movement.

Objectives

▶ Students will explain the importance of being an informed health consumer.

▶ Students will name reliable sources of health-related and fitness-related information.

▶ Students will name and describe examples of health-related and fitness-related misconceptions and quackery.

Relationship to National Standards

▶ Physical education standard 6: Values physical activity for health, enjoyment, challenge, self-expression, and/or social interaction.

▶ Health education standard 1: Students will comprehend concepts related to health promotion and disease prevention.

Opener

Introduce the lesson by using one of the following ideas:

▶ For the entire class, elicit ideas about why people are uninformed about fitness, health, and wellness.

▶ Form students into small groups and have them list the best places for finding information about health and fitness. Ask students why they believe that the sources they identified are the best.

▶ Form students into small groups and have them list the most outrageous claims they know of pertaining to fitness and dietary products and services.

Target Questions

1. You are watching television and your favorite actor shows up in a weight-loss advertisement. She claims that she lost all her weight fast by using a particular product. How would you respond?

2. Name a favorite magazine that you like to read. What types of health and fitness products are advertised in that magazine? What red flags should you look for when evaluating those product ads?

Note: Furnish reproducibles to students to use as a reference tool during this lesson.

Reproducibles

Evaluating Exercise Devices, one per student.

Fitness-Related Experts, one per student.

Question Outline to Guide the Lesson

1. What is meant by the term *quackery*?

2. Why do people become victims of quackery?

3. How can you detect quackery and fraud when evaluating claims for exercise and nutritional products?

4. What do you have to be aware of when assessing the credentials of a person making a claim about a product?

5. If you are seeking nutrition advice from a health professional or someone advertising a product, what credentials should you look for? (*Teacher's note*: If you want to learn about good nutrition you need to consider the source of that information in regard to how qualified that source is to offer sound advice.)

6. What does the term *discrediting* mean? How is it used in the selling of exercise and nutritional products?

7. Exaggerated claims about products appear in advertising and on product packaging. What are some examples of false promises made in marketing?

8. What claims are made about nutritional supplements?

9. Why should you be wary about claims made by many manufacturers of nutritional supplements?

10. What claims are made about sports supplements, and why should you be wary?

11. What is a fad diet?

12. Explain why spot reducing and passive exercise machines are considered fitness quackery.

Learning how to spot quackery in health and fitness products is important.

Super Stock

Closing Discussion

Review what is meant by the term *fitness quackery*. Ask students for reasons why quackery is so prevalent. Emphasize the importance of evaluating the credentials of the people making claims about products and services. Review many of the standard claims and false promises used to sell products and services. Ask students to provide brief examples of claims for specific products. Finish by reviewing reasons why specific claims that constitute fitness quackery continue to persist.

Adapted, by permission, from C. Corbin and R. Lindsey, 2004, *Fitness for life,* 5th ed. (Champaign, IL: Human Kinetics), 281.

MIDDLE SCHOOL AND HIGH SCHOOL

Quackery—A method of advertising or selling that uses false claims to lure people into buying products that are worthless or even harmful.

Self-motivated exercise—Becoming more physically active because of a personal need or desire to do so.

Objectives

▶ Students will evaluate health-related and fitness-related facilities.

▶ Students will describe the proper clothing and equipment that you need for physical activity.

▶ Students will evaluate printed material, videos, and Internet resources related to health and fitness.

Relationship to National Standards

▶ Health education standard 1: Students will comprehend concepts related to health promotion and disease prevention.

Opener

Introduce the lesson by using one of the following ideas:

▶ For the entire class, ask students to provide examples of products and services marketed by the exercise and diet industry. Through guided discussion, ask whether these products are effective or not and why.

▶ Form students into small groups and ask them to list criteria that they would use to determine whether a product or service has merit.

▶ Provide small groups with photos of advertisements for products and services. In their small groups, the students identify buzzwords and marketing strategies that the ads use to help sell products.

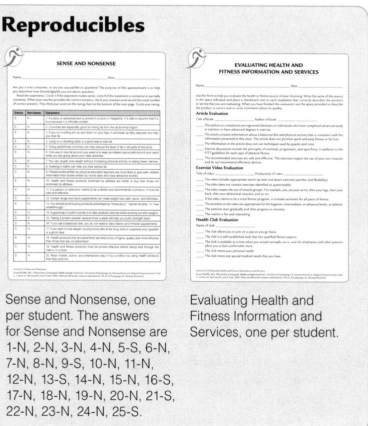

Reproducibles

Sense and Nonsense, one per student. The answers for Sense and Nonsense are 1-N, 2-N, 3-N, 4-N, 5-S, 6-N, 7-N, 8-N, 9-S, 10-N, 11-N, 12-N, 13-S, 14-N, 15-N, 16-S, 17-N, 18-N, 19-N, 20-N, 21-S, 22-N, 23-N, 24-N, 25-S.

Evaluating Health and Fitness Information and Services, one per student.

Question Outline to Guide the Lesson

1. What are the advantages of joining a fitness center or health club?

2. Being active does not require membership in a health club. What are some low-cost alternatives to expensive health clubs?

3. What are guidelines to keep in mind when considering joining a commercial health club?

4. Why should you make a trial visit to a health club that you are considering joining?

5. What are some guidelines for selecting clothing and shoes for physical activity?

6. What types of exercise equipment are available to use in the home?

7. What do you need to consider if you are buying exercise equipment to use at home?

8. What guidelines should you consider when evaluating a book or article about exercise?

9. What guidelines should you consider when evaluating a book about nutrition and health?

10. What guidelines should you consider when evaluating the value of an exercise video?

11. How can you evaluate information on the Internet?

12. What are examples of reputable agencies and organizations for health, physical activity, and nutrition?

Bananastock

Students must learn how to evaluate what products are useful and best for their personal fitness goals.

Enrichment Activity: Exercise at Home

Objective

Students will perform health-related fitness exercises using common household items. Students will learn that there are many ways to exercise and that they do not have to pay a lot of money for equipment and programs advertised on television to get a good workout.

Equipment

The following equipment is needed for the stations described on the Exercising at Home Worksheet. You can modify the stations and worksheet as needed to fit your situation.

- ▶ Several small benches or steps, for stair stepping
- ▶ Bleachers (preferable) or several benches or steps, for step push-ups
- ▶ Several towels, enough for use at four stations
- ▶ Several broomsticks, enough for use at four stations
- ▶ Several jump ropes
- ▶ Music and player

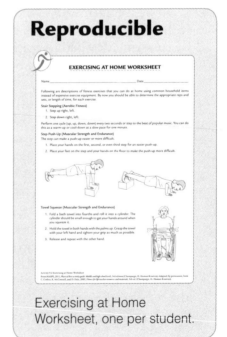

Exercising at Home Worksheet, one per student.

Opener

1. Place a sign and equipment at each station.
2. Have students do a warm-up.
3. After the warm-up, hand out an Exercising at Home Worksheet to each student.
4. Divide the class into five groups, one for each station. Assign each group to a station.
5. Have the students divide equally among the exercises at each station. Have students read the directions and then practice the assigned exercise.
6. One student from each exercise will demonstrate that exercise to the class.
7. Have each group return to their starting station and perform the assigned exercise.
8. On a signal, have groups rotate to the next station.
9. After all students have had a chance to use each of the five types of exercise equipment, have them perform a cool-down.

Closing Discussion

Review the guidelines that students should follow if they are choosing a health club to join. Ask students what they would evaluate on a trial visit to a health club. Review the variety of home exercise equipment available and highlight the advantages and disadvantages of home exercise. Review what to look for when evaluating books and articles, videos, and the Internet. Finally, provide Web sites of reputable associations for health, physical activity, and nutrition.

Adapted, by permission, from C. Corbin and R. Lindsey, 2004, *Fitness for life*, 5th ed. (Champaign, IL: Human Kinetics), 266.

Planning for a Physically Active Lifestyle

Photodisc

After students graduate from high school they will be on their own—you'll no longer be there to help them stay physically active. Therefore, you must prepare them to develop personal health and fitness plans that support a healthy and active lifestyle. The lesson plans, resource materials, and activities in this chapter will help students enhance their knowledge and skills to plan their future. See table 10.1 for a grid of activities in this chapter.

In addition to materials presented in this chapter we would encourage you to use these additional resources to help students plan for a physically active lifestyle.

▶ *Fitness for Life*—This widely used lifetime personal fitness program is designed as a foundational course in middle and high school physical education. The emphasis

of the course is helping students become responsible for their own activity, planning, fitness, and health. Self-directed activities are outlined to help students develop the self-management skills they need to create their own personal fitness programs to stay active throughout their lives. For more information go to www.fitnessforlife.org.

▶ *Physical Education for Lifelong Fitness: The Physical Best Teacher's Guide, 3rd Edition* (2011), Champaign, Illinois, Human Kinetics—chapter 2, "Physical Activity and Behavior Motivation," and appendix A contain helpful information as well as worksheets and reproducibles designed to help students set goals, develop fitness plan workouts, and monitor their activity.

Table 10.1 Chapter 10 Activities Grid

Activity number	Activity title	Activity page	Concept	Middle school	High school	Reproducibles (on CD-ROM)
10.1	Program Planning	221	Fitness profile	•	•	Developing Your Personal Plan
10.2	Sticking to a Plan	223	Nonactive versus physically active	•	•	Personal Exercise Word Puzzle
						Fitness Review Crossword Puzzle
						Overcoming Barriers
10.3	Evaluating a Physical Activity Program	225	Personal fitness plan	•	•	Reproducibles for this activity are specific to each self-assessment or activity idea.
	Self-Assessment Idea: Evaluating Your Physical Activity Program	225	Evaluation	•	•	Evaluating Your Physical Activity Program Worksheet
	Activity Idea: Perform Your Plan	226	Evaluation and change	•	•	Performing Your Plan
	Activity Idea: Your Exercise Circuit	226	Development	•	•	Your Exercise Circuit
	Activity Idea: Your Health and Fitness Club	227	Evaluation	•	•	Your Health and Fitness Club Worksheet
	Activity Idea: Heart Rate Target Zones	227	Heart rate and aerobic fitness		•	Aerobic Fitness: How Much Activity Is Enough?
	Activity Idea: Sports Stars	228	Exercise	•	•	Sports Stars Program
10.4	Schoolwide Special Event: Exercise Your Rights	230	Advocacy	•	•	Exercise Your Rights Poster

PROGRAM PLANNING

MIDDLE SCHOOL AND HIGH SCHOOL

Fitness profile—A summary of the results of self-assessments of several components of fitness.

Objectives

▶ Students will explain how to use a fitness profile to plan a personal fitness program.

▶ Students will describe the five steps in planning a personal fitness program.

Opener

Introduce the lesson by using one of the following ideas:

▶ Form students into small groups and have them create fitness profiles. Have different small groups create a fitness profile for an athlete, an unfit teen, and a middle-aged person. Guide the discussion about components to include in a fitness profile.

▶ For the entire class, elicit a list of things to consider when planning a personal fitness program. Categorize the class responses in some way, such as into personal, social, affective, environmental, and time consideration categories.

Question Outline to Guide the Lesson

Have the students use the reproducible handout as a reference tool during this activity.

1. What is a fitness profile, and how is a fitness profile used?

2. What health-related fitness components are included in a fitness profile?

3. Which activities in a fitness profile have both upper-body and lower-body ratings?

4. How is a physical activity profile used?

5. What questions might appear on a physical activity profile?

6. How can you use the Physical Activity Pyramid to make improvements to your physical activity profile? (The Physical Activity Pyramid appears as a reproducible for Activity 8.1 on the CD-ROM.)

7. What are some examples of goals that teens might have for exercise and physical activity?

8. How should the goals of a beginner differ from the goals of someone who is more advanced?

9. What guidelines should a person follow when goal setting for physical activity?

10. What factors should you consider when planning activities for different days of the week?

Reproducible

DEVELOPING YOUR PERSONAL PLAN
STEP I: COLLECT INFORMATION

Developing Your Personal Plan, one per student.

Closing Discussion

Review the fitness profile, using an example to show to the class. Highlight the key features of a fitness profile, pointing out the areas of health-related fitness that might need to

Keeping track of fitness information in class will help students gain the knowledge to continue using information after they are out of school.

be improved. Comment on the difference between a fitness profile and a physical activity profile. Review the guidelines to follow when setting physical activity goals. Finish by emphasizing the connection between program planning and goal setting: A sound program will lead to achievement of realistic goals.

Adapted, by permission, from C. Corbin and R. Lindsey, 2004, *Fitness for life*, 5th ed. (Champaign, IL: Human Kinetics), 305.

STICKING TO A PLAN

MIDDLE SCHOOL AND HIGH SCHOOL

Nonactive versus physically active—A person who is sedentary or does no physical activity versus a person who is physically active.

Objectives

▶ Students will describe the five stages of physical activity.

▶ Students will identify the strategies that help people become active and stay active at each of the stages.

Opener

Introduce the lesson by using one of the following ideas:

▶ Form students into small groups and have them discuss why they think that some people choose to be couch potatoes whereas others choose to be physically active.

▶ Form students into small groups and have them create a physical activity promotion brochure or poster targeted at people who are sedentary, or have different groups create brochures aimed at people at different levels of change.

▶ Form students into small groups and have them speculate on why people discontinue physical activity and what might be done to prevent people from discontinuing.

Question Outline to Guide the Lesson

1. Some people are extremely active, whereas others choose to be sedentary. What are the five stages of physical activity behavior (introduced in activity 8.1)?

Reproducibles

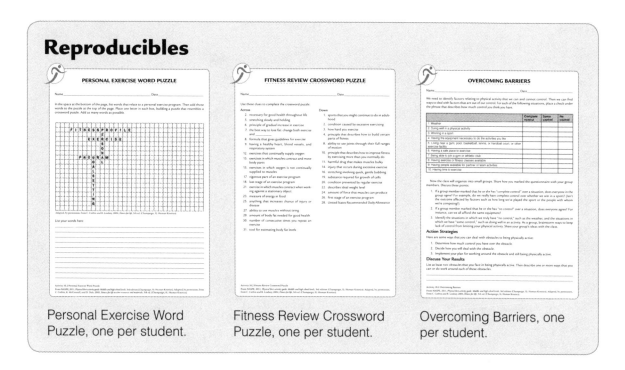

Personal Exercise Word Puzzle, one per student.

Fitness Review Crossword Puzzle, one per student.

Overcoming Barriers, one per student.

Sedentary behavior has its place during school or work hours, but an active lifestyle whenever possible should be the goal.

2. If people participate in sports in school, how likely is it that they will continue to be physically active after they leave school?

3. What are some strategies that can help people who are couch potatoes become more active?

4. What beliefs and attitudes do couch potatoes hold that influence their behaviors?

5. What strategies can motivate people who are thinking about being active to begin a physical activity program?

6. What is the difference between self-perception and self-confidence?

7. People who are planning to be physically active can benefit from strategies appropriate to people in earlier stages. What additional strategies would be helpful?

8. How can a smartphone be used to help a person increase physical activity participation?

9. What strategies are appropriate for people who are physically active on an intermittent basis?

10. Some people can be considered active for life. What strategies should these people use to help stay active?

Closing Discussion

Review the five stages of physical activity involvement. Review the strategies appropriate for each stage that can move people to the next, more active, stage.

Fitness Review Crossword Puzzle Answers

Across
2. health-related fitness
5. static
6. progression
7. diet
8. FITT
9. cardiovascular fitness
12. aerobic
13. isotonic
15. anaerobic
17. workout
18. cool-down
21. isometric
23. calorie
25. risk factor
27. muscular endurance
29. essential
30. reps
31. calipers

Down
1. lifetime
2. hyperkinetic
3. intensity
4. specificity
8. flexibility
10. overload
11. steroid
14. overuse
16. ballistic
19. nutrient
20. hypokinetic
22. target
24. strength
26. warm-up
28. USRDA

Adapted, by permission, from C. Corbin and R. Lindsey, 2004, *Fitness for life,* 5th ed. (Champaign, IL: Human Kinetics), 311.

EVALUATING A PHYSICAL ACTIVITY PROGRAM

10.3

MIDDLE SCHOOL AND HIGH SCHOOL

Personal fitness plan—Students will begin implementing their personal fitness plan.

Self-Assessment Idea: Evaluating Your Physical Activity Program

Objective

Students will perform activities from their own physical activity plan and complete a worksheet evaluating their plan.

Equipment

Select equipment needed by students for their activities. Well before teaching this lesson, you'll need to discuss students' physical activity plans to find out what types of activities students will likely want to participate in during the lesson. Their activity ideas will dictate the equipment needs.

Procedure

1. Have students perform a warm-up.

2. Have students select one day from their activity plan and perform as many of the activities as possible in class. If the activities of no single day last as long as one class period, they should supplement their workout with activities from another day on their plan. If equipment is not available, students should select an activity that is similar in its benefits and one that they will likely enjoy.

3. Students should perform activities in their plan that they cannot complete in class at appropriate times of the day.

4. On the following day, students should use the Evaluating Your Physical Activity Program Worksheet to evaluate their plan. Students should record the activities that they were able to complete.

5. If students did not complete the activities, they should record reasons to explain why they did not (for example, bad weather, homework).

Assessment

Have students put their recorded results in their portfolios or a folder or turn them in to you for safekeeping.

Reproducible

Evaluating Your Physical Activity Program Worksheet, one per student.

Activity Idea: Perform Your Plan

Objective

For students to modify one day of their personal program plan based on results from the previous lesson (Self-Assessment Idea: Evaluating Your Physical Activity Program).

Equipment

Select equipment needed by students for their activities. Well before teaching this lesson, you'll need to discuss students' physical activity plans to find out what types of activities students will likely want to participate in during the lesson. Their activity ideas will dictate the equipment needs.

Procedure

1. This lesson is similar to the previous lesson, Self-Assessment Idea: Evaluating Your Physical Activity Program. After students have completed the previous lesson and evaluated their plans, have them decide how they should change their plans based on their evaluation.

2. Have students perform the same activity plan with any modifications made because of their program evaluation.

3. Alternatively, students may choose to perform activities from a different day of their plan.

Reproducible

Performing Your Plan, one per student.

Activity Idea: Your Exercise Circuit

Objective

Students will plan a total fitness exercise circuit. This activity will help prepare students for planning their own activity programs in the future.

Equipment

► Music and player

► Several sheets of blank paper and pencils at each of four stations

► Use available equipment to create four stations for each of the fitness areas:

- Aerobic fitness
- Muscular strength and endurance (upper body)
- Muscular strength and endurance (lower body)
- Flexibility

Procedure

1. Have students perform a warm-up.

2. Give each student a Your Exercise Circuit Handout.

3. Divide the class into eight groups (two groups go to each of the four stations).

4. Assign each group to a station.

Reproducible

Your Exercise Circuit, one per student.

5. Have each group create one station for the circuit (have them create a sign for their station with the name of an appropriate exercise on the sign and the number of times it should be done). After the first round, you should have two exercises at each station.

6. Have each group demonstrate their exercise to the class.

7. Have each group return to their starting station and perform the assigned exercise.

8. On a signal, have groups rotate to the next station.

9. After students have completed all four stations, have them stay in their groups but send them to a different station than the one that they started with last time. Have them create a new circuit (with new exercises) and repeat the activity.

10. Have students cool down as a large group.

Activity Idea: Your Health and Fitness Club

Objective

To practice evaluating services and the quality of a health club, students will create a health and fitness club at school. Students will perform activities in the mock student health and fitness club that you've created. This activity will help them prepare for doing this on their own in the future.

Equipment

▶ Exercise equipment as needed for exercise stations (see instructions later)

▶ Poster board, at least eight sheets

▶ Markers, plenty for all eight groups

▶ Pens and pencils, at least one per student

▶ Music and player

Procedure

1. Give each student a Your Health and Fitness Club Worksheet.

2. Have them do the group planning (part I of the worksheet).

3. In small groups, have students set up their activity stations.

4. Allow each group two to three minutes to describe the activities that they have planned.

5. Allow students to move freely from station to station performing the created activities.

6. Have one or two students remain at their own station to explain and demonstrate the activities to other groups.

7. Rotate who remains at the stations so that all students have a chance to be a demonstrator.

8. Have students record their performances at each station (part II of the worksheet).

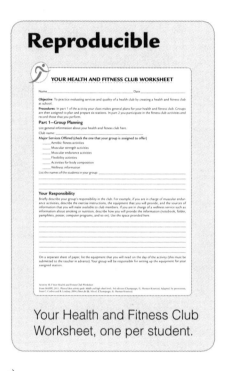

Your Health and Fitness Club Worksheet, one per student.

Activity Idea: Heart Rate Target Zones (Use for High School Level Only)

Objective

Students will determine how much physical activity is needed for aerobic fitness. This information is helpful for future program planning by your students.

Equipment

▸ Badminton net, rackets, and birdies

▸ Volleyball net and ball

▸ Basketball

Procedure

1. Mark the walking and jogging paths. Set up badminton, volleyball, and basketball areas.

2. Have students perform a warm-up.

3. After the warm-up, give each student an Aerobic Fitness: How Much Activity Is Enough? Worksheet.

4. Review with students the correct procedure for counting heart rate. Tell students to calculate their resting heart rates and record the results.

5. Have students follow the directions in part I of the worksheet to calculate their target heart rate zones, using both the heart rate range method and the percentage of maximal heart rate. Have students record their results.

6. For part II, divide the class in half and have them perform each of the jogging and walking activities (five minutes each).

7. Ask students to determine their heart rates and record them. Have students determine whether they exceeded their target heart rates.

8. Tell students to follow the directions in part III of the worksheet. Here, students can select activities (badminton, volleyball, basketball, jogging) to perform to reach a caloric expenditure of 200 calories. Students attempt to reach the 200-calorie goal by adding the calories from walking and jogging to the calories that they will expend in their chosen activity in part III.

9. Have students cool down by performing some static stretching.

Aerobic Fitness: How Much Activity Is Enough?, one per student.

Activity Idea: Sports Stars

Objective

Students can earn stars by participating in sports. This activity helps students take responsibility for finding their own activities to participate in outside of class.

Equipment

Gather equipment for the activities that you choose to play in class.

Procedure

1. Give each student a Sports Stars Program Worksheet. Have them fill in part 1 during the course of a week.

2. One week later, refer students to their worksheets again. Tell students to make a plan for the following week by incorporating changes that might help them reach their goals. Students should use the chart in part 2 to indicate which sports they will perform over the next week.

Sports Stars Program, one per student.

3. After students finish planning their week, tell them that today they are going to earn stars in class by playing a sports activity. They will earn more stars by participating in activities outside of class. They can use this activity time to start fulfilling the plan that they created in part 2 of the worksheet.

4. Have students perform a warm-up.

5. Have students choose and play a sports activity. Students should keep track of playing time and compare it to part 2 of the worksheet.

6. Have students cool down after activity.

7. Tell them to record the number of stars they earned in class.

8. Ask students to earn their remaining stars by the end of the week.

Assessment

Have students put their recorded results in their portfolios or a folder or turn them in to you for safekeeping.

Adapted, by permission, from C. Corbin and R. Lindsey, 2004, *Fitness for life,* 5th ed. (Champaign, IL: Human Kinetics), 310.

© iStockphoto/Alberto Pomares

In this activity, students get the chance to implement and evaluate their personal fitness plans.

SCHOOLWIDE SPECIAL EVENT: EXERCISE YOUR RIGHTS

MIDDLE SCHOOL AND HIGH SCHOOL

Advocacy—A schoolwide campaign to promote physical activity can lead to enhanced school programs and draw in parents and community members to help support the program and physical activity within the school and the community in general.

Purpose

To create a campaign with the students or the entire school to emphasize the importance of incorporating physical activity into the work environment. The campaign is titled "Exercise Your Rights Day."

▶ Students will recognize the benefits of taking an exercise break in their daily routine.

▶ Student will have the opportunity to advocate for physical activity as an important part of their daily routine.

Relationship to National Standards

Physical education standard 6: Values physical activity for health, enjoyment, challenge, self-expression, and/or social interaction.

Equipment

None.

Procedure

For a specified period, such as the first 10 minutes of class, an entire class period, or even an entire day, whenever a person, teacher, or student speaks the word "right" (in regular and normal conversation), the class has the opportunity to perform a physical activity of their choice for a specified period. (*Teacher's note*: Limit the number of exercise breaks to three per class period and six per day.)

For example, say, "For this class period, if anyone hears a person, either teacher or student, speak the word 'right,' please shout, 'Exercise your rights!' Then everyone must perform a physical activity of their choice (in their own space), such as the following examples. We will take no more than three exercise breaks in this class period.

▶ March in place for 10 to 30 seconds.

▶ Take three long slow breaths.

▶ Do 15 jumping jacks.

▶ Walk around the classroom once."

At the conclusion, ask students to discuss their reaction or feelings to the "break time for exercise."

Reproducible

Exercise Your Rights

Exercise is highly beneficial to health. Despite our busy lives, we still need to take some time to include exercise. In fact, exercise can also be beneficial to academic performance. Taking an exercise break allows the mind and the body time to rest and rejuvenates the creative juices required to succeed in school.

Health Benefits:

Enhances blood circulation and strengthens cardiopulmonary functions

Burns calories and helps maintain healthy body weight

Helps relieve stress

Finding time to exercise requires some commitment and thoughtful planning. Here are some suggestions.

During school try the following:
1. Walk or ride a bicycle to school.
2. Carry your books using proper form.
3. Stretch tense muscles periodically (without interrupting others).
4. Take a walk during lunchtime after your meal.

After school try the following:
1. Get involved in an after-school activity.
2. Spend less time watching television.
3. Dance to your favorite music with a friend.
4. During holidays, plan some time to explore outdoor activities in your area.

Exercise your rights to be physically active!

Activity 10.4 Exercise Your Rights Poster.
From NASPE, 2011, *Physical Best activity guide: Middle and high school levels, 3rd edition* (Champaign, IL: Human Kinetics).

Exercise Your Rights Poster.

Teaching Hints

▶ Include insights that make this activity easy to understand and execute.

▶ It is best to set rules for this campaign by creating a list of appropriate activities to minimize any safety considerations.

▶ Another recommendation is to create this list and a poster explaining the rules, using students' input.

▶ Limiting the amount of time for each activity and the number of occasions during any one class period will minimize academic interruptions.

For example, say, "There will be no more than three 'exercise your rights' benefits during any one class period."

Sample Inclusion Tip

Students with verbal difficulties can use alternative communication devices.

Variations

▶ Advocate for "Exercise your rights"—Allow students the opportunity to campaign for this type of event to the entire school environment. Provide guidelines for students to petition classroom teachers and the principal and to create a campaign brochure to implement an "Exercise Your Rights Day."

▶ Assign groups of students to create brochures and pamphlets about the benefits of exercise.

Students must learn that taking the time necessary to be physically active is important, wherever they are.

▶ Assign students to create an informational flyer to report the many benefits of including an exercise break in their daily activities. The flyer must include

• the health benefits of exercise and

• exercise options during the work day.

Home Extension

Ask students to try this activity with their families and report the results to class.

Assessment

▶ Evaluate the students' comments about taking an exercise break.

▶ Evaluate the assigned pamphlets or brochures for accurate information.

▶ Discuss the reactions to the information flyer; for example, have students write down their impressions and the reactions of other students and staff. Have students interview other students and staff members to determine whether the campaign enhanced their awareness of the need to be physically active.

APPENDIX
NATIONAL OBSERVANCES RELATED TO PHYSICAL ACTIVITY

FEBRUARY

American Heart Month
American Heart Association
www.heart.org

First Thursday
Girls and Women in Sports Day
Women's Sports Foundation
www.womenssportsfoundation.org

MARCH

National Nutrition Month
American Dietetic Association
www.eatright.org

APRIL

National Youth Sports Safety Month
National Youth Sports Safety Foundation
www.nyssf.org

April 7
World Health Day
American Association for World Health
www.thebody.com/content/art33029.html

First full week
National Public Health Week
American Public Health Association
www.apha.org

MAY

National Physical Fitness and Sports Month
President's Council on Physical Fitness and Sports
www.fitness.gov

National Bike Month
League of American Bicyclists
www.bikeleague.org

National High Blood Pressure Education Month
National Heart, Lung, and Blood Institute
www.nhlbi.nih.gov

First week
National Physical Education and Sports Week
National Association for Sport and Physical Education
www.aahperd.org/naspe

First Wednesday
All Children Exercise Simultaneously Day (Project ACES)
Youth Fitness Coalition, Inc.
www.coordinatedfitnesssystems.com/yfc_page/hjsyfc.html

First Saturday
Parents and Children Exercise Simultaneously Day (PACES Day)
Youth Fitness Coalition, Inc.
www.coordinatedfitnesssystems.com/yfc_page/hjsyfc.html

Second week

American Running and Fitness Week

American Running and Fitness Association
www.americanrunning.org

Third Wednesday

National Employee Health and Fitness Day

National Association for Health and Fitness
www.physicalfitness.org

Fourth week

National Water Fitness Week

U.S. Water Fitness Association, Inc.
www.uswfa.com

JULY

National Recreation and Parks Month

National Recreation and Park Association
www.nrpa.org

Third week

National Youth Sports Week

National Recreation and Park Association
www.nrpa.org

SEPTEMBER

National Cholesterol Education Month

National Heart, Lung, and Blood Institute
www.nhlbi.nih.gov

Third week

National Turn Off the TV Week

Center for Screen-Time Awareness
www.tvturnoff.org

Last Sunday

Family Health and Fitness Day

Health Information Resource Center
www.fitnessday.com/family

OCTOBER

Family Health Month

American Academy of Family Physicians
www.aafp.org/online/en/home.html

Walk to School Month

National Center for Safe Routes to School
www.saferoutesinfo.org

First weekend

American Heart Walking Event

American Heart Association
www.heart.org

First Monday

Child Health Day

National Institute of Child Health and
Human Development
www.nichd.nih.gov

Third Sunday

World Walking Day

Trim and Fitness International Sport
Association (TAFISA), Frankfurt, Germany
www.tafisa.net

NOVEMBER

American Diabetes Month

American Diabetes Association
www.diabetes.org

REFERENCES

Ainsworth, B.E., Haskell, W.L., Whitt, M.C., Irwin, M.L., Swartz, A.M., Strath, S.J., O'Brien, W.L., Bassett, D.R., Jr., Schmitz, K.H., Emplaincourt, P.O., Jacobs, D.R., Jr., & Leon, A.S. (2000). Compendium of Physical Activities: An update of activity codes and MET intensities. *Medicine and Science in Sports and Exercise, 32* (Suppl): S498–S516.

Ainsworth, B.E. (2002, January). *The Compendium of Physical Activities Tracking Guide.* Prevention Research Center, Norman J. Arnold School of Public Health, University of South Carolina. http://prevention.sph.sc.edu/tools/docs/documents_compendium.pdf.

American Academy of Pediatrics (AAP). (2001). Strength training by children and adolescents. *Pediatrics, 107*(6): 1470-1472.

American College of Sports Medicine (ACSM). (2009). *ACSM's guidelines for exercise testing and prescription,* 8th ed. Philadelphia: Lippincott, Williams, and Wilkins.

American College of Sports Medicine (ACSM). (2000). *ACSM's guidelines for exercise testing and prescription,* 6th ed. Philadelphia: Lippincott, Williams, and Wilkins.

Baechle, T.R., & Earle, R.W., eds. (2008). *Essentials of strength and conditioning,* 3rd ed. Champaign, IL: Human Kinetics.

Bar-Or, O., & R.M. Malina. (1995). Activity, health and fitness of children and adolescents. In *Child health, nutrition, and physical activity,* ed. L.W.Y. Cheung and J.B. Richmond, 79-123. Champaign, IL: Human Kinetics.

Blair, S.N., Kohl, 3rd, H.W., Barlow, C.E., Paffenbarger, Jr., R.S., Gibbons, L.W., & Macera, C.A. (1995). Changes in physical fitness and all-cause mortality: A prospective study of healthy and unhealthy men. *Journal of the American Medical Association* 273: 1093-1098.

Bompa, T.O., & Carrera, M. (2005). *Periodization training for sports,* 2nd ed. Champagin, IL: Human Kinetics.

Boreham, C.A., Twisk, J., Murray, L., Savage, M., Strain, J.J., & Cran, G.W. (2001). Fitness, fatness, and coronary heart disease risk in adolescents: The Northern Ireland Young Hearts Project. *Medicine and science in sports and exercise* 33: 270-274.

Boreham, C.A., Twisk, J., Savage, M., Cran, G.W., & Strain, J.J. (1997). Physical activity, sports participation, and risk factors in adolescents. *Medicine and science in sports and exercise* 29: 788-793.

Cooper Institute. (2004). *Fitnessgram/Activitygram test administration manual,* 2nd ed. Champaign, IL: Human Kinetics.

Corbin, C.B., & Lindsey, R. (2005). *Fitness for life,* 5th ed. Champaign, IL: Human Kinetics.

Darst P., & Pangrazi R. (2009). *Dynamic physical education for secondary school students,* 6th ed. San Francisco: Benjamin Cummings.

Hass, C.J., Feigenbaum, M.S., & Franklin, B.A. (2001). Prescription of resistance training for healthy populations. *Sports medicine* 31(14): 953-964.

Joint Committee on National Health Education. (1995). *National health education standards: Achieving health literacy.* Atlanta: American Cancer Society.

Knudson, D.V., Magnusson, P., & McHugh, M. (June 2000). Current issues in flexibility fitness. In *The President's Council on physical fitness and sports digest,* series 3, no. 10, ed. C. Corbin and B. Pangrazi, 1-8. Washington, DC: Department of Health and Human Services.

Malina, R. (2006). Weight training in youth-growth, maturation and safety: An evidence-based review. *Clinical Journal of Sports Medicine,* 16: 478–487.

National Association for Sport and Physical Education (NASPE). (2004a). *Moving into the future: National standards for physical education,* 2nd ed. Reston, VA: Author.

National Association for Sport and Physical Education (NASPE). (2004b). *Physical activity for children: A statement of guidelines for children ages 5-12,* 2nd ed. Reston, VA: Author.

National Association for Sport and Physical Education (NASPE). (1992). *Outcomes of quality physical education programs.* Reston, VA: Author.

National Dance Association (NDA). (1996). *National standards for dance education: What every young American should know and be able to do in dance.* Reston, VA: Author.

National Strength and Conditioning Association (NSCA). (1985). Position statement on prepubescent strength training. *National strength and conditioning association journal* 7: 27-31.

Roberts, C.K., Freed, B., & McCarthy, W.J. (2009). Low aerobic fitness and obesity are associated with lower standardized test scores in children. *Journal of Pediatrics,* 156: 711–718.

Rowland, T.W. (1996). *Developmental exercise physiology.* Champaign, IL: Human Kinetics.

Shaw, B. (2001). *Beth Shaw's YogaFit,* 2nd ed. Champaign, IL: Human Kinetics.

Tanaka, H., Monahan, K.D. Monahan, & Seals, D.R. (2001). Age-predicted maximal heart rate revisited. *Journal of the American College of Cardiology* 37(1): 153-56.

U.S. Department of Health and Human Services (USDHHS). (2008). Physical activity guidelines for Americans. www.health.gov/PAguidelines/guidelines/chapter3.aspx.

U.S. Department of Health and Human Services (USDHHS). (1996). *Physical activity and health: A report of the Surgeon General.* U.S. Department of Health and Human Services, Centers for Disease Control and Prevention, National Center for Chronic Disease Prevention and Health Promotion. Atlanta, GA: U.S. Department of Health and Human Services, Government Printing Office.

Weiss, M. (2000). *Motivating kids in physical activity.* President's Council on Physical Fitness and Sports. SuDocHE 20.114:3/11.

Winnick, J.P., & Short, F.X., eds. (1999). *The Brockport physical fitness training guide.* Champaign, IL: Human Kinetics.

Xiang, P., McBride, R., Guan, J. & Solomon, M. (2003). Children's motivation in elementary physical education: An expectancy-value model of achievement choice. *Research Quarterly for Exercise and Sport* 74(1): 25-35.

ABOUT THE AUTHOR

The National Association for Sport and Physical Education (NASPE), a nonprofit professional organization, is an association of the American Alliance for Health, Physical Education, Recreation and Dance. NASPE is dedicated to educating the general public about the importance of physical education for all young people. Through its members as well as corporate and public partnerships, NASPE develops and supports sport and physical activity programs that promote healthy behaviors and individual well-being. NASPE's 15,000 members include K-12 physical educators, college and university faculty, researchers, coaches, athletic directors, and trainers.

Physical Best is a comprehensive health-related fitness education program developed by physical educators for physical educators. Physical Best is designed to educate, challenge, and encourage all children in the knowledge, skills, and attitudes needed for a healthy and fit life. The program helps students move from dependence to independence and take responsibility for their own health and fitness. Physical Best educates all children regardless of athletic talent or physical and mental abilities or disabilities. This program is implemented through high-quality resources and professional development workshops for physical educators.

HOW TO USE THIS CD-ROM

You can use this CD-ROM on either a Windows-based PC or a Macintosh computer.

Windows

- ▶ IBM PC compatible with Pentium processor
- ▶ Windows 2000/XP/Vista/7
- ▶ Adobe Reader 8.0
- ▶ Microsoft Office PowerPoint 2003 or higher
- ▶ 4x CD-ROM drive

Macintosh

- ▶ Power Mac recommended
- ▶ System 10.4 or higher
- ▶ Adobe Reader
- ▶ Microsoft Office PowerPoint 2004 for MAC or higher
- ▶ 4x CD-ROM drive

USER INSTRUCTIONS

Windows

1. Insert the *Physical Best Activity Guide: Middle and High School Levels* CD-ROM. (*Note:* The CD-ROM must be present in the drive at all times.)
2. Select the My Computer icon from the desktop.
3. Select the CD-ROM drive.
4. Open the file you wish to view. See the 00Start.pdf file for a list of the contents.

Macintosh

1. Insert the *Physical Best Activity Guide: Middle and High School Levels* CD-ROM. (*Note:* The CD-ROM must be present in the drive at all times.)
2. Double-click the CD icon located on the desktop.
3. Open the file you wish to view. See the 00Start file for a list of the contents.

For customer support, contact Technical Support:

Phone: 217-351-5076 Monday through Friday (excluding holidays) between 7:00 a.m. and 7:00 p.m. (CST).
Fax: 217-351-2674
E-mail: support@hkusa.com